STRIP-SET

Fly-Fishing Techniques, Tactics, & Patterns for Streamers

George Daniel

Published by
STACKPOLE BOOKS
5067 Ritter Road
Mechanicsburg, PA 17055
www.stackpolebooks.com

Printed in the United States of America

10 9 8 7 6 5 4 3 2 1

First edition

Photos by the author except where noted
Illustrations by Amidea Daniel
Instructional sequences and fly pattern photos by Jay Nichols

Library of Congress Cataloging-in-Publication Data

Daniel, George.
Strip-set : fly fishing techniques, tactics, patterns for streamers / George Daniel. — First edition.
pages cm
Includes index.
ISBN 978-0-8117-1297-2
1. Streamer fly fishing. 2. Streamers (Fly fishing) I. Title.
SH456.25.D36 2015
799.12'4—dc23

2015025573

Contents

Acknowledgments

It takes a fly-fishing community to produce a book, and if I were to list everyone who helped me in this endeavor, these acknowledgments would take up five full pages. Instead of doing that, I've done my best to provide credit within the pages of this book—anyone mentioned in the main text or shown in a picture has contributed to this effort in some form. The fact is, anyone I've fished with has provided me with a streamer lesson.

Additionally, Robert Humston and Will Travis helped me collect scientific journals in reference to predator and prey behavior. Thank you, guys!

An old Chinese proverb says, "The journey is the reward." Working on this book has shown me that nothing could be more true. Over the last three years, I have been given an incredible opportunity to travel all across the United States and fish with some of the country's best streamer anglers. The knowledge I've obtained while fishing with the anglers mentioned within these pages has been my greatest reward. So to everyone listed in this book, thank you!

Of course, I do need to specifically mention two people who made this book possible. First, I want to thank Jay Nichols for his advice, photography skills, and his willingness to work on another project with me. Second, I want to thank Tony Gehman, president and owner of the TCO Fly Shop, for his continued support over the years. Guys, this project wouldn't have been possible without your support.

Finally, I want to thank my wife, Amidea, for her unwavering support during our thirteen years of marriage. Amidea, you had faith in my crazy dream of entering the fly-fishing industry when others thought I had gone mad. You have given me everything I wanted in life, and I'm forever in your debt. The family we've made together is the reason I try to live life to the fullest. Thank you!

Foreword

When my friend George asked me to write this foreword, I was both shocked and honored. I was shocked because I certainly didn't fit the mold of the usual cast of characters who have written forewords for the hundreds of books out there on the subject of angling with the fly. But I was honored that he would ask and that I could now be a part of that group.

Thinking about it in hindsight, though, it is that very thought process that makes George the angler he is and that made *Dynamic Nymphing* the definitive book on the subject. It's the same thinking that will ultimately make this book the definitive work on streamer fishing. George doesn't just stick to the usual way of doing things. He doesn't leave well enough alone. He experiments, he tinkers, he plays with and breaks convention, and he forces people outside their comfort zones—all in an effort to catch more fish.

I thought *Dynamic Nymphing* was the end-all be-all of nymph-fishing literature, but then I started spending time on the water with George. Since then, I've probably compiled enough new material from him with my notes to help him make

Don Trump Jr. and his son pursue rainbows on the swing during a recent trip to Alaska. DON TRUMP JR.

Don Trump Jr. with a East Branch Delaware River brown trout taken during high water. DON TRUMP JR.

a pretty solid run at a sequel. I couldn't believe how much more there was to learn and how much more George could adapt the various techniques, or break from the competition rules he followed for so many years as a competitive angler, to make any given fishing situation easier. The bottom line is that George can adapt and excel in any fishing situation, yet despite being a virtual vacuum cleaner on the river—and perhaps America's most accomplished competitive angler—you wouldn't know it from George's demeanor. He is truly one of the nicest and most humble gentlemen I have had the pleasure to share a boat with.

I got into the outdoors somewhat by luck, and it has kept me out of a lot of trouble I would have otherwise gotten into. My grandfather was a blue-collar electrician from what was then Communist Czechoslovakia, who from an early age took an interest in the way that my siblings and I were brought up. While he fully appreciated the potential benefits of growing up among family in New York City, he also seemed to understand the pitfalls associated therewith. Starting when I was five, he would take me with him to Czechoslovakia for six weeks or so every summer and just set me loose in the woods. I spoke the language fluently and made friends fast, and I came to realize that the life I led in New York was very different from that of the average kid my age anywhere else. My grandfather taught me the basics of the outdoors: campcraft, woodsmanship, air guns, archery, and fishing. I learned fast that the novelties I experienced at home were just that, and that people got by with much less and were just as happy, if not more so, than many of the people I grew up around. The woods were our playground, the campfire was our TV, and the memories and friendships made there were truly unforgettable. It was these formative years that led me to a lifelong pursuit of all things outdoors. It was a great lesson in humility, and it taught me to not take the other things I had been blessed with in life for granted. In the end I think that was all my grandfather had in mind, and those lessons stuck.

My grandfather passed away when I was twelve, but he had lit the kindling of the proverbial fire that was my love of the outdoors. As I was now on my own for outdoor pursuits, being from a family where no one else was an outdoorsman or -woman, I did what I could. I read, and I asked questions and took advice wherever I could find it. At thirteen I went to boarding school in eastern Pennsylvania, and there is where it all took off. One teacher introduced me to the shotgun sports and wingshooting, taking a total novice under his wing, and another taught me the basics of the fly cast. The latter was largely self-taught, as evidenced by the fact that for the first few years of my fly-fishing journey, I reeled in my line like a conventional reel rather than stripping it in. Other than these two gentlemen, at the time all I had to learn from were books. It was before the Internet and YouTube, and the popular outdoor publications only gave a passing glance to fly fishing compared to the more commercialized fishing pursuits.

I got to know George Daniel a few years ago, shortly after the publication of his *Dynamic Nymphing*. Being an avid fly fisherman since the age of thirteen, I've constantly tried to better my game. I've bought, read, and even highlighted—while taking notes in the margins—virtually every fly-fishing book that has come out since the publication of Izaak Walton's *The Compleat Angler* in 1653. After doing the same with *Dynamic Nymphing*, I knew this was a man I had to spend some time with on the water. *Dynamic Nymphing* was not the usual how-to book on fishing; it wasn't the same book we have seen time and time again, written by a different author under a different title but ultimately regurgitating the same information that's been out there for the past few decades. This book was different. It was cutting-edge, and it went into extreme detail, covering the minutiae that journeymen anglers wouldn't possibly think of and setting off lightbulbs even in truly experienced anglers.

The personal introduction I was looking for ultimately came by way of another great angler friend, Paul Weamer, who was one of the first people I got know when I started calling New York's famed Delaware River system in the Catskills my home away from home. I knew he and George worked together in Pennsylvania, so I reached out to Paul to see if he would make an introduction. A few weeks later, I was on the water with George. While I always felt I could hold my own with a fly rod, I realized quickly that George was in a league of his own. It was like fishing with a vacuum, albeit a very precise and deliberate one. After spending some time with George on the East and West Branches of the Delaware, the Beaverkill, and the Willowemoc, as well as on his home waters in Pennsylvania, I can truly say that no other experience has helped improve my game or my catch rate as much as my time on the water with George.

Two of my good friends, Catskills guides Ben Rinker and Rob Lewis, are asked by clients what to expect to catch on "The D"—the Delaware. They somewhat jokingly tell their clients to "expect to catch nothing—that way you won't be disappointed." I say they do this "somewhat jokingly" because anyone who has fished the Delaware knows how great it can be—as well as how quickly it can get tough. However, since I started adopting the mind-set and the lessons I have learned from my time on the water with George, those slow or fishless days seem to be a thing of the past. That's not a coincidence. I'm fishing water I would have overlooked in the past, and I am hitting each stretch of water a few different ways, not just with the same old methods. In doing so, I have been able to turn water that had for the past decade been barren for me into some of the most trout-rich water on the system.

For the past few years, George has fully immersed himself in streamer fishing, employing these flies even when convention would dictate not to. Trying, testing, and disproving (at least some of the time) every old wives' tale out there about streamers, George does not take his research lightly—though given what he gets to do while collecting said research, I am sure none of us feel all that bad for him. I know *Strip-Set* will do for my streamer game what *Dynamic Nymphing* did for my nymphing. While I have had the pleasure of fishing streamers with George, I know there is much that both you and I will get from this new book. I know George has made countless trips to all parts of the country and the world to research this book, as well as spending thousands of hours perfecting each and every technique and cast—all so he can shed new light on the art of streamer fishing.

While the modern proverb that a bad day on the river is better than a good day at work certainly holds true, I would be lying if I said I didn't think actually catching a few more fish makes any day on the water better. I escape the craziness of daily life by going to the river; I love the scenery and the tranquility, but catching a few more fish in the few precious hours of free time I have definitely adds to the experience. I have George to thank for much of that additional enjoyment.

Donald J. Trump Jr.

One good thing about streamer fishing is that you should not lose many flies. Tommy Lynch holds a Pere Marquette trout that fell prey to his Drunk and Disorderly pattern, which had been fished for three months before fooling this trout.

Introduction

Every year I offer a variety of fly-fishing classes at the TCO Fly Shop in State College, Pennsylvania. Several years ago I decided to teach a streamer class. Streamer fishing was and still is an art misunderstood by many, so I wanted to show its effectiveness on our local waters. E-mail blasts were sent and posters were hung in the store to promote the event.

Several days into the promotion, one of the shop's favorite characters stopped by, and as he walked in, I noticed his hesitation as he read the poster plastered on the door. He continued into the shop and sat down on a bench near the wader section. We exchanged pleasantries, and before I got another word in, he asked, "Who in their right mind is going to pay you to teach them how to strip a Woolly Bugger down and across the stream?" I asked him what he meant. He replied, "Honestly, how many ways can you strip a Woolly Bugger?" I tried to explain the various streamer methods, but he wasn't buying anything—be it store inventory or my streamer approach.

I understood that this exchange was meant to rattle my chain in a good-natured manner, but I also realized that this was the only method he thought about when considering streamer fishing. Unfortunately, many anglers believe stripping a Woolly

Moments like this are why we fly-fish. My hope is that you're able to learn a few tips here that will increase your enjoyment of your time along the stream.

I believe catching trophy-size trout is 10 percent skill and 90 percent luck. Having a good skill set is essential, but being at the right place at the right time is even more important. I caught this trout while anchored in a Southern tailwater; I was waiting for the push of water and blind casting a streamer to kill time. From out of the shadows, this beast struck and inhaled my small streamer during a period of low and clear water.

Fall is a great time to swing streamers for steelhead. Timing is everything; understanding when to target steelhead with a streamer and when not to may be the difference between catching a fish and catching nothing.

Left: Streamer tactics are effective for all trout species, including stocked rainbows, and can produce great results year-round, from the coldest days of winter to the warmest summer months.

Anglers prepare to fish a lake in the Italian Alps. Many of the streamer lessons within these pages have come from spending time with great stillwater anglers.

Bugger across-stream is the only streamer method. To me, it's similar to hearing an angler contend that placing a nymph under a bobber is the only nymphing method. It's baffling since there are so many streamer fishing methods, and successful streamer anglers need to have the same mind-set as those who match the hatch while dry-fly fishing. As with any major hatch, each baitfish has its own unique features that an angler needs to understand before deciding on tactics. While a trout's brain is small, its ability to judge whether a fly's movement is natural is sharp.

The other problem with the gentleman's comment is that the category of flies called "streamers" is way more complex than just a handful of Woolly Buggers. The term *streamer*, at least to me, encompasses a broad range of patterns and techniques, ranging from swinging baitfish imitations to dead-drifting leeches to waking mice patterns across the surface. This catchall category is probably best defined by what it is not (dead-drifting a small dry fly or nymph), but more or less anything other than that can likely fit into the streamer category. Perhaps as fly fishing evolves, we will continue to refine the term, but in this book I define streamers and streamer fishing as anything that involves relatively large forage items that are not aquatic insects and are most often imitations of fish, crayfish, leeches, and other foods such as small rodents and amphibians.

Yet, despite all the nuances, little has been written about streamer fishing. One important book, Kelly Galloup and Bob Linsenman's *Modern Streamers for Trophy Trout*, reenergized the streamer game thanks to the authors' countless hours of underwater research and their development of a wounded baitfish approach, but in my opinion, there is still a lot of ground to cover—even beyond this book.

At times, streamer fishing can be as effective as nymphing or dry-fly fishing, and I have experienced a number of occasions where streamer tactics have outfished both nymphing and dry-fly tactics by a wide margin. But as with any fly-fishing approach, the key is to know when to use it and when to leave it. Streamer fishing can also, at times, be the most unpredictable approach. I've fished few rivers where nymphing and dry tactics couldn't at least capture a couple trout, especially nymphing. However, there have been many times when I couldn't get a trout to chase down my streamer. In my experience, trout can be ready to engage streamers, or they can completely ignore their presence. But on those days where I've only had a few fish engage my streamer, they were big enough to get my blood flowing.

This adrenaline rush is a large part of the allure of streamer fishing. What makes someone stand in a river for hours, casting

There is no wrong way to fish a streamer. One good approach is dead-drifting a large streamer in the head of a fast run just as a nymph fisher would drift a large stonefly pattern. CHRIS DANIEL

large flies and heavy rods, hoping that a trout will chase down the streamer? I think there are at least two reasons. First, it's because you have a chance to observe a large trout leave its cover and chase down your fly. Speaking for myself, a trout may only be 10 inches, but it's still exciting to watch when it chases my fly, even if I don't hook it. Second, the "thump" you feel when a fish takes your fly is a sensation like no other—it's what keeps streamer junkies coming back for more. The tug is the drug.

My goal here is to share with you the exciting world of streamer fishing and to help you develop a set of streamer fishing skills that will be effective anywhere in the world, whether you are wading or floating. This book's focus is on trout tactics, but much of the material is applicable to other fish species. If you're looking for a beginner's book to streamer fishing (i.e., a book that lays out a couple simple steps to catching a fish with a streamer), this is not the book for you. Instead, I want to provide a wide range of ideas and concepts for you to think about and from which you should draw your own conclusions. I will share streamer approaches and concepts that work for anglers across the United States. That's my idea of a good fly-fishing technique book: one which provides some general direction, but which, more importantly, forces the angler to think deeply about his or her approach.

For this project, I traveled the country and sought out some of its top streamer anglers. I wanted to learn from them, just as I learned from many European anglers as I researched and wrote my first book, *Dynamic Nymphing*. My goal was to create a systematic streamer approach that would allow me to deal with varying stream conditions, year-round, on not only my local waters, but also on new waters. I gained incredible insight from these great anglers, and borrowed different aspects of each of their approaches for a system that fits my needs. I'll continue to build my streamer system as I travel and fish new waters with different guides, and this is what I would like for you to do with the information that I share with you. I do not want you to take everything I write in this book as gospel. Instead, I want you to question my theories, test them, and over time, develop your own streamer system that you have confidence in. After fishing with so many great streamer anglers, many of whom are guides, I know that many different methods and flies work, even on the same stretch of water. The best guides will tell you that the key is to find fly patterns and presentations that *you* believe in.

Listen to the guys on the ground. I put great stock into what the local guides are recommending on their home waters before planning my own strategies. This is also why I hire the best guides I can afford when fishing new or unfamiliar waters. In Michigan, I make an effort to hire Tommy Lynch or Russ Madden (pictured) when fishing either the Pere Marquette or the Upper Manistee Rivers. Russ introduced me to a sophisticated streamer game in 2002. He is also the creator of patterns such as the Circus Peanut, Kraken, and Mad Pup. Guys like Russ respect traditional methods but find ways to tweak them, which is why fly fishing continues to move forward. JON RAY

Once a trout reaches a certain size, it relies on larger food items to satisfy its daily energy needs. Such fish are looking for larger meals, making streamers a useful tool for targeting them. LANCE WILT

An angler works his streamer at first light on a magnificent October morning along Montana's Madison River. CHRIS DANIEL

Streamer System Tools

1

So often, anglers look at streamer fishing as a backup plan—a last resort when all other tactics have failed. But streamer tactics can be just as effective as dry-fly or nymph fishing, and in some cases even more so. The key is having a general idea of when to fish streamers and how the current conditions will dictate your approach.

The beautiful thing about fishing is that you can create your own experience. If you want to catch a couple fish during prime streamer time, all you need is a Bugger and the ability to strip it across the stream. However, if you want to successfully fish streamers under all conditions, you need to change your streamer system to match the demands—this includes everything from line types to leaders to streamer designs to retrieves, all of which should vary based on the fishing conditions. Streamer fishing is not mindless. There are as many presentation possibilities with streamers as there are with nymphs, drys, and wets.

The streamer system that I share here is one that I've spent fifteen years developing. It works great for me and the waters I fish. I've been fortunate enough to spend hours with anglers who are some of the best streamer fishers in the industry,

Lance Wilt ties on a streamer during an early-morning float. Streamer fishing is often done during low-light periods, and amber lenses allow for better fishing during such times while also offering eye protection—essential when casting large streamers.

specifically the Michigan boys. I know I may take some heat for saying that, but of all the states I've traveled to and fished in, the average Michigan angler is the most deadly with a streamer. So much of my system is based on information I've gleaned from these Great Lake State anglers and then carefully refined based on my own experiences and observations to create something that works for me.

I feel my limited success is mostly due to the confidence I have in the system I have built for myself. This is no different from those anglers who only have confidence in fly patterns they tied themselves. Therefore, I don't want to you replicate my system; instead, build a streamer arsenal that works for you. Just as nymph fishers will create different leader formulas for fishing the same piece of water, I have found that streamer fishers will also use different lines and rigs to fish the same piece of water. And guess what? They all work. These are the tools I use to deal with an ever-changing stream environment, and they should provide a solid foundation for your own streamer system. Over time you can experiment and tweak your streamer system to match your home waters.

RODS

You don't need to carry a big gun (a 7-weight or higher) all the time to fish streamers. Rod choice really depends on the waters you fish and the size of the flies you are fishing. I use a 5-weight for most of my streamer fishing near my home waters in Pennsylvania. However, central Pennsylvania limestone streams are small to medium in size with an average depth of less than 4 feet, and patterns' length average 3 to 4 inches. For bigger water or larger flies, you might opt for a heavier rod and line. I'm a minimalist, so I like to find one rod than can handle everything from nymphing to dry-fly to light streamer tactics. A 9- to 10-foot 5-weight makes a great all-around rod. There have been many occasions where I've started with streamers early in the morning, nymph-fished before the main hatch, and then finished with drys—all within a five-hour period. A 5-weight coupled with several line-and-leader setups will allow you to adapt to a changing stream environment and will meet most streamer-fishing demands.

That said, if I'm targeting large trout and casting larger or wind-resistant flies, then I will bring my 8-weight with accompanying lines to better match the conditions. I throw 8-weight rods when I'm presenting big patterns (greater than 3 to 4 inches) and have an opportunity at trout larger than 20 inches. The increased rod backbone allows me to play larger fish and cast bigger flies with less fatigue. I've thrown large double-articulated streamers with my 5-weight, but it's a lot of work—such casting is much easier when using a rod suited for a heavier line weight.

Another reason I prefer the 8-weight over a 7-weight is that it allows me to throw a wider variety of grain weights. Instead of purchasing multiple fly rods to match specific grain weights, I use a rod that allows me to comfortably throw grain weights as low as 150 and as high as 400. While matching line weight to rod action will allow for easier casting for beginners, it's not essential for the intermediate to advanced caster. A decent caster using a single line-weight rod (such as an 8-weight) can adjust the power and timing of the cast to match the grain weight. For instance, if the only line you have available is a 150-grain, but you are fishing a rod rated for a 300-grain head, you can make several changes to your casting approach. First, you'll need to use more force (stronger movements to speed up the rod tip path) in your casting stroke to load the rod. You can also use a longer casting stroke, which will create greater force and increase rod load.

Any rod can quickly be converted into a streamer stick. While fishing the Sulphur hatch on the South Holston River, the water levels began to rise due to generation. I quickly clipped my dry-fly leader off this 10-foot, 4-weight rod and added a long, level tippet to the only streamer I had in my box. This trout took it on the second cast, proving that you should never make an excuse that you didn't have a big enough rod to fish a streamer. Use what you've got.

While I don't recommend it, there are times when I will bounce between dry-fly/nymphing tactics and streamers. When doing so, I use the rod holder flap (standard on most vests) to hold one rod while the other is in use. I only do this when I know I will be continually switching rods.

As with nymphing, I use a longer rod (9 to 10 feet) to enable longer casts and better line and leader control, especially when fishing broken water. A longer rod allows you to reposition the line by mending on the water. And there's another important aspect to consider: A trout is most likely to jump on a vertically moving pattern at the end of the retrieve when the fly begins to swing upward. This last stage of the retrieve is deadly, but only when you can position yourself far enough away from the fly to avoid spooking the trout.

A long rod helps you sell the figure-eight retrieve (see page 226) or implement the hang. You do these maneuvers at the end of the presentation when you can't retrieve the line in any farther; they are a last-ditch attempt to keep the fly moving when a trout is following the streamer. Too often, an angler implements this tactic too close to his or her position. As a result, the trout notices the angler and scurries back into the depths. The advantage of a long rod and a good reach is that you can implement this tactic from farther away.

I also prefer longer rods because I enjoy fishing larger rivers. These waters require long casts to cover a wider arc, and this is where I go against my normal belief of "keep the cast short." A good approach to streamer fishing is to cover the largest amount of water in the least amount of time while still exercising total control. Not all trout in the river are aggressive or hungry enough to chase down a forage fish; this is where nymphing has the advantage, as most fish are willing to snack. By covering more water, you increase your chances of finding aggressive fish, and I feel a longer rod aids in my ability to make longer casts. Even if you only fish small- to medium-size streams, you should use as long a rod you can get away with. Rarely do I drop below an $8^1/2$-foot rod.

Rod action is a personal preference because it relates to how you cast and fish. I use my rod tip to impart motion into the streamer during the retrieve, so I'm looking for a fast-action rod with a little wiggle. The faster the action, the more motion I'm able to impart into the fly during the retrieve. As soon as I twitch the rod tip on the retrieve, I want to impart that same motion into the fly. A rod with slower action bends too much during this twitch, which forces me to sweep the rod tip through a longer motion to create the retrieval action.

When I use the rod tip motion to twitch the fly during the retrieve, this short but powerful rod movement not only imparts movement to the fly, but also creates additional momentum to aid with the hook set. A faster-action rod creates more momentum than a slower-action rod, which in turn creates more energy to set the hook on the fish. All a faster-action rod needs is a short, sideways movement of the forearm to create enough energy to retrieve and set the fly. A slower-action rod (which has increased rod bend) requires more movement from the rod hand to achieve the same results. I prefer to conserve my energy during all aspects of the retrieve and hook set.

REELS

Over my time managing the TCO Fly Shop, I have come to one conclusion: Almost everyone makes a great reel these days. Mid- to large-arbor and fully sealed drag systems, which can handle anything from steelhead to tuna, are the norm these days. So I'm not going to discuss what reel manufacturers and drag systems are superior for streamer fishing, since just about any of today's reels will get the job done.

That said, there's one style I feel is useful for the angler who carries multiple streamer lines: cassette reels. These reels have come a long way since their inception. Today's cassette reels have dependable, fully sealed drag systems; a large-arbor option; and less expensive but still durable polycarbonate spools. You can buy these extra spools at a fraction of the cost of a traditional spool. They are lighter and take up less storage space. For these reasons, I use the cassette design for all my streamer line storage. My Hardy 5000 CL Ultra reel system is rated for 5- to 7-weight lines. This is perfect for me, since all my trout lines are either 5- or 7-weights. This means I only need two reels, and I simply purchase the number of cassettes needed for all my lines. There's a dial on the side of the spool that allows me to determine the line weight and sinking design, so that I can quickly identify the line class and sink type of each spool.

I also prefer large-arbor reels because they store fewer coils of line on the reel when compared to small- and mid-arbor reels. This is very helpful when dealing with full- and sinking-tip fly lines, as both lead- and tungsten-coated lines have a tendency to tangle.

LINES

Lines are probably the most underrated tool in the streamer fisher's kit. Because of the seemingly infinite number of ways to present a streamer—dead drift, up-and-across, down-and-across, straight upstream—and the importance of the level and path of retrieve, I tend to carry a variety of lines and heads to deal with changing conditions. Because trout are not always in the mood to move a good distance for your streamer, you need to present the fly in the trout's kill zone.

I tend to fish my streamer patterns up-and-across stream. This is by far my favorite tactic and the one I use well over 50 percent of the time. However, there have been many times when this approach has failed terribly and I had to switch to another

If you plan to streamer fish with a variety of fly lines, then a cassette system may be the most economical way to go. The spare cartridges cost a fraction of what a machine's spare spool costs and are easier to store.

TEXTURED LINES

I find myself looking to textured lines when streamer fishing. These lines differ from traditional lines in several ways. Textured lines go through a second process where divots (depressions) are grooved into the fly line. This process reduces the surface area of the line, which allows it to pass through the guides with less friction.

Fly line companies market textured lines as better casting tools, and this may be true, but their greatest value as a streamer tool lies with their increased sensitivity during the retrieve. I find that textured lines become less tacky over the course of the day, especially when fishing the limestone streams of central Pennsylvania. There's nothing more frustrating than losing sensitivity in the retrieve due to a tacky line, and I'm all about any small advantage I can get—especially for detecting subtle takes. Remember, trout will not always smash the streamer; sometimes a trout will simply inhale it, creating nothing more than a slight degree of tension on the line. Some anglers who use textured lines complain that they are rough on your hands when stripping line all day. To prevent wear and tear on my fingers, I use stripping gloves.

While I enjoy the slickness and retrieval sensitivity of textured lines, many of my favorite streamer lines are not available in this line design. As a result, I take extra care of nontextured line by cleaning each line after every use. You'd be surprised how a little dirt or mud on the line can decrease the line's retrieval sensitivity. After every fishing session, I clean the fly line in a sink using mild soap. I'll place one pump of liquid hand soap in a gallon of water, mix the soap into the water, pull the line off the reel, and let the line sit in the water for five minutes. Then I'll moisten a soft cloth with fresh water and pull the wet line through the cloth. Try not to create too much tension while pulling the line through the cloth; doing so will likely take some of the coating off the fly line. When done correctly, this process cleans the line of any dirt or grime that has accumulated. ■

tactic. This usually entails switching to a different line or a sinking-tip line in the hope of achieving a different retrieve action. Remember, the best plans are flexible, so carrying a variety of lines will ensure that you're prepared for most conditions.

While I recommend carrying multiple lines, I recognize that some anglers may carry only one line with them while wade-fishing, so changing lines or rigs as one moves up and down the river may not be feasible. A good angler can adjust his or her approach to make any line or rig work for most scenarios. I don't expect you to carry every line and rig I discuss in this book. However, I wouldn't advise fishing the same rig or line across a wide range of conditions if you have the ability to carry multiple rigs. Drift boats provide the option of carrying multiple rods; some of the best guides I know carry a small variety of setups to deal with varying conditions as they float down the river. Cassette reels allow you to easily carry a small variety of line types to make quick adjustments. Additionally, you can carry a variety of weighted flies to deal with a wide range of conditions.

While there is no bad time to streamer fish, many prefer the fall. While autumn streamer fishing is full of chasing fish, I personally find that winter through early spring provides just as good, if not better fishing. LANCE WILT

These are the lines I carry with me when I am focused on fishing streamers and leave my dry-fly and nymph equipment at home. I specify the manufacturer and the type of line not for advertisement but to clearly explain the pros and cons of each line as I see them. There are subtle but important differences between brands and the lines they produce. Some lines will have a shorter sinking portion and a better floating line to better deal with mending. Other lines will have a density-compensated (DC) sinking section, where the sinking portion uniformly sinks at the same level. With that in mind, this is a list of my favorite lines, along with reasons why I feel each line is important. (It should be noted that I have not fished all lines on the market today.) I break lines into three categories: floating, full-sinking, and sinking-tip lines.

Floating Lines

The most versatile lines in the arsenal, floating lines can be fished in any direction (upstream, downstream, and across). I mostly fish weighted streamers with full-floating lines, except when I want to fish a streamer pattern immediately below the surface.

Floating lines offer an advantage because they give you the ability to easily mend or reposition the line on the water,

Brian Wilt holds a nice brown that ate a sculpin pattern headfirst. I prefer articulated hooks because you never know which end of a pattern a trout will eat or from what angle it will attack. I've had trout come from behind, eat headfirst, and even T-bone my streamer. When possible (and allowed in the waters you fish), I keep both hook points on articulated streamers. If I'm only allowed one hook point and I'm fishing upstream, I'll likely cut the back hook off because I will be pulling my streamers toward the fish. When fishing upstream, the trout will most often eat the streamer headfirst. If I'm swinging a pattern and holding it in front of me at a downstream angle, I will cut the front hook off, as I've experienced more trout attacking the rear side in this scenario.

whether by changing the retrieval direction or reducing or increasing tension in the system. Have you ever tried mending a sinking line that is positioned 4 feet under the water? Floating lines are easy to mend since they sit on the water's surface (as compared to sinking lines, which are anywhere from several inches to several feet under the surface).

I enjoy fishing streamers at an upstream angle, which requires that I focus my attention on the top portion of my fly line that is lying on the water; I'll look for subtle takes or clean up any slack that may inhibit my ability to sense a take. My preferred floating line is either a RIO Indicator Line or an Orvis Easy-Mend Line. Both lines have an aggressive front taper that makes it easier to turn over heavy and wind-resistant flies. Both lines contain a long belly taper, which lets you reposition the line on the water anytime during the drift and allows for roll-casting of larger flies. Finally, these two lines come with a bright orange tip, which I use to track my fly's position relative to the drift (the orange tip points toward the fly). Not only does this aid in strike detection, but it also helps me determine if the drift has too much or too little slack. While any floating line will get the job done, these bright-tipped, long belly lines are designed to better handle the widest array of conditions.

If you're just starting to fish with streamers, I recommend beginning with a floating line (or a short sinking tip) for one main reason: line control. Using a floating line when streamer fishing is like using a suspension device (traditional indicator) when nymphing—as soon as the floating line lands on the water, the surface currents create immediate tension and pull the floating line downstream. This immediate line control helps beginner streamer fly fishers as they practice stripping line. This is in contrast to sinking lines, which cut below the water's surface and lie in slower-moving water, forcing you to strip in line fast enough to stay in touch with the fly. If you throw too much slack with a sinking line, you'll spend the first several strips just trying to regain control of the line. In comparison, if you throw too much slack with a floating line, the immediate tension created by the surface currents will help you regain control of the drift.

Orvis Bank Shot. As streamer tactics become more popular, manufacturers are developing both sinking and floating lines to deal with specific situations. For example, the Orvis Bank Shot line is a full-floating line with an aggressive 23-foot head that can deliver big flies with minimal backcasts. You could almost call this a switch line, as it sports a very aggressive head with running line. While I prefer a floating line with a longer belly, Bank Shot is a great tool for throwing big flies to the bank or in windy conditions. It also works for casting long distances when there is little room for a backcast. By keeping only the short 23-foot head out of the rod tip, you can sling shot this line a great distance.

There are several disadvantages to this line. One downside is that once you get the 23-foot head out onto the water, it is difficult to manipulate the remaining 77 feet of running line because thin running line has little mass and is difficult to mend on the water. The other disadvantage is the massive diameter of the head. The greater surface currents caused by this larger diameter create additional drag, which means the fly can be pulled off the bottom more quickly and move faster than you want.

RIO Ultimate Euro Nymphing Line. Designed by Steve Parrott and RIO for European-style nymphing, this is also a great tool for jigging streamers. Essentially this line is nothing more than backing with a fly-line finish and a level .022 diameter. There's no taper in the line—it's a straight .022 throughout the entire line. Because of the thin diameter, there's less sag in the line, which allows you to hold a long length of line.

RIO Gold Lumalux Floating Line. Designed for low-light and nighttime fishing conditions, this line literally glows on the water. It's a great tool for reading currents at night, when you can't see the current's interplay with the fly line. (It's difficult enough to read microcurrents in the daytime.) Streamer-fishing takes are more often felt through the tension a trout puts onto the line during the attack, rather than through being able to see the take. The only way I know to ensure line control and sensitivity for the take is to eliminate slack in the line and leader. If there's slack in the line, there's less chance you will register the take. Instead, I keep the entire system (line, leader, and fly) under slight tension. This often means there's a tension loop in the system where everything from the line on the water to the fly is under varying degrees of tension. This ensures that I will feel any resistance on my line, whether it's a trout inhaling the fly or the fly getting stuck on the bottom.

The difficulty of fishing a non glowing line at night is that we don't always see what the currents are doing to the fly line. We can often feel (with our hand) if the fly is under tension or not, but rarely can we see how microcurrents are affecting the drift of the fly. A glowing line will show up in complete darkness, allowing you to see the degree of slack that occurs

An angler prepares a jig on Italy's Isarco. A long leader (up to 20 feet) can be useful for approaching each pocket from a distance while keeping line and leader off the water. A heavily weighted streamer is needed so that it will quickly anchor itself in the turbulent water.

When fishing timbered stream bottoms like those on Michigan's Pere Marquette River, a sinking line in combination with a buoyant streamer is a good choice. The sinking line lies across the stream bottom, and the shorter leader keeps the buoyant streamer riding just above the wood—keeping the pattern in the strike zone without fouling on the bottom.

during the retrieve. I have found that anglers who prefer not to night-fish feel this way because they feel they're not able to read the water at night. Using glow-in-the-dark lines will allow you to read every microcurrent in the water.

Sinking Lines

Just as I do when fishing a dry fly or nymph, I look at the size of the river, the water depth, and the average length of the cast to give me an idea of how long my leader should be. Because I often use uniformly short leaders (3 to 5 feet) with full-sinking or sinking-tip lines, I tend to match the sink rate and line style, just as one would design a leader to fish a particular stream. Generally, the faster sinking the line, the shorter the leader, especially when fishing buoyant streamers. The idea is to keep the fly and the line holding at about the same depth and within several feet of one another.

Keeping the lines and leader at roughly the same depth maintains a better connection between angler and fly. Think about using a super-fast, full-sinking fly line, a 12-foot leader, and a buoyant streamer while fishing a deep pool. After you make the cast, the sinking line begins to sink toward the stream bottom, while the buoyant streamer remains high in the water column. When fishing a slow, deep pool where little current exists, there's a chance the buoyant streamer could be riding 8 to 12 feet above the sinking line. This separation creates too much slack and causes a loss of control when fishing moving water. However, you can fish a heavily weighted streamer with a long leader and superfast-sinking line, as the sink rate of the fly better matches the sink rate of the line—keeping fly and line within several feet of one another. The greater the difference between the sink rate of the line and the buoyancy of the streamer, the shorter I tend to keep my leader. You don't need to keep the line and fly at the exact same level, but you do need to position them in a manner that allows you to fish the fly at the correct level and maintain control throughout the retrieve.

The same holds true when choosing a sinking line. While it's true that good anglers can make any style or length of sinking line work for the conditions they face, I feel that looking at several variables will help you pick a better tool for the conditions:

- Do you plan on mending? Maybe a better way to phrase this question is, are there protruding boulders or other obstacles within the presentation area that will force you to reposition the line on the water in order to move the fly around the obstacle and not get stuck? I'm referring to mends that occur later in the drift, after the sinking portion has dropped in the water column. Full-sinking lines can be mended, but usually only at the beginning of the drift before the line has sunk too deep. Mending sinking portions becomes difficult once the line sinks more than a few inches under the water.

If you plan on repositioning throughout the entire presentation, then you're going to need enough floating line on the water to implement the mend. Let's say you're fishing a large flat with exposed boulders. If you were to cast directly across-stream to the other side and retrieve straight back, you would snag several boulders with the fly line. One way you can avoid snagging boulders is by repositioning the belly of the line so that the streamer retrieves on a path that moves it away from the boulder. This is the reason that, when fishing broken pocketwater, I often use a full-floating line or a short 7- to 14-foot sinking-tip section. I'll continuously reposition the line on the water so the streamer slides past each boulder or likely trout holding spot.

Because of rocks and other obstructions, the line has to be repositioned to move both the fly line and fly away from any potential snags. However, I use a full-sinking streamer line on bigger flats or pools with uniform currents (scenarios where less mending is needed), in situations where less repositioning is needed because of the lack of snags, or if I want to simply keep the streamer moving without mending.

- What's the average length of the cast? If I'm fishing a 30-foot-wide stream with strong currents and lots of depth and I need to mend the line continually, I don't want a sinking section that is 30 feet long. This is because the average length of the cast may only be 30 feet, which means that nothing but sinking line will be lying on the water and the floating section will remain on the reel. Again, this is only important if you need to mend the line throughout the entire drift (i.e., as the fly line continues to sink during the presentation). On small streams where I want to mend, I'll choose a shorter sinking-tip line or simply add a short sinking poly leader to the fly line via a loop-to-loop connection.
- Are you planning on fishing weighted or unweighted patterns? Everyone has an opinion on this. Your decision will dictate what line you need to fish.
- How much time do you have to get the fly to the fish's zone before the end of the presentation? Just as with nymph fishing, the shorter the drift (the distance fly travels from presentation to pick-up), typically the faster the sinking line you need. When fishing a cut or a drop-off on a river system, where the water depth goes from shallow to deep within a couple feet, you need a line that can achieve depth quickly. However, on longer runs where there's a more gradual increase in water depth, you can use a slower-sinking line if the cast is placed far enough upstream to give the line and fly enough time to settle to the correct depth. If you're drifting on big water, and your presentation is short and trout are holding deep in the column (a maximum of five or six retrieves), then you may consider fishing a faster-sinking line.
- How fast do you want to fish the streamers? If you plan to fish the streamers slower (such as during a cold snap in the winter when trout are not actively chasing down prey) on a relatively shallow piece of water, the last thing you want is a fast-sinking line. This is why my preferred winter streamer line on central Pennsylvania trout streams is a full floater. By changing the weight of the streamer, I can fish the fly as slowly as I need to during periods of low trout activity. A fast-sinking line, when fished slowly, will quickly sink and snag bottom on every cast. However, if you're fishing shorter presentations and you need to get down quickly, a faster-sinking line is necessary.

Full-Sinking Lines

As the name implies, the entire full-sinking line is designed to sink. These lines allow me to achieve a more level retrieve (one in which the fly moves horizontal to the current rather than vertical) in deeper water. The fly follows the path and depth of the line belly; if the line belly is anchored deep in the water, the fly will ride deep in the water. If you're fishing deep water with a full-floating line and a heavy streamer, a long pull or retrieve will move the fly at an upward angle, which is often the desired

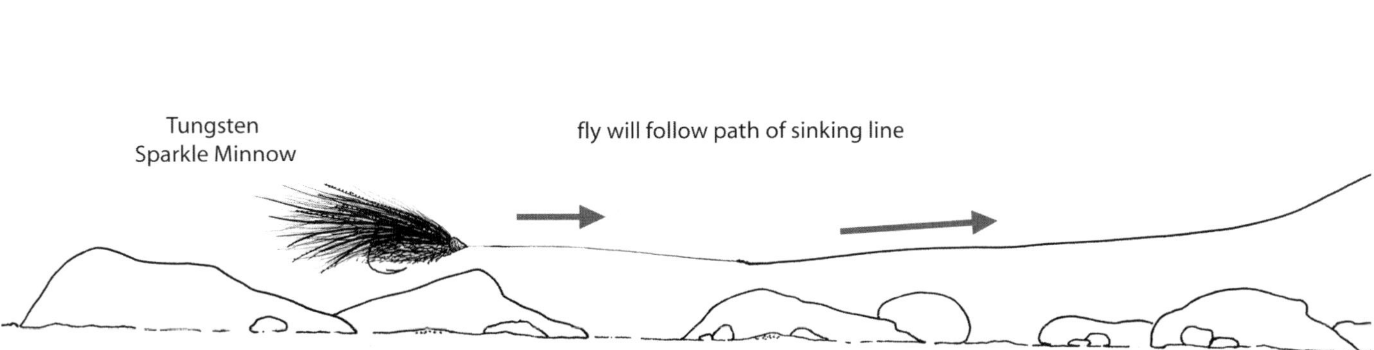

Sinking line and a weighted streamer allow for a deeper ride along the bottom—sometimes a good tool for cold winter fishing. This is one of my favorite approaches for situations when I need a deep retrieve along the stream bottom (for example, during a cold snap when trout are holding tight to the bottom).

STREAMER CRAFT

Whether fishing a stillwater or a river, a boat allows you to cover water and find aggressive fish. The more water you can efficiently cover, the greater chance you have of moving a larger trout. ■

Josh Day shows off a nice brown taken while floating a small stream from a Gheenoe. Such watercraft allows you to cover miles of water, skipping less promising sections and focusing on hot spots.

Josh Greenburg pilots an Au Sable River boat down the Miracle Mile stretch. These longboats date from the timber days and today are employed by anglers on the river's upper reaches.

Below: Covering large expanses of water is helpful when attempting to locate larger fish on the hunt. So many times I've drifted for several hours only to move a single large fish. If you don't know where a large fish is located, then thoroughly covering a large area of water may be a good approach.

Lance Wilt tests his jet boat before a morning float on Arkansas's White River. When allowed, a jet boat is a great tool for focusing on hot spots. Compared to a drift boat, which is difficult to move quickly back upstream, a jet boat allows you to make multiple passes over likely holding areas.

approach. However, in conditions where trout are not moving vertically in the water column to chase down prey, a full-sinking line will keep the pattern in the kill zone for a longer period of time and increase your chances of moving a trout. Full-sinkers reach depths faster than floating and sinking tips since the entire line will sink below water's surface, where the fastest currents are typically located.

The reason I'm not fond of wade-fishing with this line is that I often make casts longer than 30 feet, which means the retrieved sinking section will sink to my feet rather than stay on the surface. Unless you're using a stripping basket or have a way of capturing the line, the retrieved line will sink to the bottom, catching on your boots or on rocks. However, there are times when wade-fishing with a full-sinking line may be the best option.

Not all full-sinking lines sink at the same depth from rear to front. There are lines that are classified as density-compensated (DC), where the entire length of the line will sink at the exact same rate. Remember that most sinking lines have a taper (one section thicker than another); because of the larger surface area, the section with the larger diameter will not sink as fast as that with the smaller diameter unless the line is rigged with a weighting material (such as lead or tungsten) that increases or decreases density throughout the line. This is what is referred to as density-compensated, where the thickest section of the line will sink at the same rate as the running line. This level sink rate creates a straight-line path for the fly to follow during the retrieve. This was my line type of choice prior to the recent development of streamer-specific lines. These days I tend to use DC lines solely on stillwaters, where I may be looking to maintain a level retrieve.

Fly-line companies have recently begun creating streamer-specific lines like the Scientific Anglers Streamer Express and the Orvis 3D Depth Charge. I tend to fish this line style in moving water or from a boat more than I do DC lines. These fly lines have full-sinking sections that are approximately 24 to 50 feet and that transition into a thin running line. These hybrid streamer lines often possess an aggressive front taper that allows you to cast larger flies with ease, as compared to the DC lines often used for stillwater fishing. These lines are often designated in grain weights instead of line weights.

Compared to a sinking-tip line, in which the sinking section transitions into a larger floating section, the sinking section of these streamer-specific lines transitions directly to a smaller-diameter (floating or slow-sinking) running line. Because the running section possesses a smaller diameter, there's less surface drag, which allows the streamers to sink faster. Unlike density-compensated fly lines, where the entire line sinks at the same rate, the running line section isn't as likely to sink fast enough to grab your fishing boots. This is especially

Joe McGinley and Montana guide Greg Bricker show off a respectable brown taken while dead-drifting a size 8 Sparkle Minnow under a Thingamabobber. While it's exciting to feel a trout tug on your line, I prefer any technique that's going to land me a good fish. Dead-drifting a streamer under a suspender is a great tactic for keeping your streamer deep in the water column.

The wood-strewn bottoms of the Manistee River are great for a sinking line and buoyant streamer. This combination allows you to work the pattern tight to the stream bottom with less chance of a hang-up.

helpful for anglers who want to wade-fish, as the running line is slower to sink as they retrieve line. Unless you're using a stripping basket, the slack retrieved from a density-compensated line will sink like a rock near your feet. The result is that you may step on the fly line with studded boots or the line may snag on the bottom.

I mostly fish unweighted streamers with full-sinking lines, except when I'm fishing exceptionally fast or deep sections of water. I feel that the combination of a weighted fly and a sinking line creates more movement. Because the sinking line is acting as an anchor, the unweighted pattern moves up and down in the water column more naturally. However, it's important to note that while this combination creates more natural movement, you need deeper water to fish these lines. I live around trout streams where the average depth is less than 2 feet. I fish either DC or streamer-style lines only during high-water events when there are stronger currents and greater depth. Otherwise, these sinking lines would continuously grab the stream bottom, causing snags or shredding the line as it's being pulled over sharp rocks. Streamer fishing isn't exactly like nymph fishing, where you often want your patterns close to the stream bottom. With streamer fishing, we're looking for aggressive fish that are willing to move several feet off the bottom to inhale a large morsel. This is no different than a person who is willing to bend over and grab a quarter off the sidewalk yet will refuse to use the same amount of energy to pick up a penny. I look at sinking lines as a solution for getting my fly down just deep enough to pull a trout off the bottom or away from structure.

Line and leader management is more difficult with full-sinking line. The line sinks below the surface currents, so you need to retrieve at a speed that doesn't allow the line to drop too fast and snag the bottom. This is especially true with ultrafast-sinking lines. Unlike a full-floating or sinking tip, where the belly portion floats on the surface and keeps tension on the rig, the entire line sinks below the surface. If the line is a fast sinker and you cannot retrieve line fast enough, the line and fly will snag bottom.

Orvis 3D Depth Charge Fly Line (30-foot sinking section). A textured (streamer-specific) fly line with an aggressive 30-foot sinking head. This is my all-around streamer line for regular conditions when the water is neither too low nor too high. The core of these sinking lines is made of multifilament instead of mono or braid. As a result, the line functions well in both cold- and warmwater conditions, tangles less, and has less memory than any other sinking line I've ever owned. Also, because of the line's longer taper, it can be mended on the water immediately following the line landing on the water.

I own three of these lines. I'll use the 150-grain weight (4.5 inches per second sink rate) when fishing calmer waters where I need a more delicate presentation. Too often, I've used a heavier grain weight in low water and noticed I was spooking trout as far as 20 feet away from where my fly was landing. Remember, the heavier the grain or line weight, the greater the force of the presentation. I prefer to use the 150 on my 5-weight because it better matches the rod action. However, if I'm using my 8-weight and need a milder presentation, the 150 will still work on the rod.

A 250-grain line (5 inches per second) is used for fishing the majority of medium-size streamers (3 to 5 inches) and for fishing medium to strong currents. The 250-grain Depth Charge is my go-to line when casting medium-size streamers or when dealing with normal springtime flows on medium to large rivers.

Rarely do I cast excessively large streamers for trout or fish big water, but when I do, a 350-grain weight (5.6 inches per second) is about as big as I go. The 350 handles most big-water conditions, even when I'm fishing waters like the White River in Arkansas during high water generation and casting 7- to 9-inch flies.

Scientific Angler Streamer Express (50-foot head). Developed by Kelly Galloup, this is a longer version of the Orvis Depth Charge. It's a favorite of mine when making longer casts on rivers that possess uniform currents. Because of the long 50-foot sinking section, the fly maintains a level retrieve through a longer range of motion. This line is rated to sink at approximately 6 inches per second.

RIO's Outbound Custom Line. A favorite for when I'm float-fishing big water and I need my lines to sink like a rock. For example, during peak generation times on the White River, the baitfish are pushed close to the bank where trout feed. Because of the extreme flows created by the dam release, fishable pockets of water may be found only 2 to 5 feet off the bank. If the trout are holding closer to the bottom near drop-offs and I am fishing from a moving boat, my drift will be short enough that my fly will be at the trout's feeding level within one or two strips of the retrieve. I use this specialty line in these kinds of extreme conditions. This line only comes in two sizes: T11 (11 grains per foot) and T14 (14 grains per foot). T11 is rated to sink at up to 8 inches per second while T14 sinks up to 9 inches per second. Each line has a head length of 35 feet, which means you need to cut the head length to match the line weight of the rod. For example, if I am using T14 (14 grains per foot) and need 350 grains to match the action of my 8-weight rod, I'll fish a head of approximately 25 feet (350 divided by 14). Because of the thin running line and short, aggressive head, this line is difficult to mend. Instead, it is designed to cast bigger flies with ease and to quickly drop your presentation into the trout's kill zone.

Dropping a small nymph off a streamer is a system I rarely use, but I see friends such as Lance Wilt use it with continued success. I enjoy fishing with anglers who have different views on streamer approach. Doing so always provides me with a piece of humble pie and reinforces that my approach isn't always the best method.

Sinking-Tip Lines

Sinking-tip lines are great tools when wade-fishing or fishing right off the banks. As the name implies, the tip of the fly line has a sinking head that transitions into a floating rear section. Sinking tips come in a variety of sink ranges (intermediate to type 7) and lengths (4-foot tips through 24-foot tips). The advantage of sinking tips lies in the angler's ability to mend the floating line section anytime throughout the drift. Full-sinking lines can be mended immediately after the presentation (before the line sinks too deep), but sinking tips can be manipulated any time during the presentation. This is important for any angler who wants to quickly change the path of the retrieve for presentation effect or to move it away from an obstacle.

For fishing central Pennsylvania's medium-size streams where shorter casts are necessary, I prefer to use a sinking-tip section no longer than 15 feet. This length of sinking tip gives you the ability to reposition the floating section to achieve a different retrieval path or to increase or decrease tension through mending. At least 4 or 5 feet of floating line needs to be on the water to mend/reposition the line. If I'm casting approximately 20 feet and my sinking-tip section is 24 feet, this means the entire length of line on the water is sinking, which will not allow me to mend throughout the retrieve as the line continues to sink toward the bottom.

I'll typically use sinking-tip lines for swinging streamers down-and-across rather than fishing directly upstream. The problem with fishing these lines upstream is that a large part of the fly line is below the surface, which creates less tension and thus less contact with the flies. Remember that the faster currents are near the surface and that a full floating line lies entirely on those faster currents, creating more downstream drag. This is good when fishing streamers upstream, because the increased tension creates a better connection with the streamers. A sinking-tip line is smaller in diameter, so it creates less tension because of the smaller surface area and because the sinking section is positioned lower in the slower currents. It should also be noted that the two levels where the fly line is positioned (sinking and floating) can create an upward angle during faster or longer retrieves.

The same characteristics that limit sinking-tip lines' ability to fish upstream make them great tools for slowly swinging streamers down-and-across stream. There are times when trout prefer to have a slower-presented fly, and a sinking-tip line is able to slow the swinging speed down because part of the fly line is anchored in the slower currents lower in the water column.

RIO StreamerTip Fly Line (15-foot sinking tip) in both a type 3 (3 inches per second) and type 6 (6 inches per second). The 15-foot sink tip is also useful when working streamers deep around boulders. The short sinking section allows you to present your streamer deep, and it's short enough that the sinking portion won't wrap around every boulder.

Sinking-Line Alternatives

If you don't want to purchase multiple sinking tips or carry a variety of sinking tips with you along the stream, using poly leaders or any manufacturer's add-on sinking tip is a decent alternative. One reason I feel some anglers fail to capitalize on optimal streamer conditions is because they're caught without the right tools. However, poly leaders can turn any floating line into a sinking tip, and they take up very little space in your leader wallet. Using a loop-to-loop connection, a poly leader, or any sinking leader can get you fishing your streamer deeper in the water column within a minute. While Orvis isn't the only manufacturer selling this product, I've been very pleased using the company's three sinking versions of poly leaders: intermediate (1.9 inches per second), fast (3.9 inches per second), and ultrafast (6.1 inches per second). While convenient to carry and easy to take on or off the line, the line/leader connection can create a kick in your presentation, unlike a manufactured sinking-tip line where the sinking section is smoothly integrated into the floating line.

Stretching the line reduces memory and allows for easier line management. If you don't have a fishing buddy to hold onto your line, impale the streamer on a soft piece of wood. Strip out the length of line you plan on fishing with, pinch the line between the rod hand and the cork, and pull on the line, keeping it stretched for 20 to 30 seconds. This will reduce line memory and make for easier line management.

The streamer game often includes casting and retrieving long lengths of line. One of my biggest frustrations comes when line tangles during and after the cast. While stretching line isn't a total remedy to tangled lines, it greatly reduces its occurrences, especially for tungsten-coated sections. You can use a tree to stretch out the line or have a friend help you. The key is to create enough tension on the line that you feel the line stretching out like a tight muscle. When I find myself getting tangled on every other cast, I take a few minutes to stretch out the line. JAY NICHOLS

GET A GRIP

Little things make a difference, and this is one of the small preparations that allow for better streamer hookups: When you are strip-setting (using the line hand to set the hook), your thumb, index finger, and middle finger on the line hand need to create enough force to set the hook. If the land hand is too smooth or slippery, you may not get a good enough hold on the line to set the hook. This is why I rarely put lotion or any type of covering on the top half of my thumb and index and middle fingers. I don't want the line to slip through my fingers. Instead, I want enough friction on my fingers so I get the best grip during the hook set. During the winter my hands get so dry that I have to apply lotion to keep them from cracking. But winter is also my favorite time for streamer fishing, and I noticed in the past how the line kept slipping through my hands when setting the hook. I simply couldn't get a good enough grip, since my line fingers were coated with lotion. As a result, I now refrain from placing lotion on the insides of my fingers, which keeps them dry like sandpaper. The result is a better grip on the line during the strip-set and better hook sets. ■

LEADERS AND TIPPET

Streamer leaders are simple in design when compared to dry-fly and nymphing leaders. This is because streamer anglers use a variety of specialized fly lines to get the fly down to a specific level and to achieve a specific type of retrieve. They're not relying on the leader's taper to turn over the fly—the weight of the fly line or the fly itself does that. Most of my leaders comprise two or three sections of heavy fluorocarbon or Maxima. The latter is a nylon material that many anglers feel is just as good or even better than fluorocarbon, and it's the only nylon material I would recommend for streamer fishing. Even larger-diameter nylons will abrade quicker when being pulled over boulders and other sunken obstructions. Maxima has both the knot strength and abrasion-resistance of fluorocarbon, but it's far more visible when in the water. When you're retrieving 6-inch streamers through the water column, a trout's hunger and aggressive instincts can peak to a point where the fish doesn't have time to inspect the pattern and will thus use less caution during its approach. Remember, streamers' drifts are often faster than those of nymphs or dry flies.

I use fluorocarbon for its knot strength and abrasion-resistance. Buying and tying flies both cost money, so I do everything I can to protect my investment. Spending a few extra dollars on fluorocarbon will save you time and money by reducing unnecessary breakoffs.

I feel fluorocarbon tippet may be more effective when fishing streamers at a slower pace during low and clear water conditions. When building leader mid and butt sections, I use P-Line Fluorocarbon, which you can purchase in 250-yard spools. For most trout fishing, 25-, 20-, and 15-pound weights suffice. Very rarely should you break off a fly while streamer fishing. Basically, you're fishing a larger fly and fishing it at a speed that permits you to use "rope," since the trout doesn't have time to fully inspect the presentation.

A nonslip loop knot allows the fly to slide freely around the knot. Every bit of additional movement is helpful.

If you fish a sinking line with an unweighted streamer, choose a leader length that corresponds with the stream's pockets or holding lies. In this turbulent pocketwater, I would choose to fish a short leader (2 to 3 feet) to ensure both line and fly are positioned in the same current. The wider the distance between current seams, the longer the tippet length that you can use successfully. I'm not overly concerned with the fly being located too close to the fish in pocketwater, as the trout often has a short period in which to make a decision on whether or not to strike.

The other advantage of heavier-diameter fluorocarbon is abrasion-resistance. Streamer retrieves are aggressive, with the angler sometimes ripping the leader and tippet material over rocks and other obstructions. While I don't recommend it, there was a period where I fished the same 0X fluorocarbon streamer rig (leader, tippet, and fly) for two weeks straight without changing tippet or fly.

However, when fishing smaller streamers or during low-water conditions, I'll use RIO Fluorocarbon Plus in 0X through 3X diameters. While the RIO 0X is rated for 15 pounds, it's significantly smaller in diameter than the P-Line material. On the flip side, if I'm retrieving streamers along a stream bottom laced with sharp rock edges, I'll go with a thicker-diameter line such as P-Line's 15-pound line over the RIO Fluorocarbon Plus 0X because it will hold up better to abrasion.

When I fish light tippets (2X and 3X), it's only during times when the water is low or clear, or when I need to fish my streamer very slow. Fishing small flies on a slow retrieve allows the trout more time to look over the presentation before deciding whether or not to strike. Most often, streamer anglers are fishing their patterns at speeds that allow for significantly heavy tippet materials, including 0X and larger diameters.

In my opinion, streamer leaders are pretty straightforward. I categorize streamer leaders into three categories:

1. **Level tippet:** I use a piece of level (straight-diameter) tippet when fishing sinking lines with patterns 6 inches or larger. Patterns of this size (weighted or nonweighted) normally have enough mass to propel themselves to the target without needing the taper of the leader to assist.

2. **Two-section tippet:** I use two-section tippets when fishing medium-size streamers 3 to 5 inches in length and when fishing either a floating, a sinking-tip, or a full-sinking line. While flies of this size do possess significant mass, I find that a tapered leader helps when presenting the fly to the target. This leader formula is right from *Modern Streamer Strategies* by Kelly Galloup and Bob Linsenman.

3. **Three-section tippet:** When fishing microstreamers (those 2 inches and smaller), I find that a three-section tapered leader is needed to create enough energy to present the fly along with a smaller-diameter tippet to delicately lay the fly on the water. I've used this three-section leader for both floating and sinking lines.

nail knot
tippet ring

When you want a shorter leader (2 or 3 feet), use a straight piece of tippet, as there's no need for a tapered leader at that length. There are two possible methods for fishing a short leader.

The top illustration shows the loop cut off from line, where a short 8-inch section of 30-pound Maxima Chameleon or Ultra is connected to the line using a nail knot followed by a medium-size (3/32-inch) tippet ring. The tippet ring will allow you to continue to add or take off tippet without cutting back on the line.

The bottom illustration shows the angler using a loop-to-loop connection between the line and the straight leader section. I prefer to only use a loop-to-loop connection between the line and leader when using a heavy diameter tippet (15-pound or higher). Smaller diameter tippets and leaders connected with a loop-to-loop have a tendency of cutting through the coating. If you prefer to use a smaller diameter leader or tippet, consider using the method in the top illustration.

loop to loop

Shorter leaders on a sinking line create better contact between the angler and fly, as there is less slack. However, this shortening of the leader also results in less diving motion, as short leaders (say, 2 to 4 feet) cause both the line and fly to ride at approximately the same level. This relationship causes less diving action and a more parallel retrieve.

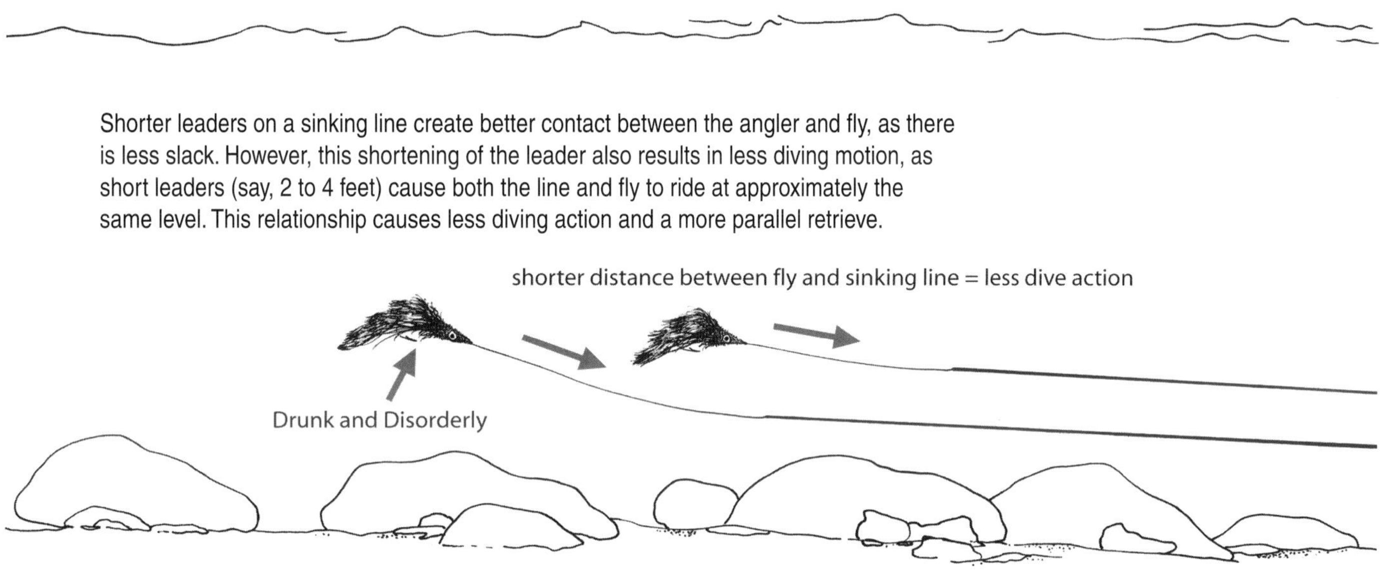

shorter distance between fly and sinking line = less dive action

Drunk and Disorderly

Length of leader will determine how close a streamer rides to stream bottom. My preferred approach is a sinking line with a buoyant streamer, as the streamer will ride above the sinking line and move downward during the retrieve. The fly will not ride as deep as a weighted fly and sinking line, but it will have more movement.

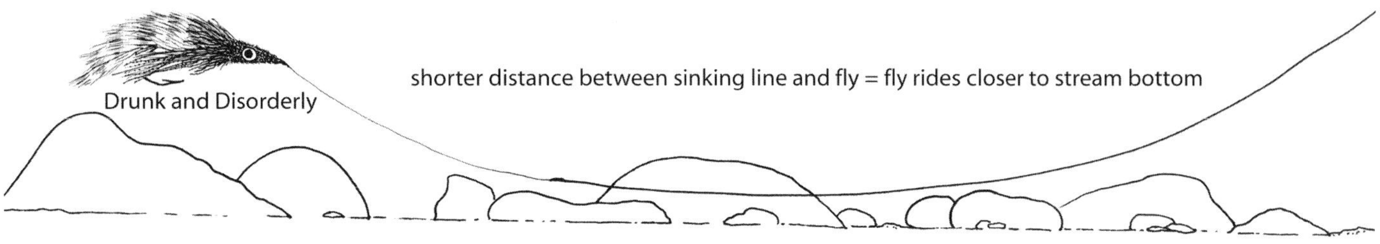

Drunk and Disorderly

shorter distance between sinking line and fly = fly rides closer to stream bottom

nail knot triple surgeon's knot

4' 20 lb. 4' 10 lb.

This simple design for long leaders with a heavy streamer and sinking or floating line comes straight from Kelly Galloup. When fishing large or heavily weighted streamers, a simple two-section leader is often all you need to present the fly, especially with heavily weighted streamers where the weight of the pattern will help carry itself toward the target. Again, I prefer to use Maxima Chameleon or Ultra Green for the butt section along with a fluorocarbon tippet. When using longer leaders on either floating or sinking lines, I use a leader anywhere from 8 to 10 feet. A nail knot is used in this illustration to connect the leader to line. While I still use the nail knot to make this connection, I've begun using the loops on certain fly lines. For example, as of this writing, the Orvis lines have (in my opinion) one of the most durable loops on the market. As a result, I've begun to use loop-to-loop connections, as this allows me to exchange leaders without cutting back on the line.

It's personal preference, but when using a smaller streamer (size 8 or smaller), I prefer a tapered leader to help turn over the fly, especially if it's lightly weighted. You can use a standard knotless tapered leader or build your own. I choose to build my own streamer leaders and use three sections. I prefer to use Maxima Chameleon or Ultra Green for the top two sections, followed by a medium 3/32-inch Anglers Image Tippet Ring. This tippet ring is heavier in diameter and designed to fish heavier rigs, including streamers. Then you can connect a straight section of fluorocarbon tippet to the tippet ring, using your favorite tippet-to-fly knot. This is my standard leader when fishing smaller streamers on either floating or sinking line, and it runs between 9 and 10 feet.

ACCESSORIES

The right accessories are a must-have for any streamer angler. Accessories allow you to deal with any situation along the stream, whether its sharpening hooks or needing a new nail-knot after a snag rips off the original knot. When choosing a pack for streamer fishing, think about how you fish. While I prefer to keep my accessories to a minimum, there are a handful of streamer tools I carry at all times.

Hook hone. One of the most common mistakes in streamer fishing is not sharpening your hooks, so a hook hone is a must-have piece of equipment. It's inevitable that hooks will become dull when being stripped past boulders. The thumbnail test will determine if you need to sharpen your hooks: To test your hook, slide the hook point over your thumbnail. A sharp hook will create a small groove on your nail. If this doesn't happen, then you should sharpen the hook. I have lost so many fish because I didn't take the time to sharpen my hook points. You need to check the hook and make sure its point is sharp anytime you snag bottom. Another consideration, especially if you are fishing from a boat and have the storage space, is to use a cordless Dremel with a file. A few of my friends who are muskie fanatics use this tool to keep their flies sharp at all times.

Besides carrying a hook hone while along the stream, I also sharpen my hooks before fishing each fly. For whatever reason, I've found that not all hooks are equally sharp coming from the factory. As a result, after de-barbing each fly, I take a moment to resharpen the hook before placing it back into the box.

You should pay attention to your hook point before, during, and after fishing. A hook hone is a must—it's my favorite streamer tool. I will sharpen the point of even top-quality hooks straight out the pack. Make sure to purchase hooks with points that allow for easy maintenance. Test the sharpness of the hook; the point needs to be able to stick into your fingernail with little pressure.

Eyewear. By now everyone knows about the advantage good polarized optics give you in reading the stream bottom. However, with streamer fishing I look at glasses more as eye protection. This is due to the nature of the patterns I fish, with their heavy dumbbell-style heads and large hooks. A great

When fishing from a boat, a large net is an absolute must for landing larger fish. I've lost too many fish while trying to land them by hand from a moving boat. A net allows you to land larger fish with speed, which means getting the fish back to the water quicker.

example of how optics work as eye protection while streamer fishing comes from my friend Tommy Lynch. Tommy is a streamer fanatic who also runs mousing trips under the cloak of darkness in Michigan, and he makes his clients wear clear safety glasses at night to protect from the frequent bad casts.

You need to see and read the stream the same way a nymph fisher reads the water—noticing the drop-offs, looking for depressions, or picking up any location from which a trout could ambush prey. Since the best time for streamer fishing often occurs during low light, I prefer a lighter-colored lens to help illuminate low light and help me read the water. I'm currently using Smith's Low Light Ignitor glasses anytime during low-light conditions. Other options could include a yellow or amber-colored lens, which allows more light to reach your eyes.

Line cleaner. A clean line that moves smoothly through the guides is an absolute necessity, not just for better casting but, more importantly for me, for a smoother and more sensitive retrieve. I've already detailed my line-cleaning routine at home, but in the field, I carry a handful of single-use line cleaning pads. They pack easy and require no preparation—just run the line through the pad, and you're ready to fish.

Nail knot tool. When fishing heavy tippets, I've had nail knot connections fail before the tippet material broke. This tool ensures that you'll be able to reattach a leader to your fly line in the event that either the nail knot or the loop breaks off.

Leader materials. I prefer fluorocarbon to nylon for several reasons. First, fluorocarbon has a greater resistance to abrasion than nylon. This is an important thing to consider when pulling streamers in shallow but rocky stream bottoms, where your leader and tippet are running over rock edges. Second, fluorocarbon has approximately 30 percent stronger knot strength over nylon once wet. Third, it's stiffer than most nylons, which I believe provides greater connection to the rig. I carry four sizes of fluorocarbon with me for most of my streamer work: 20-pound, 15-pound, 12-pound, and 10-pound, all of which I carry on a single tippet post. These four sizes allow me to build any streamer leader, whether I'm targeting monster brown trout with a triple-articulated streamer pattern on Arkansas's White River or chasing small brook trout on central Pennsylvania mountain streams.

Interchangeable sinking tips. These allow anglers to easily convert any floating line into a sinking tip via a loop-to-loop connection. While I prefer to have a seamless transition from sinking head to floating line, these are useful for the minimalist or for those who don't wish to purchase a separate spool and sinking-tip line. Most manufactures who make this product offer a short (approximately 7 feet) and a long (12 feet) sinking-tip portion that ranges from intermediate (an approximately 1 inch per second sink rate) to type 6 (6 inches per second).

Fly boxes/storage. I use two types of boxes for my streamer patterns: storage and working boxes. For storage, I

Make sure to check your leader for abrasions after every hang-up or snag. It only takes one big fish lost due to laziness to remind me to keep checking my rig for any potential issues.

own three large briefcase-style boxes to organize my flies into small, medium, and large categories. These are my organized storage facilities, from which I can pull all the flies needed for the day. My "small" case contains microstreamer patterns in sizes 8 to 12. My "medium" box holds all flies from size 4 through 6, while my "large" box holds all flies size 4 and larger, along with all my articulated streamers. These three boxes are normally stored at my house or in my car. Only if I'm fishing from a boat—where I have ample storage—will I carry these boxes with me.

For a working box, I carry an Umpqua Pro Guide (UPG) streamer-style box. This single box can hold up to twenty articulated streamers—more than enough to last me half a season. The aspect I like most about UPG boxes is the Zerust insert, which reduces and controls rust. Streamer patterns are expensive and time-consuming to tie, so the last thing I want is to open up my box to find that all my hook points are rusted. Zerust is especially useful for protecting streamer patterns, which are bulky and hold moisture more than other patterns. This is important for the angler who is constantly changing streamer patterns, especially those tied with natural materials like bunny and wool.

Leader wallet. This older fly box style has a lot of utility for streamer patterns. Today's streamer boxes are wider to accommodate the larger patterns modern anglers are fishing.

You shouldn't lose many streamers along the stream. Instead of stocking one style, carry a variety of sizes and types to deal with varying conditions.

When you develop confidence with a particular streamer, make sure to tie it in several colors and sizes to match varying conditions.

Many of the tactics discussed in the book can be applied to any gamefish. Here Blane Chocklett shows off his most recent innovation—the Game Changer. The Game Changer is similar to the Clouser Minnow in the sense that it can be adapted to target certain species. JAY NICHOLS

A leader wallet fits easily into any pocket and can carry upward of a dozen streamers. I use my leader wallet as a working streamer box and rarely find myself reaching for my sling pack. This wallet has two compartments for carrying several spools of tippet, which is all I need when streamer fishing. JAY NICHOLS

Right: To reduce the odds of impaling yourself when tightening a knot to the fly, use a pair of pliers to hold the streamer when cinching the knot.

These bulkier designs do a good job of accommodating larger patterns, but often are difficult to fit into vests and packs because of their size. Leader wallets, on the other hand, will hold a small variety of streamers and can be worn around the neck or slid into a pocket. When you're done fishing, it's important to open up the wallet and allow it to dry. The wallet's one downfall is that the slim design will compress your flies. The leader wallet I use was designed by Vedavoo. It fits easily into any pocket and takes up very little space when compared to a traditional streamer box.

Window patch dryer. When I'm wade-fishing with my streamer pack, I use a large foam insert as my working bench. Most packs on the market today have this foam insert. This "bench" will hold recently used flies and those that I plan to fish with. Velcro strips are attached to the bottom, allowing me to move it from my pack to my car's dashboard to dry. I keep this insert inside my pack—not on the outside—because I have the tendency to knock these flies off the insert into the water while fishing or walking through the woods.

I will normally carry two patches, one for darker colors and another for lighter ones. Anyone who has fished and put a soaked black Woolly Bugger next to a white one will remember that dyes do run. I hate to throw away an otherwise perfectly fine streamer that has been tie-dyed. Separating wet streamer patterns in the field will save you time and money in the long run. Immediately after the fishing trip, I will take each of these inserts out of my box and place them on my dashboard or other area to dry.

Sling pack. I don't think there is one perfect pack for all conditions, so I own several styles of packs and vests. For the days when I am committed to fishing streamers, I use a sling pack, which allows me to carry enough gear yet stays out of the way when fishing. You can position the sling on your backside when fishing, which keeps everything away from the moving line and line hand. Think about the continuous hand motion needed when retrieving streamers; now think about how any item (forceps, lanyard, tippet posts, and so on) hanging in front of you becomes a potential snag for line. Too often I have failed to execute a strip-set because my line wrapped around the tippet caddy hanging on my vest. By having all my gear stowed away in the back, it opens up space for both my rod and line hand to move without colliding with equipment on my chest. (I'm normally not concerned with this when fishing dry flies or nymphs because the line hand will move in a slower and more controlled manner.) Streamer tactics often call for fast and furious line-hand movements, where line is near the chest or waist

A sling pack is a great tool for the streamer angler because it can be stowed away from the action of the rod and line hand. I prefer to keep my chest and stomach area free and clear of any potential snags, and a sling offers me the option of keeping all my gear stowed on my back while fishing. I use the eye of my zipper to hold my streamer in place when I need to use both hands for another job like pulling a fly box from the depths of my sling. JAY NICHOLS

area. That's why I prefer to have all my equipment positioned on my backside or stuffed in my waders.

I currently use the Orvis Guide Sling Pack. Its large capacity allows me to stow several streamer boxes, extra spools, and ample tippet along with other miscellaneous accessories. I enjoy the pack's clean design, which minimizes the chance of the line snagging. When streamer fishing, I want the area below my chest to be clear of any snags, and this style of pack offers me that luxury.

Stripping guard. During a streamer retrieve, the line can pass over one of the lower fingers on your rod hand as your line hand pulls in the line. If the line is textured, this increases the rate of the line cutting through your finger. Even nontextured lines being quickly pulled over a finger enough times will create a cut. This item slides onto your finger where the line passes over and protects your finger from cuts and grooves.

Hot Hands. Nothing is more frustrating than not having your hands work when retrieving a streamer during cold weather. I'll slide a pack of Hot Hands down each of my fingerless gloves during cold conditions. Although they add additional bulk to your gloves, the Hot Hands have kept my hands functioning during the coldest weather conditions.

Fish hand net. Instead of carrying a net, I've begun using a fish hand net to secure larger fish. This tool's mesh allows you to securely grab the fish's tail and hold the fish while you safely remove the fly without having to touch any additional part of the trout's body. If done correctly, you'll take less slime away from the trout and likely place the fish under less stress.

Use a system you have confidence in. My friends Richard Strolis and Matt Grobe (pictured) both prefer to use a floating line with weighted streamers. Experiment with a variety of rigs, and find the one that best suits you and the waters you fish. Confidence is everything. No matter how good the rig is, your efforts will be marginal if you lack confidence in your tools. ANDY GROBE

A good rubberized net is easier on the fish and often makes retrieving a fly easier as well—allowing you to release the trout with greater speed. Pictured is Paul Weamer holding a nice brown.

Left: Always have a spare rig ready when fishing sinking lines. I've accidently stepped on sinking lines with cleats and have severed a sinker when working streamers near rocky bottoms.

Predator and Prey

Predicting trout behavior is about as difficult as predicting the weather—you're never going to get it right every time, but often you guess correctly. Some may claim to have a pretty good handle on trout behavior, but I do not. I approach the trout stream with theories rather than absolutes. My approach is based on what I believe is going to happen (based on my experience, information from other anglers, and scientific research) rather than what always does happen. It's important to remember that we can't call our shots like Babe Ruth.

The trout will tell you what they want, and you will have to adjust your tactics to meet their needs. My friend John Stoyanoff says it best: "You cannot dictate to the trout." Meaning, you must first try to develop a streamer approach to match the conditions you're faced with. It's far more of a guessing game than an exact science. However, having a basic understanding of both the predator (trout) and its prey (baitfish) allows you to ask fewer questions and find a quicker path to success. It's like a successful relationship between two people, one in which one

The early bird gets the worm. One of my favorite things is to be on the water before daybreak and get an hour of fishing in before the family wakes. Large trout prefer to feed in low light, and the first thirty minutes of daylight have provided some of my best streamer sessions. Although many know this, I rarely see another angler on the water at daybreak, even during prime season.

On streams like Michigan's Muskegon River, an angler may mistake a riseform like the one in this illustration for a trout taking an insect off the surface. In early May 2006, I made the same mistake while fishing the Muskegon, where I noticed trout surfacing along the edges of slack water. A local guide told me these were the riseforms of trout eating salmon fry near the surface. He instructed me to swing a floating line, a long 10-foot leader with either a single or double lightly weighted fry pattern. Immediately, I began moving fish—thanks to that local angler who shared his advice.

person first thinks about the other person's feelings before making a decision. The best strategy I can think of is to put myself in the trout's position, think about its needs and wants, and develop a strategy to satisfy the needs of the trout.

For all the research that has been done concerning trout behavior, the modern angler is still left with as many questions as his predecessors. Studies have been conducted to determine preference in food colors, trout movement, feeding behaviors—the list goes on. Yet I have never had a day when I was able to predict the entire day's events. All I have to work with each time on the stream is what little knowledge I've retained over the years through my own experiences, through reading fishing literature, and by listening to knowledgeable anglers. My goal with this chapter is to share with you my knowledge regarding predatory trout behavior, to the point where your streamer playbook leads you to slightly more wins than losses.

Trout are like any living creature—they take advantage of feeding opportunities. While the focus of this book is salmonids, especially trout, the information here can be applied to other predatory fish species. Understanding trout feeding habits and behavior is the first step in becoming a decent streamer angler. Some of the best streamer guys I know behave like a military sniper—after carefully sneaking into position, they study the movements and behavior of the enemy. While I don't consider trout to be an enemy, to be a good streamer angler, you must study the movements of predatory fish. And when I say predatory fish, I'm speaking about any size fish that will attack a baitfish or similar-size prey.

In addition to exhibiting feeding behavior, trout will also attack your fly out of aggression. There are periods when trout hunt and periods when they rest. Typically, low-light periods are when piscivorous trout are hunting for prey, as that is when a trout's prey is hunting insects. Then there are times when a trout is resting and the streamer pattern invades its personal space, causing the trout to strike out of pure aggression.

Resting often occurs during periods of high illumination (i.e., when the sun is brightest). But then there are several days every year when during high sun you can't keep the trout off your fly. These are the days that make me scratch my head trying to understand. What triggers a stream's entire trout population to begin hunting baitfish on a sunny day? I have yet to find those answers.

Finally, there a couple days each year when you come across a phenomenon that really leaves you guessing. There have been several occasions where I've caught several nice brown trout measuring in the mid to high teens, with crayfish or sculpin already hanging out of their mouths. We're talking about food items that measure one-fifth of the total length of the trout—more than enough to keep a trout satisfied for several days. You can feel the trout's belly is full of prey, which makes you wonder: Was the fish hungry, aggressive, or opportunistic? Trout are not on the same meal plan as the predatory anglers that chase them. Trout don't have the privilege of stopping at a local fast-food joint or a restaurant where they can order anytime. They don't know when their next meal is going to happen, and so they will often capitalize on the next feeding opportunity.

This chapter aims to provide a picture of the general behavior of both predatory trout and some of their favorite forage. Understanding trout behavior will aid you in developing a better approach as it relates to where to fish, because predatory trout will hold in specific ambush locations to feed. Variables such as time of year, amount of sunlight, and water clarity will affect when predatory fish move into such locations. There are always a few surprises, but having a basic understanding of where predatory fish hold will allow you to isolate likely holding spots, which will reduce the number of casts you make to unlikely holding water.

Understanding the behavior of specific baitfish will allow you to develop patterns and presentations that mirror the actions of the natural. This is similar to matching the hatch. For example, mayflies come in a variety of sizes and colors. Mayfly nymphs are classified as swimmers, burrowers, or clingers. Each insect thrives in its own environment and behaves in its own manner. As a result, fly fishers tie and fish patterns to match the naturals. The same is true with baitfish. Not all baitfish behave the same or live in the same water types. Understanding the basic shapes, movements, and general behaviors of the different types of baits provides anglers with some direction when picking a pattern, rig, and presentation. Basic information such as color, shape, habitat, and behavior will provide a general idea of the tactics and tools needed to increase success.

So much of my streamer approach came from my experiences fishing with live minnow and spinner anglers. (Joe Humphreys always talks about the lessons he learned from the live minnow men of Penns Creek, Pennsylvania.) One of my greatest streamer mentors is my father-in-law, Walt Dickey. Walt was and is (at times) a minnow fisherman. I believe it's almost impossible for a streamer fly fisher to keep up with a good live minnow fisher; a good live minnow fisher is a large trout's worst nightmare. One of the first lessons I learned from Walt came while watching him fish live minnows and sculpins on a local stream. His approach with the live minnow was the opposite of my streamer tactic. Instead of casting across the stream and retrieving at a fast pace like I was doing with my fly rod, Walt would cast directly upstream. He would hold the rod

The great thing about fishing from a boat is that you don't need to carry your gear. Instead, you can keep everything stowed in your boat box.

Chris Willen shows off a quality muskie. The tips in this book will help you catch any apex predator. LANCE WILT

tip high in the air and allow his minnow to drop to the desired depth. (In this case, it was winter, and Walt was sinking his minnow close to the bottom before retrieving.) Once the bait achieved the desired depth, he would slowly reel in the slack line as the minnow was drifting downstream. He wasn't retrieving the minnow—he was simply taking in the slack as the current carried the minnow. His drifts were long (averaging 80 to 100 feet) in comparison to the 15- to 20-foot retrieves I was making.

The one thing I will say for Walt was that he showed no mercy toward his future son-in-law. One would think that Walt would take it easy on me after he was up ten fish to none. But no, he continued to pound fish until I was willing to modify my rig, attach a heavier streamer, and begin casting upstream. Eventually I hooked into a couple fish, learning the value of going against the normal protocol of casting over-and-across the stream.

UNDERSTANDING THE FISHERY

What works on one river system may not prove useful on another. Michigan's famed fisheries—the Muskegon, Pere Marquette, Au Sable, and Manistee—are by far my favorite streamer waters. These lower-gradient waters snake through the northern parts of Michigan's lower peninsula and contain impressive collections of wet woody debris (aka logjams). Because of the abundance of cover, availability of baitfish, and heavy fishing pressure, fish in these rivers hold tight to the bank, even during low-light conditions. Streamers often need to be placed right off the bank, fewer than 6 inches off-target. You need to present tight to cover to encourage a take. The opposite is true on my home waters near central Pennsylvania, where less in-stream structure is present and where the larger predator fish will hold midstream throughout the day. As a result, you don't need to place the fly 2 inches off the bank—many of the larger fish will be holding closer to drop-offs or deeper waters.

While habitat influences where fish hold, the amount of food in any given stream also influences where you should be focusing your fishing efforts. When fishing healthy, biodiverse streams like Spring Creek—where aquatic insects, vegetation, and larger prey are living in every conceivable location—I find on-the-hunt trout everywhere. The rich aquatic life spreads bugs throughout the entire river, which in turn spreads sculpins and other larger prey throughout the water. As a result, I find I need to cover more water because there are fewer distinct locations to target trout with streamers. This is no different than when an angler nymph-fishes streams like the Bighorn, where trout can hold in every square inch of the river. An effective angler will slowly work each section of water.

When nymphing these types of waters, I'll divide the water into a grid of 3-foot-square sections. However, when streamer fishing these same waters, I'll double the grid. I've found trout are a little more willing to chase down a streamer than a cressbug. However, it's important to note that I'll focus my presentation longer on promising stream reaches than when angling streams with fewer trout. Why? Even with streamer fishing, trout living in rich streams have an abundance of larger prey available to them, meaning they don't have to chase down streamer patterns. It pays to cover all possible holding lies because trout will hunt throughout all water.

This is in contrast to the poorer fisheries, including some sterile freestone streams I fish, where much of the aquatic life is centered in the riffled sections during low-light periods when trout are hunting larger prey. This concentrates all levels of the food chain in those places and increases your odds of locating hunting trout. While trout will hunt in nonriffled sections, the majority of their feeding will occur where the baitfish are hunting insects in the riffled sections. While it may be more effective to focus on the riffled sections, you still need to present your streamer in other areas such as banks and tailouts; larger trout prey can be found in these areas. The only difference is that I make fewer casts into these areas, as trout in these streams are more competitive for food and more willing to chase down their prey.

It may seem like common sense, but the key to becoming a successful streamer fisher is to find fisheries where the trout population feeds on baitfish and other foods that you can imitate with streamers. For instance, on Spring Creek, cressbugs constitute a large portion of the trout's diet, but a healthy sculpin population has created an environment where 10-inch trout are also looking to eat baitfish. A number of years ago, I was running a nymphing class on Spring Creek when all of a sudden, my client asked me to show him some streamer tactics. It was a bright, sunny day and the water was low—typically not a good scenario for fishing streamers. I reiterated that the conditions would make it difficult to move even a single fish. However, after three casts I had moved and hooked two fish. Thinking it was a fluke; I went back to Spring Creek during similar conditions and experienced identical results. Even though I found that rainy days and higher water make better streamer days overall, fishing streamers here can be effective just about any time of the year. I believe this is because these trout are conditioned to feed on both insects and other fish year-round.

There are also streams I have fished where I believe the trout feed primarily on larger forage. There's a lesser-known stream in Pennsylvania I frequent that has an incredible minnow population with a mediocre macroinvertebrate (bug) population. This stream is also fished a lot by live minnow guys who keep their catch. Even though I promote catch-and-release, I do ask to watch as the live minnow guys clean their catch. In this particular stream, trout ranging from 13 to 19 inches contained mostly small minnows with very few bugs. In order to survive, the trout population in this stream had to learn how to become piscivores.

Tailwater Streamers

Johnson, Coghlan, and Harmon demonstrated in a March 2007 study of the diets of brown trout on the Little Red River tailwater in Arkansas ("Spatial and temporal variation in prey selection of brown trout in a cold Arkansas tailwater") that piscivorous feeding among larger brown trout was minimal. Cold water being released from the tailwater created a lack of forage opportunities for larger baitfish, such as minnows and sculpins. Instead, sow bugs constituted a large portion of the brown trout's diet. This is not to say that large tailwater trout will not eat a streamer, because they will. But trout in such locations have to be in the right mood to feed on larger food items.

These large tailwater trout feed mostly on smaller food items because they are not well trained to feed on larger food items. They have to position themselves in the primary currents, which are transporting smaller invertebrates. As a result, these fish are not holding in an ambush position, ready to attack the next passing forage fish. Typically, I have found the best times to approach these fish is during low light, when the bigger fish hold in shallows or near the bank in ambush mode. Of course, this is likely the best time to fish for any large trout. However, I have had far less success catching larger trout with streamers during daytime hours on similar tailwaters, where trout are likely to be looking for floating invertebrates (small bugs).

Bernie Taylor's book *Big Trout* (Lyons Press, 2005) details another study conducted on Arkansas's White River, another tailwater within two hours of the Little Red. According to

Rob Kinkopf caught this trout while using a floating line with a heavy jig fly along the edges of a weed bed along a South American spring creek. Streamer fishing doesn't always require a sinking line.
LANCE WILT

An angler transitions from daytime to nighttime on Colorado's South Platte River. The last thirty minutes of daylight can provide some of the best streamer action of the day. Larger trout (aka predatory fish) begin hunting the moment the sun sets.

Left: You can turn any nymph into a streamer by changing the presentation. Chris Daniel switched from suspending a Hare's Ear Nymph and began stripping with immediate results.

Taylor, local fisheries biologists classify the White River system as oligotrophic, meaning the river does not sustain a diverse food chain. Instead of focusing their feeding on sow bugs, as larger trout do in the Little Red, the White River trout begin to feed on sculpins and crayfish once the trout reach 13 inches. Taylor suggests that streamer fishing may be a better tactic (on average) on the White River rather than the Little Red, since trout are conditioned to feeding on larger prey.

The Allegheny River in Pennsylvania is another great example of how streamer tactics may not be the best tactic for targeting larger trout. This tailwater in the northwest section of the state is known for its large trout, but Damon Nepher, who knows the Allegheny better than anyone else, says that while he enjoys fishing streamers, he finds that nymphing is the most consistent method of catching the river's larger trout. While I haven't found any studies on Allegheny River trout, my suspicion is that fish in similar tailwaters spend more time feeding on smaller insects than they do chasing down larger food items due to the lack of available food items. This is not an uncommon occurrence with tailwaters.

Understanding Home Range

Trout behavior is difficult enough to try to predict. An angler will never "dial in" the fishery 100 percent of the time. Compounding this are studies that have shown contrasting behaviors between trout species. A 1997 study conducted on Idaho's Silver Creek by Young, Wilkinson, Phelps III, and J. S. Griffith ("Contrasting movement and activity of large brown trout and rainbow trout in Silver Creek, Idaho") analyzed the difference in home ranges between brown and rainbow trout. It was found that rainbows have a large home range (median of 606 meters) versus the brown trout (median of 131 meters). This suggests that the home range of a Silver Creek brown trout is slightly longer than a football field. In theory, this could mean that once a trout is spotted chasing your streamer, the trout will likely be holding in approximately the same location during the next fishing trip.

Streamer fishing is a tool for locating bigger fish. While holding in its resting area, a trout will still chase away prey or another large fish. The larger trout doesn't always strike your pattern, but it does give away its location. Building on the findings of the Silver Creek study, this may suggest you can come back during the periods of low or little light and likely have that same fish feeding within a short range of where it revealed itself. I have found similar results while fishing streams with a healthy food source. A stream rich in fish food means trout don't have to travel far to find their next meal. On one limestone stream that I fish about 120 days a year, I took one 16-inch brown trout about five times in one season (during both day and night), all within a 50-meter radius.

However, this isn't the case for all rivers. Several studies have documented the movements of the Au Sable River's brown trout. They've reported a range from 100 to 930 meters among the test subjects. Also documented was the fact that larger trout traveled a farther distance to feed during low-light periods. What does this mean for the angler? While the Au Sable is a healthy fishery, I would argue that many spring creeks and tailwaters possess a larger biomass of prey for trout, including the limestone stream that flows near my house. While considered a healthy trout stream, studies have shown that larger trout in the Au Sable River have a larger range than trout in other fisheries. This may make it more difficult for anglers to target a specific fish during the daytime. It's also worth noting that the Michigan study showed that most movement occurred during low-light periods as the trout was moving to its hunting grounds. This may suggest that an angler who moves a fish on a streamer pattern during the daytime may find it difficult to locate the same fish during lower-light periods. In the case of the Au Sable, the trout's hunting grounds could be up to 900 meters away from where you pulled it away from its resting spot.

An impressive brown trout taken from the Au Sable River in Michigan. This fish made short strikes several times before committing, which is typical of a prespawn brown trout. The moral of the story: If you hit and miss a fish during the fall, there's a good chance the same fish will come back on a follow-up attempt.

STREAMER ENVY

Some trophy trout hunters stick with fishing big flies, and if this is your goal, then fishing a large fly all day, often without a fish in the net, might be what is called for. But I like to catch fish, and that often means fishing smaller streamers on my local waters. One factor to consider when developing your streamer strategy is that you must first understand the biomass and the average size of the fish in the water you are hunting. Lately, I've developed a love affair with fishing large (4 to 7 inches long) Double Deceivers while fishing famed water such as the White River in Arkansas, the East and West Branches of the Delaware River in New York, and the South Holston River in Tennessee, along with many of the famed Michigan streams. However, my enjoyment of fishing those large streamers ends when I come back home to central Pennsylvania to fish. While this region is home to some of the best trout fishing in the East, there are a number of surveys confirming that we are not blessed with large populations of big predatory trout. There may only be a handful of trout in my home waters large enough to actually attack those big Double Deceivers, and attempting to throw these large flies would greatly reduce my chances of catching any fish.

Streamer design has become a competition to develop the largest or nastiest streamer pattern instead of considering how to catch fish with streamers. This recent craze has fly tiers developing the most amazing triple and even sometimes quadruple articulated patterns, some exceeding 7 inches. I enjoy fishing large articulated flies more than anything, but there's a time to fish them and a time to keep them in the box. While there is a correlation between big trout and big food items, not all big fish eat large food items all the time.

I have friends who only throw large flies in the hope of targeting large fish. And they do catch large fish, but there are times when they will go hours and sometime several days without moving a fish. But when do they move a fish, the size of the specimen is likely going to be substantial. I admire and respect these anglers, as they have far more patience than I do. They are essentially "trophy hunting" for large trout. I, on the other hand, simply enjoy retrieving streamers and feeling the tug of any trout. While I catch smaller fish than some of my trophy-hunting friends, I do occasionally connect with a large trout using smaller patterns. Just as with humans, large trout will snack on smaller food items (especially if larger prey isn't available), and I feel smaller streamers not only allow me to catch more fish but also large fish.

When playing a big fish and forced to keep the rod tip at a higher position, lock the rod butt against your forearm as you would when casting. Again, this anchors the rod into a fixed position and allows you to keep steady pressure on the fish. When you want to change direction, simply slide your forearm to another position. Steady forearm movements maintain tension on the rig and reduce the chances of creating a moment of slack, which I believe is the number one cause for lost fish. JAY NICHOLS

TIMING IS EVERYTHING

There are two known times when trout will strike a streamer. The first is when they are on the hunt and willing to eat a fly. I find this is the period when the trout are far more committed to inhaling your streamer pattern rather than striking it in the tail. This is the time streamer anglers enjoy the most, as trout that are hunting are not willing to play with their food. Anglers sometimes miss a fish on a streamer, getting a hit but not connecting. I've gotten buck fever several times, causing me to accidentally pull the fly out of the trout's mouth before it had time to inhale the fly.

Then there are periods when trout are more interested in resting than hunting food, which can trigger a different response. When another fish enters a trout's resting spot, it may strike out of aggression. A trout may inhale a pattern at this time, but more often than not, the trout will nip or short-strike at the baitfish as a means of keeping it away from the trout's holding area. For me, these short strikes occur more often during midday, when many piscivorous trout are resting. At times, the only response you get is a trout chasing your fly—only to move your fly away from your area and not eat it.

On average, low-light periods are hunting periods for trout and are more consistent times for the streamer angler. Macroinvertebrates and forage fish are photosensitive. The bugs that trout and forage fish eat are more active during periods of low light. Streamers imitate trout prey items that are higher on the food chain than these bugs, so several things have to happen before prime conditions for streamers exist. First, small insects need to come out from hiding and begin feeding on phytoplankton or in-stream vegetation. Then prey fish need to begin feeding on the insects eating the phytoplankton. Finally, the next level of predator—trout—needs to begin feeding on the prey fish.

Some of the best streamer fishing occurs when you are fishing at the exact time trout are chasing forage fish. Have you ever noticed that sculpins appear to be far more active during low-light periods? There have been a number of occasions while night-fishing when I shined my flashlight on a spot to see several sculpins in the open, yet they usually hide under in-stream structure during the day. Have you ever noticed there are low-light days where the stream bottom is covered with active crayfish, and these are the days when your hookup percentage is better? If smaller prey items leave their hiding areas to feed themselves, there's a good chance trout are also on the hunt, and that is a prime time to be fishing a streamer.

Lance Wilt holds a solid brown trout taken midstream during generation on the White River. When water levels are up, weighted heads (in this case a Fish Skull) in combination with fast-sinking lines help drop the streamer to the correct level, especially during periods when trout are holding tight to the stream bottom.

An early-morning view of the South Holston River during low flow. Although the water levels are low and clear, the early-morning light offers you a short period of opportunity to catch large trout before the fish head back to their daytime resting locations.

On these active hunting days, the trout is committed to eating your streamer pattern because it is on the hunt and hungry when chasing your food item. I miss far fewer fish during low-light periods compared to bright-light conditions. Why? I believe if a trout is hungry while chasing your streamer pattern, it will suck in your fly. This is why I prefer to streamer fish from right before dark to all the way through early morning, when there's a high probability that trout are actively hunting forage fish.

Midday streamer tactics are another story. Trout hold in resting lies and feeding lies; throughout the daylight periods, piscivorous trout are likely to hold in a resting location where there's little current—places like back eddies, deep pockets behind boulders, undercut banks with little or no current pulling through, and most slack water with any depth. The slack-water sections are often the areas anglers walk right through to get in position to cast to the other resting spots. But these are areas you should target, especially during daytime hours, as larger trout will seek slack water during nonhunting periods. I've found trout holding in resting spots are more likely to chase away your streamer instead of attempting to eat it. In this respect, daytime provides a great opportunity for you to locate larger trout by watching them move out of their resting spots to chase down a streamer.

However, even during the day, you can experience terrific streamer fishing. For example, think about your favorite tailwater fishery on a sunny day when it begins to release water. The increased water volume dislodges insects and moves them downstream. As a result, forage fish begin to eat the dislodged insects, and soon the piscivorous trout begin to hunt. All this occurs during the brightest period of the day.

Another example of excellent streamer fishing conditions during bright days is when you're downstream of a road project, where the road crew is digging close to the stream and disturbing the earth. Such a situation happened one day below my house when I was fishing a favorite section of water with nymphs. It was a sunny morning when suddenly the water began to turn off-color. We live along a trout stream, and for whatever reason our neighbors bought a flock of domestic ducks for their children. These ducks would often swim toward our house to be fed by our kids. One day in late September during a drought, all the trout were stacked in one pool below my house. This is also the same spot where my daughter and son fed the ducks. Before the ducks heard my kids calling for them, we were able to spot a large number of both forage fish and trout hugging the bottom. Soon the ducks arrived and my kids began feeding bread to the ducks. Before the ducks arrived, the water was almost static due to the low flows. As the ducks began feeding and fighting for each piece of bread, they began to disturb the stream bottom. Silt rose and soon the forage fish began to move into the cloudy water to feed on the insects. Within 30 seconds, a 16-inch trout that was holding at the rear of the pool quickly moved right up to the edge of the murky water and suddenly inhaled a feeding baitfish. All of this happened with my entire family standing 10 feet away on the high bank.

While you cannot always guess what days in the calendar are best for streamer tactics, there are some constants. For example, we know when dusk and dawn will occur every day. Trout, particularly larger trout, need to feed even during the summer months when flows are low and clear—not typically the best streamer conditions. However, sculpins and other bait-fish become active during this time, and streamer fishing can actually be excellent, but only if you are fishing the time period when trout are hunting forage fish. This is not new information—we have known for years the best time for streamers tactics is early and late in the day. Yet most of us don't take advantage of these prime forage fish feeding times.

Another item you should look at when deciding to streamer fish is the changing of lighting conditions. Trout like constants. They don't have eyelids or sunglasses to help them deal with sunlight. Their eyes will adjust to the changing light, but the process takes upward of thirty minutes. This becomes an issue when light conditions change every five minutes, such as on a partly cloudy day, when the sun lights up an area for a few minutes and then disappears and then appears again shortly

This fish, along with several others, was taken during one of the coldest days of the year, when water temps were around the mid-30s and air temps were below freezing (there was slush floating in the river). While there may be some general rules to follow in regards to conditions and trout behavior, there are just as many occurrences that tell me humans will never be able to predict how good the fishing will be. As they say: "The best time to fish is when you have time to do so"—you may find everything you've been told about ideal fishing conditions isn't always factual.

Postspawn is a great time to work a streamer, as trout are trying to replenish their body fat heading into the winter. This is the time I find trout more willing to eat a streamer.

Right: Small mountain streams are not only for the dry-fly enthusiast. Some of my most memorable days have been stripping small streamers in the mountain streams.

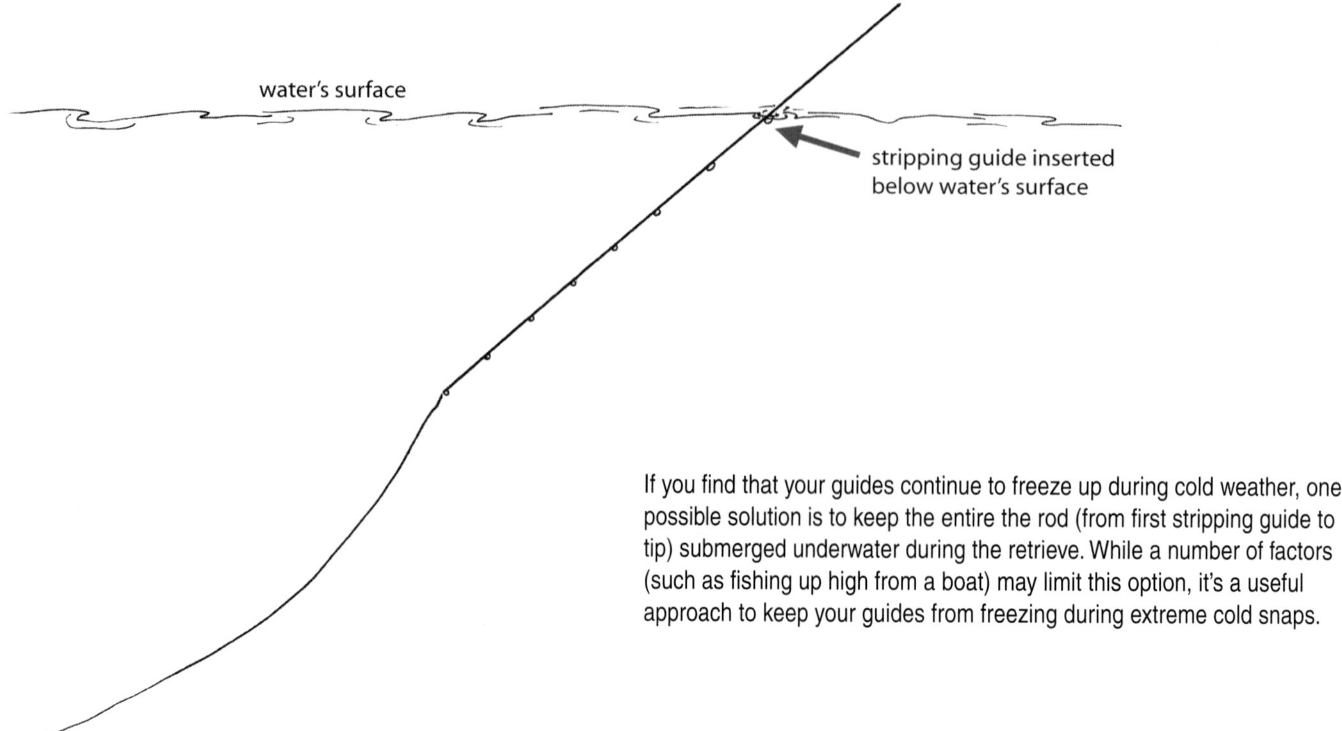

If you find that your guides continue to freeze up during cold weather, one possible solution is to keep the entire the rod (from first stripping guide to tip) submerged underwater during the retrieve. While a number of factors (such as fishing up high from a boat) may limit this option, it's a useful approach to keep your guides from freezing during extreme cold snaps.

thereafter. Trout will continue to feed but at a less consistent pace, especially when chasing larger prey items. Streamer tactics can still produce during these times, but they seem to be less consistent when compared to nymphing strategies.

The streamer angler who matches the type of retrieve to the trout's mood will produce better results. This is also true for nymph fishing, where there are times when insects are hatching and trout are looking for these emergers. The angler who creates a vertical drag in his nymphing presentation to mimic the insect movement that the trout are keying on is likely to catch more fish than the angler who is dead-drifting his pattern. When trout are in stalking mode (i.e., more likely to follow a fly before attacking) during the fall or any other time this mood occurs, you will be better off retrieving the pattern all the way back to the rod tip.

Serious streamer anglers are willing to give up fish numbers for an opportunity to feel the tug of a trout taking their fly. I've had many fishless mornings when fishing thirty minutes before work, but I was committed to feeling the tug of a trout. As my best friend Brian Wilt constantly reminds me in regards to mouse fishing at night, "It only takes one cast." However, there are periods when trout will not chase down a streamer, either for consumption or out of aggression. Very rarely will I fish a streamer midday in summer with low-water conditions. I enjoy the streamer game, but there are times when you need to be logical.

In my experience, springtime is when trout in central Pennsylvania are most committed to eating the fly. Since I have streamer fished these streams year-round (under a myriad of conditions) for the last twenty years, I feel confident in this statement. Whether it's due to the trout trying to catch up on their calorie counts after cold winter water temps or because the rest of the food chain is more active, trout appear to chase less during this period, and commit faster. We don't get the long follows where a trout will shadow your fly from the bank all the way back to your feet or boat, without any sign of attempting to kill the pattern. Instead, when I see a fish flash during the spring (indicating that it's moving toward my fly), a take normally occurs immediately thereafter. My friend Tommy Lynch says that when streamer fishing the banks in the spring, he usually has his clients pick up the fly after a couple good strips off the bank. As his countless hours guiding on many of the famed Michigan waters has taught him, springtime trout are more aggressive to eat at first sight—they attach almost immediately. As a result, he finds that fewer fish will stalk their prey all the way back to the boat and eat the streamer at the last minute. This is not always the case when fishing during the fall months.

In the fall the complete opposite scenario plays out. This is a theory, but I believe fall is when trout begin to focus more on procreation rather than food. As a result, it appears trout become more aggressive than hungry during this period. The trout isn't as likely to eat the streamer at first sight, but it will chase it. Too often, anglers make a couple retrieves, pick up their line, and fire right back to the bank. This may be good approach for the springtime, but this tactic will not be as effective during the fall months, where I've seen trout follow a fly 30 feet and finally commit to eating it when directly under the boat. Lynch has his clients fish their flies all the way back to the boats during this time because he finds fall trout will stalk their prey longer. This is not always the case, as there are days when fall trout commit immediately. This is just something I've witnessed, as have some of my best fishing friends, over the last twenty years of streamer fishing.

TROUT PREY

There are countless possible forage items to imitate when streamer fishing. For example, there's approximately seventeen species of minnows in Pennsylvania. We also have two sculpin families, along with other potential fish forage, including perch, baby suckers, and trout—just to name a few. It's not logical to attempt to represent every potential baitfish within a certain reach of water. However, these are some of my favorite forage fishes I feel trout will prey upon, and thus, items streamer anglers should pay attention to. It's important to know the size of the baitfish available to trout in the water that you are fishing and let that guide your decisions about how large a streamer you should fish.

Sculpins

Sculpins feed in low light and can be found in trout waters throughout North America. Although most members of the sculpin family are saltwater oriented, numerous freshwater species (including mottled and slimy sculpins) inhabit many of my local trout waters and provide trout with a high-protein meal. I don't feel it's necessary to tie patterns that exactly match each individual species. However, it is important to understand the behavior of each before designing and fishing streamers. For example, sculpins lack an air bladder—an organ that can inflate or deflate, allowing a fish to move vertically in the water column. Trout and other fish use an air bladder to move off the bottom and grab food at the surface. Sculpins can't move up and down the water column since they lack a swim bladder. As a result, this trout prey can only move horizontally on the stream bottom. This suggests that sculpin patterns should be fished close to the stream bottom via a heavily weighted streamer or with a fast-sinking line. Just as trout are conditioned to seeing spent mayfly spinners lie motionless on the water, they are also used to seeing sculpins move close to the stream bottom. That's not to say that trout will not eat a suspended sculpin pattern, because they will, but it's important to fish and tie streamers that provide the same look the naturals show to the trout.

Sculpins are robust, with a thick front portion that tapers down to a thin tail. They possess a broad head and large pectoral fins, giving them impressive girth for such a small fish. Many of the most effective sculpin patterns mimic this wide profile and slender taper. Sculpins are similar to chameleons in that they will change color based on the stream bottom. Some color schemes work better in certain fisheries. In central Pennsylvania the limestone bottoms of the spring creeks are often covered with dark green vegetation. As a result, sculpins in this region will also take on a dark olive appearance, which explains why "sculpin olive" is a favorite color for central Pennsylvania streamer anglers. This is in contrast to many of the famed Michigan streams, which have sandy bottoms and where sculpins take on a lighter body color. You don't have to carry ten different shades of sculpin patterns, but you should try to match the color of stream bottom you're fishing.

Sculpins spawn in the spring and will turn almost black, with orange bands around the pectoral fin. I'll find myself throwing a black-and-orange pattern like the Autumn Splendor or any black sculpin pattern with orange rubber legs. I use a fluorescent orange conehead to act as a hot spot during the sculpin spawn, similar to fishing a hot spot on a nymph pattern.

Blacknose Dace

Part of the minnow family, the blacknose dace inhabits some of the best headwater streams in the Eastern United States. Blacknose dace prefer moving waters and average 3 inches in length. The telltale sign of the blacknose dace is the long, horizontal black pinstripe along its lateral line. In Pennsylvania, the live minnow fishermen call them redfins. Many of the large trout in our local streams got big by eating 3- to 5-inch baitfish, and I've yet to cross paths with a large brown trout that would pass up a 5-inch meal.

Longnose Dace

Although found throughout North America, the longnose dace is more common in the East. The longnose dace prefers faster-moving waters than its cousin the blacknose dace, and it can reach up to 5 inches in length. It possesses a downward-sloping nose that helps it position and hold in faster-moving waters. During the five years I worked as a Fisheries Biologist Aide for the Pennsylvania Fish and Boat Commission, we identified and released back into the water an incredible number of longnose dace on the faster headwater trout streams in northcentral Pennsylvania.

Smaller Trout and Salmon (Fry)

My first significant understanding of the effectiveness of fry patterns came in 2007 on Michigan's Muskegon River while I was competing in a regional event for Fly Fishing Team USA. It was early May and I was part of a small group out on the water before the event. With little knowledge of the watershed, we began fishing nymphs with limited success. We heard trout rising on the surface, especially in the slack water. But we couldn't see any noticeable hatches, and it got to the point where I was using my net to seine the river to find what the trout were feeding on. Still I had no answers.

Leaving the river disappointed, we went to an evening gathering where all the competitors were drawing beats for the next day's competition. Luckily we sat at a table with two local guides, who listened to our story about the rising fish. They told us the trout were not feeding on insects, but instead were likely crushing salmon fry near the surface. As we found out, salmon fry will hold tight to the slack water near the edges during high water. This concentrates the fry along the slack water, which explained why most of the surface disruptions occurred near the bank. We took the guide's advice and tied a selection of 1½-inch salmon fry using chickabou. The next day we targeted the slack water with lightly weighted fry patterns on a dry line and had instant success. At least on the Muskegon River, a fry pattern is a good tool between mid-April and early June. This is another example of a local anomaly that streamer anglers need to be aware of anytime they're fishing streams with stocked or wild salmon runs.

GALLERY OF TROUT PREY

Profile is another important consideration when designing patterns. For example, the longnose dace is designed to hold in fast currents. Its "long nose" and narrow-bodied design are key features of this potential trout prey and should be replicated. The thin-bodied design will also reduce surface drag and allow you to fish the pattern more effectively in faster currents where the naturals live and are preyed upon by trout. ROB CRISWELL

Crayfish are known for stepping backward with their pinchers facing toward a potential predator as they try to escape. With this in mind, it may be useful to place the pinchers on the tail end of the hook. U.S. FISH AND WILDLIFE SERVICE

Top Right: Blacknose dace are a popular baitfish throughout my home waters in central Pennsylvania. You not only need to best represent the color, but also the size. Spending time capturing live bait with several live minnow fishermen near my home has shown me that the average size of the blacknose dace is approximately 3 to 5 inches. As a result, many of my dace patterns are also tied in that length range. ROB CRISWELL

Bottom Right: Try tying duller imitations of young rainbow trout. So many small rainbow patterns have excessive amounts of bright pinks and greens, which are more fitting for adult rainbows. ROB CRISWELL

Understanding trout prey is the first step to success. For example, sculpins lack a swim bladder, meaning they cannot create an air pocket and move vertically in the water column. Instead, they move horizontally. As a result, when fishing sculpin patterns, it often pays to fish your patterns closer to the stream bottom.

Streams that possess salmon parr, like Michigan's Muskegon River, are good candidates for fishing smaller streamers (size 10 to 12), which better represent the actual size of the parr. Notice the barring of the natural; materials like barred chickabou do a great job of imitating this natural pattern. U.S. FISH AND WILDLIFE SERVICE

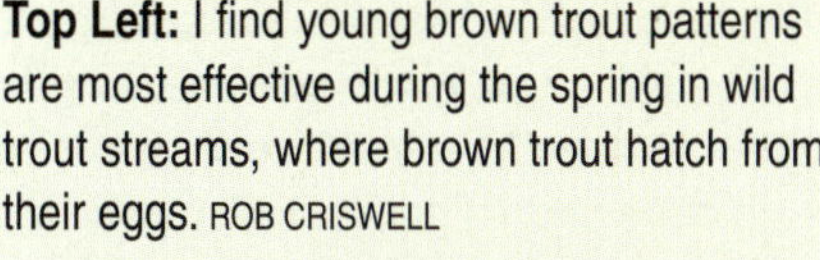

Top Left: I find young brown trout patterns are most effective during the spring in wild trout streams, where brown trout hatch from their eggs. ROB CRISWELL

Bottom Left: Suckers are bottom dwellers that feed with a subterminal mouth, literally sucking food off the bottom. When tying a sucker pattern, use materials and a design that allow you to fish the pattern along the stream bottom. Suckers are often found near the bottoms of deep pools. U.S. FISH AND WILDLIFE SERVICE

The chickabou salmon fry pattern is also a great fly to fish when trout hatch from their eggs. In Pennsylvania, brook trout hatch between February and March, and they stay within the gravel they hatched from until the egg yolk is used up. After the yolk is gone, the fry leave the safety of the gravel to feed on plankton and other small insects. This occurs between March and April, and this is the period when trout begin to prey upon the fry. While the average fry may only be $^3/_4$ to 1 inch in length, trout will readily feed upon these juvenile trout. I first realized this when growing up as a bait angler in northern Pennsylvania. When I was eight years old, I would barter filleted brook and brown trout for baked goods from several older ladies in my hometown of Germania. I would find tiny fish (likely brook trout fry) inside the stomach contents of the 8- to 10-inch brook trout. Even today, when I fish small brook trout mountain streams in Pennsylvania during the early spring, I'll fish micro Buggers to imitate newly hatched fry. When I move from a small stream to a larger river, I'll fish two fry patterns in tandem to cover more water.

Both fingerling and regular trout stocking locations are good places to start using small trout imitations. In fisheries like the ones in central Pennsylvania, where fewer large predatory trout are found, fishing smaller fingerling-size (3- to 5-inch) imitations is more effective than imitating catchable (7-inch-plus) trout. However, when fishing the Au Sable River's Mio section, larger 6- to 9-inch trout imitations can be effective because that stretch of water harbors a bigger population of larger trout. Again, the idea is to (approximately) match your imitation to the stream's natural food source.

One of my favorite microstreamers is the Michigan Fry, which is constructed from yellow/olive chickabou. Another favorite is a Micro Slumpbuster constructed with micro pine squirrel Zonker strips. Both patterns use material that creates a barred look, which represents the parr marks of a young trout. Think about the additional forage fish (suckers, sculpins, fall fish, etc.) in your fisheries, along with the times when their young hatch from the eggs. These young fish may provide a substantial food source to trout. As with salmon fry, trout fry hold in slow or still river sections.

Frogs

My good friend Josh Greenburg owns and operates Gates Lodge on Michigan's Au Sable River. One day while floating the Au Sable's Holy Waters, we were discussing large trout food and the application of frog patterns. Josh traps in the off-season to help reduce the number of natural trout predators, and he told me about a 19-inch trout he found dead several years ago while checking traps. He examined the stomach contents and found five frogs inside the trout. While the only experience I've had fishing frog patterns was during nighttime, frogs may be a viable food option for your fishery.

Mice

While the mouse is technically a rodent, anglers have for years been using streamer tactics to imitate this creature. Instead of sinking the patterns and retrieving them below the surface, anglers will fish their rodent patterns right in the surface film. Although many anglers swing mice during the daylight in areas such as Alaska, New Zealand, Kamchatka, and Chile, mice are most active during the night. Although there are some anglers who have effectively fished mouse patterns during daylight in the Lower 48, a nighttime approach remains best. Mice are active almost year-round except during extreme cold weather, when they seek nests for warmth. This explains how Tommy Lynch could produce some big trout while mouse fishing the White River in Arkansas in February.

IMITATING WOUNDED BAITFISH

I've heard many people say that the best approach for imitating a wounded baitfish is to cast upstream and pull your pattern with the current. A wounded baitfish is likely to flow with the speed of the current because it's on its last reserve of power, and it doesn't have the energy to move against the current. It will kick, flip upside-down, and try to right itself back to a normal position in the water. This behavior will trigger movement from predators, who are hard-wired to weed out the weakest link (the old, the wounded, or the young). So when you're trying to imitate this natural occurrence, I feel a presentation where you cast upstream, then allow your streamer to be fished downstream while incorporating the kicks, flop, and turns of a wounded baitfish is one of the best approaches for triggering a strike from a predatory trout. I think the key is to move the pattern in a manner that tells the predatory trout that your pattern is in trouble. I believe that panic can inhabit a trout's mind, just as it does with a human being. Panic forces the fish to behave in unpredictable manners, such as swimming across or upstream against the current, erratically moving back and forth, or trying to jump out of the water. You can see this behavior, known as nervous water, in schools of baitfish in both fresh and salt water.

A panicked baitfish can move in any direction—sideways, downward, upward—and you need to think about presenting your patterns in another dimension. Some believe there is an absolute way to represent naturally moving wounded and panicked baitfish. While there are some approaches that I feel strongly about, I want you to keep an open mind regarding your methods. Learn to mix it up a bit. Think about a past experience where you were suddenly spooked, whether it was a car crossing into your lane or a friend coming from behind to scare you. Now think about what your reaction was. You may have frozen still, or jumped up and screamed, or instinctively turned around and hit your friend. My point is that there's no certainty as to how you're going to react in each situation, and I believe the same is true for a trout under duress. There is no set standard as to how you should move your streamer pattern, and this is why I believe varying retrieves, directions, and depths is the most effective approach.

Reading the Water

When streamer fishing, I read a trout stream the same way I would when fishing nymphs, wet flies, or dry flies. I look for likely trout-holding areas to present my streamer to. If you can keep your streamer moving through prime holding waters, you increase your chances of moving a fish. While we have an idea of the areas where larger trout normally hold, the truth is we don't always know where big trout are likely to show up. Too many times on my own home waters, I've been surprised by where I find bigger trout. My limited years as a fly fisher—and my time spent with live minnow fishers and spin fishers—tell me I need to cover all water types when fishing with large food items. Streamer tactics have caught trout in all water types during all times of the day. The key is being able to read likely trout water, assemble a correct streamer rig to match the conditions, and accurately present the fly.

In my opinion, a trout may not know it wants to eat a sculpin until it sees one swim. While floating the West Branch

Think before making the first cast; the first cast is usually the most important. Establish where you suspect a trout is holding, and then develop a plan on where to cast and how you want to move the pattern. CHRIS DANIEL

Hutch Hutchinson casts directly behind a man-made fish structure. Such structures create a scouring effect, where the bottom is dug deep by the narrowing currents. As such, many of the larger fish will rest in the depths during the daylight hours. An upstream approach allows you to cast upstream, giving the fly ample time to drop to a greater depth before beginning the retrieve. The key is to conduct a countdown before beginning the retrieve. Too often anglers begin the retrieve before their pattern reaches the correct depth.

of the Delaware River one April morning, Ryan Furtak, Lance Wilt, and I came upon several trout that were feeding on Blue-Winged Olive duns. Earlier that day before launching the boat, we agreed to commit ourselves to fishing streamers all day. We left all other patterns and equipment in the vehicle. This meant we only had streamers to offer the rising trout, so as we slowly drifted, Ryan suggested that we should at least target the risers with the streamer. It was a slow day, and seeing the rising fish at least gave us a target to cast to. It's also worth mentioning that we had gone over four hours without moving a fish. Ryan said that he had seen this approach work before on the West Branch's trout population, so I placed my streamer 4 feet above the rising fish. Within two pulls of the line, the line went tight, and I was hooked into a healthy brown trout. The trout was taking advantage of a larger meal while snacking on Blue-Winged Olive duns. While this strategy doesn't always work, it's worked enough times to show me that trout can quickly switch from eating bugs to eating forage fish (and vise versa). I've never been able to determine 100 percent accurately, by looking at the water, if the trout are going to chase streamers. All I can do is locate likely trout water and present my streamer.

I'm not a trophy trout hunter, but rather an angler who enjoys catching trout on streamers. I enjoy catching larger trout but realize that you need to fish your streamers in all water types. The result of fishing all water types is that you'll inevitably catch smaller fish while in pursuit of the larger ones. While I understand streamer fishing increases your chances of catching larger trout, I enjoy the application of streamer fishing above all other fly-fishing tactics. This is the same reason why dry-fly anglers will sit along a riverbank all day waiting for a rising trout—it's their preferred method of hooking a trout.

While seasoned anglers who have fished a river long enough have a good handle on where to find larger trout, they still get surprises from time to time. Blake Boyd knows how quickly a river can change. Blake spends over 290 days a year on Tennessee's South Holston River, and I had the pleasure of spending two days on the water with him. Blake mentioned to me that he rarely fishes other rivers since he feels the South Holston changes often, and his job as a guide requires him to have a good handle on the stream conditions. If Blake can spend 290 days a year fishing the same water and tell me he never has the fish 100 percent dialed in, it never hurts to place your streamer into an unlikely holding spot. I believe that any trout water is worthy of a cast with a streamer, though variables including water temp, turbidity, and amount of light may dictate when certain water types will produce strikes.

Many great books have been devoted to reading trout streams, so my plan is not to repeat what has already been written. Instead, my thought is to break down a trout stream from the viewpoint of a streamer angler. It's thought that there are several designations of trout lies: lies where trout feed (feeding lies), where they rest (resting lies), and others where they accomplish both (prime lies). However, I believe the rules of the game change while streamer fishing, especially when it comes to resting lies.

When trout typically position themselves in a holding lie, they are resting without the intent of eating. We've all seen large trout holding motionless near the bottom of a slow-moving pool. Repeated attempts with both dry flies and nymphs receive no interest from the trout. In this case the trout is resting and may feel that the small drifting food item isn't worth its effort to chase. However, drifting a streamer normally results in the trout moving toward the streamer, for two reasons. First, the trout may be an opportunistic feeder that wants to take advantage of a free large meal. Second, the trout may be trying to protect its turf and ward off any potential competitors. In either scenario trout are known to strike a streamer, giving you an increased chance of moving a resting fish. On the other hand, I've seen streamers spook fish from their resting spots. Regardless of whether they become spooked, hungry, or aggressive, I feel streamers evoke more reactions from resting trout than any other tactic and can turn a resting fish into a feeding fish. I'm not saying you can't catch a resting trout with other tactics, but I feel the intrusion of a streamer pattern into a trout's resting spot has a better chance of turning it into a chasing fish.

Streamer tactics are useful during the brightest time of day for at least one reason—they allow you to locate bigger trout. While larger trout will feed throughout the entire day, most of the large trout I've caught have come during the lower-light periods (nighttime, early morning, or periods with significant cloud cover). However, a large trout may aggressively protect its turf during the brightest periods of the day when a larger streamer invades its territory. Sometimes the large trout may charge the streamer at full speed. Other times the trout may slowly slide across the bottom and follow the streamer from a distance. Then there are times where the trout will do nothing but instinctively flinch toward the fly and create a large flash in the water. Either way, the trout may not eat the streamer, but it gives away its location and provides you with a future target, whether with a streamer or nymphs. Sometimes I fish streamers solely to locate a bigger fish that I will ultimately try to catch with nymphs, but keep in mind that some trout move great distances from their holding lies to feeding grounds.

In this chapter I provide a wide range of possible scenarios a streamer angler may encounter, along with my thoughts on how to approach each situation. The examples are general representations of how to read and approach each section of water. Again, it's important to understand there could be a more than one acceptable approach to each situation. All I'm able to do is recall past experiences, both positive and negative, and impart the advice I've received from so many great anglers over the years to provide what I believe is a good streamer approach.

I worked for five years as a biologist aide with the Pennsylvania Fish and Boat Commission's Stream Habitat Division. During that time, I learned how water hydraulics affect a trout's resting and feeding behaviors. While looking at each of the following scenarios, my hope is to pass along some of the great bits of information I received from my two former habitat managers.

Don't hesitate to place a streamer where you see a fish rising. A rising fish is an actively feeding fish, and it is likely willing to chase down a streamer. This Delaware rainbow was feeding on Sulphur duns but decided to chase down a small Slump Buster I placed near the rising trout.

GALLERY OF WATER TYPES

Logjams are often hunting grounds of larger trout. Woody debris attracts aquatic insects, which in turn attract smaller fish (including baitfish), which attract larger trout. But not all logjams are trout magnets. What makes this an attractive location is the slow to medium current moving toward the bank, where trout don't have to fight the current. Also, notice the deep cut immediately in front of the logjam, where larger trout are protected from fighting the current. Finally, notice the two slow pockets directly in front of and behind the logjam.

During high water, focus most of your energy on the inside bends. Smaller fish will not remain on the outside bends unless there are soft pockets; they will instead move toward the inside, where slack water occurs. Think about where the small fish will locate during such events, and you will find larger trout.

Remember with deep cuts along wooden logs to allow your fly to settle to the trout's level before beginning the retrieve. When trout are holding in deep cuts, a short countdown may be useful to allow the streamer to drop to the appropriate level before beginning the retrieve.

Even during complete darkness, trout will position tight to wood structure, so you need to make sure your presentation is spot-on. If you're not snagging wood from time to time during the night, you need to fish more aggressively. Make sure you know the water well enough in the daytime before fishing at night.

When the sun is out, large fish are more likely to be resting than feeding. The dark edge directly underneath the log is an ideal location to cast downstream, swing, and hold a streamer directly in front of a log to entice and aggravate a resting fish. I have no problem holding a fly in an area for an extended period of time if I believe there's a large trout resting in the darkness. At this time of the day, I'm likely trying to encourage an aggressive/territorial strike, not a hunger strike.

Not all fish will move toward the bank when a tailwater is generating. However, 90 percent of the anglers will target the bank. Unless I'm one of the first boats floating downstream, I prefer to fish farther off the bank. Submerged islands, especially their downstream sides, are hotbeds for feeding trout. Even during full generation, the downstream side offers a hydraulic soft spot for a fish to rest and feed.

Where there's small fish, larger trout are likely to be within striking distance. In this case, fallen trees or shrubs are great spots for small or young fish to hide from predators. When fishing in low light, find where small fish feed, and you will find larger trout.

A tributary dumps muddy water into the South Holston after a hard rain. Focus your efforts on the transition between muddy and clear water, as larger trout will feel protected by the turbidity and feed during the daytime.

GALLERY OF WATER TYPES

A typical situation on a northern Michigan trout stream: a shallow sand flat transitioning into deeper water. I always try to retrieve my flies into the shallow sand flat and hold there for several seconds before recasting. On too many occasions I've seen large fish follow my streamer and stop along the dark edge before springing out and attacking the fly. Fish your fly all the way to the end of the retrieve and allow it to swing all the way to the surface before picking up and recasting.

Here lies a log angled downstream with a deep cut underneath. Every time I approach a similar situation, I remember Russ Madden's words to me: "Let the fly drop below the contours before stripping." Meaning, I need to allow the line and fly to drop below the level of the log so it is in the trout's vision before beginning the retrieve. Think about "bringing the fight to the fish"—putting the fly right at the trout's eye level to encourage an aggressive follow.

When fishing dirty water, you can smack the fly hard on the surface to gain the trout's attention. In a soft pocket of water like that pictured here, only one good cast (with a smack on the surface) is necessary before moving on to the next spot.

Notice the multiple-speed currents below this rock dam. This is a prime spot for casting directly upstream or downstream (in line) with the current. Casting across-stream would mean placing your fly in myriad various-speed currents, creating a series of S-curves in your line and putting you out of touch with your streamer.

The shallow backside of an island is a great spot for a large predatory trout on the hunt, but only during the right conditions. Such locations hold trout during low-light periods or when water is off-color. However, I would rarely find a trout on the hunt on the backside of islands during periods of high water, as pictured here. As soon as the low light sets in, such areas will usually hold a larger trout on the hunt.

A slower retrieve is often useful when fishing riffles or any fast-moving stream with off-color water, as it allows the trout more time to find your pattern. The opposite is true in slow and clear water—I find myself fishing faster to give the trout less time to investigate my presentation.

Prime water for a heavily weighted streamer on a floating line or short sinking tip. Notice the submerged boulders. I would stay away from a full-sinking line, as there's a chance the line could accidently wrap around the rock, resulting in a hang-up or a sharp rock edge cutting your sinking line. A floating line, long leader, and heavily weighted streamer enable you to mend the floating line—allowing you to slow down the drift and give more time for the fly to drop to the correct depth.

When fishing a boulder-strewn area, think about where trout are likely to hold when planning to ambush prey. This Pennsylvania limestone stream holds trout that know to wedge themselves tight to submerged boulders. As a result, I prefer to cast and drift my fly parallel along the rock face, so the pattern is moving through a trout's kill zone.

POCKETWATER

This is likely one of the least-targeted areas with streamer patterns. Why? One reason could be the extreme differences in surface current speed as it relates to surface drag. Traditionally, streamer anglers often lay their entire line on the water, keep their rod tip close to the water, and strip in line. While this approach works for water types with uniform surface currents, laying down a good length of line in pocketwater often results in excessive drag as sections of the line and leader make contact with currents of various speeds. This excess drag works to pull your fly out of the pocket and doesn't give the trout enough time to find it.

To combat this, I prefer fishing streamers in pocketwater with a method similar to nymphing. I keep as much line off the water as possible and use either a longer leader or level fly line, along with a heavily weighted fly. Using either a long leader or a level line with a shorter leader allows you to hold excess line off the water, which reduces surface drag and allows you to hold your streamer in the pocketwater for a longer period. Think of this technique as similar to tight-lining a pocket; hold the rod tip higher to keep as much line and leader off the water as possible. The other difference is you're likely to place tension on the fly through a jigging of retrieving action instead of dead-drifting through the pocket.

I rarely use sinking lines and unweighted or lightweight streamers in pocketwater, since I need so much of the line to be lying under the surface to keep my streamers riding deep. Instead, I want to focus my weight into one specific area to reduce unwanted drag and to get my flies down to the kill zone as soon as possible. Although trout are often willing to move farther to pick up a baitfish than a small nymph, you still need to get the fly close enough to a trout's kill zone to evoke a reaction.

Lance Egan shows off a brown trout caught during later runoff in the Italian Alps. The stream section was choked with boulders, so Lance used a microstreamer with a long nymphing leader to jig the patterns in the small pockets.

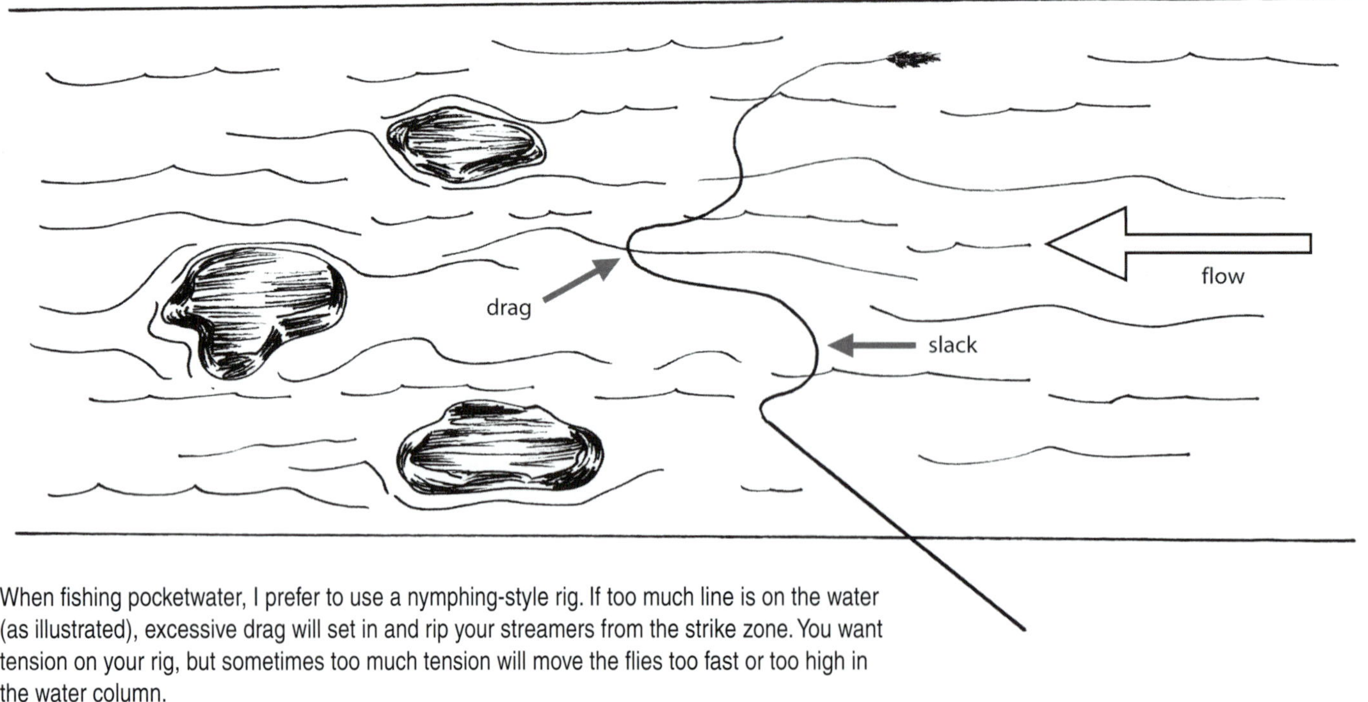

When fishing pocketwater, I prefer to use a nymphing-style rig. If too much line is on the water (as illustrated), excessive drag will set in and rip your streamers from the strike zone. You want tension on your rig, but sometimes too much tension will move the flies too fast or too high in the water column.

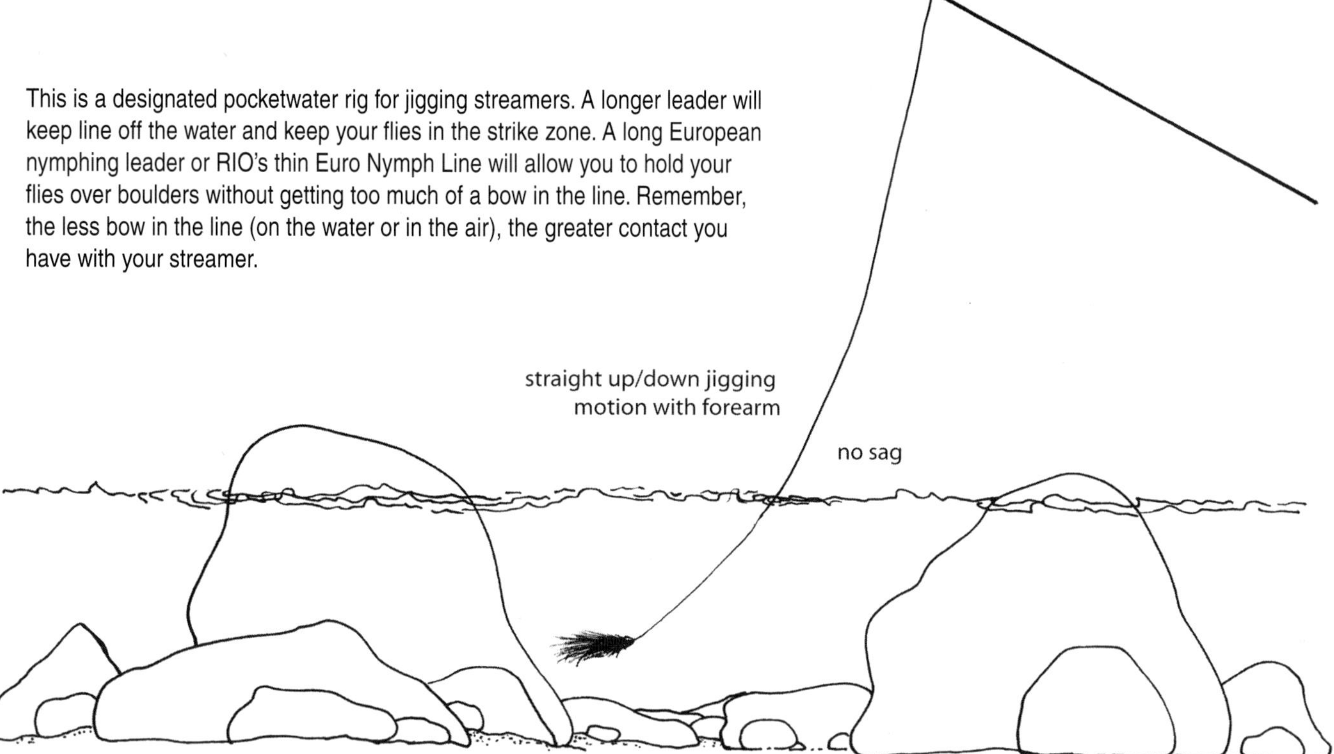

This is a designated pocketwater rig for jigging streamers. A longer leader will keep line off the water and keep your flies in the strike zone. A long European nymphing leader or RIO's thin Euro Nymph Line will allow you to hold your flies over boulders without getting too much of a bow in the line. Remember, the less bow in the line (on the water or in the air), the greater contact you have with your streamer.

While some anglers prefer a long leader, I prefer a thin-diameter line. My current go-to line for jigging streamers in pocketwater is the RIO Euro Nymph Line designed by Steve Parrott. While originally designed for European nymphing tactics, this thin-diameter line allows you to hold a long length of line outside the rod tip without too much belly. The advantage this line has over a long leader is that you can grab hold of the line, which results in better line control when retrieving or stripping in the line. Too often when fishing a long leader, my hands would slip during the retrieve, strip, or hook set.

Another advantage of the RIO line is its bright orange tip, which can provide additional strike detection when jigging, along with providing a depth gauge. If I'm fishing a deep pocket and need to get my streamer deeper in the water column, I'll lower the heavily weighted streamer into the pocket (allowing the tip of the fly line to drop closer to the water's surface) before I begin retrieving the flies. Having to lower your flies in pocketwater is a rare occurrence, as most trout living in pocketwater are often very aggressive feeders. The few times I've had to drop a streamer deeper into a pocket occurred while fishing depths that exceeded 4 feet or on excessively cold, or bright, days. Normally, when fishing pocketwater up to 4 feet, active trout are willing to move a considerable distance (1 to 3 feet) to chase down a streamer.

John Horsey, one of the England's most decorated competitive fly fishers, once told me that because trout normally look up for food, when he's retrieving nymphs or streamers on stillwaters, he often starts higher in the water column and works his way down. If John feels trout will be feeding higher in the water column, he won't let his fly drop too low before retrieving. However, if conditions force the trout to take up a position deeper in the column, he'll count down his flies and let them sink deeper before the retrieve.

Tight-lining streamers is also a great tactic during high water, when wading is limited. This line system with a heavily weighted jig allows you to fish pockets up to 40 feet away without having to place any line and leader on the water. And besides, if you were to lay line and leader down on the raging water, the flies would quickly be swept away as immediate drag set in.

While I prefer to keep as much line and leader off the water as possible and jig my flies in pocketwater, this isn't always possible. Conditions may force a longer cast that results in line and leader lying on the water. If this is the case, a floating line with a long head is my first choice, as I want the ability to mend my presentation around rocks and exposed obstructions. I'm not a fan of short, aggressive tapers, as they are difficult to mend and roll cast once the head of the line is outside the rod tip. I use RIO Steelhead Taper floating line, which has a long head (approximately 66 feet) that makes it easy to both roll cast and mend line from a distance. Other options, including traditional double tapers and indicator lines, are also good choices for fishing streamers in pocketwater.

Flies for Pocketwater Streamer Fishing

The short retrieves in pocketwater require a fly with a tungsten conehead, bead, or dumbbell eye to achieve a quick penetration into a pocket. Just as with nymph fishing, I'm not only looking for a heavily weighted pattern but also a pattern that is slim in diameter, so it quickly drops to the bottom. Because I'm using the rod tip to retrieve the streamer via a jigging motion, the rod

Work the wood. Even in higher water, trout will hold tight to structure. Here Lance Wilt is dropping (not casting) a jig-style streamer in between several submerged trees. As my mentor, Joe Humphreys, always told me, "It doesn't have to be pretty. Just find a way to get the fly to the trout."

will absorb much of the resistance created by the take of a fish. I want a pattern that doesn't feel like I'm jigging a wet sock across the bottom. This is why I stay away from material such as wool and large strips of rabbit, or any similar products that absorb water and decrease my connection to the jigging fly. One of my favorite pocketwater streamers is a GD Sculp Snack, which is a slight variation of a Woolly Bugger with a tungsten conehead. This pattern is slim in profile with rubber legs and a marabou tail, and it slices through the water.

While dumbbell eyes can obviously be used for jigging pockets, I prefer to use a conehead on my pocketwater streamers. I feel the bullet-shaped head allows me to stay in better contact with my streamers as I use the rod tip during the retrieve. Dumbbell eyes create more drag during the retrieve and decrease the sensitivity I have when feeling for a take while jigging.

If you plan to bounce the bottom while jigging your streamer, consider using jig-style hooks (those with a bend). The reason is the hook rides upside-down and reduces snagging. You can purchase jig hooks that already have lead molded on, or you can purchase a bare jig hook and add either a slotted tungsten bead or slotted tungsten conehead.

The idea when fishing heavily weighted flies in pocketwater is that you're fishing a pattern that is heavy enough to anchor itself in the water (it would sink straight to the bottom if tension wasn't applied to the fly). This allows you to control the speed the fly moves via the jigging action of the rod tip. Basically, you are dragging in a desired direction, normally parallel with the current. I'm not too concerned with drag in this case for at least two reasons:

1. Baitfish, minnows, and other larger prey items do not always drift or move at the same speed as the current. Instead, they swim, dart, and dive with the current, sometimes moving faster—making a "drag" presentation more natural than dead-drifting.
2. In pocketwater, the window trout see through is broken and doesn't provide ample time to inspect an angler's presentation. This allows us to use heavily weighted patterns, which don't move as naturally through the water as unweighted patterns but can be held longer in broken water—giving trout more time to find the pattern.

Whether you're fishing a pocket from downstream, upstream, or from across, it doesn't matter as long as you're in position to hold your streamer in the pocket without having your line or leader grab nagging currents. That said, if I had the option of fishing from any angle, I would choose fishing upstream and jigging my streamers back to me. This approach offers several advantages: First, remember that trout most often face into the current. By positioning yourself downstream of the fish, you pull the fly directly toward the fish's mouth during the hook set rather than away from it.

Besides using a hook hone to keep the point sharp, also consider using a point that is both thin in diameter and durable. The larger the diameter of the hook point, the more force is needed to set the hook. When jigging patterns, the action of the rod is responsible for creating the hook set more so than the strip-set. Although the forearm creates a forceful movement during the hook set, the rod flexing absorbs much of the created energy. While it seems logical to lower the rod angle (point the rod tip more directly at the fly) and strip the fly in, rather than use the rod tip to jig to transfer more energy during the hook set, lowering the rod tip will place more line and leader on the water. And more line and leader on the water, when fishing pocketwater, will create unwanted drag and give your streamers less time in the pocket.

It's important when jigging the pattern that you use your forearm rather than your wrist to set the hook. The forearm can create more tension during the hook set than the wrist, which creates a more secure hookup. When using the wrist to jig, this motion creates too much slack in the system and puts you out of touch with your streamer. Instead, use a steady up-and-down lifting motion with the forearm to jig your flies. This is why using a faster-action rod is useful, as the rod tip is what you'll use to set the hook during the lifting movement.

Another advantage of this system is that it gives you the ability to hold your streamer in an area for an extended period of time, which is an advantage when fishing exceptionally cold periods or while fishing muddy water. With muddy water and low visibility, trout do have the ability to find food, but their visual window is shortened. As a result, trout need more time to find your pattern.

Casting and presenting a streamer from a downstream position with a fly heavy enough to anchor itself in the water allows you to take advantage of drag. Because water's tension wants to move the streamer downstream, you can control the depth of the fly by the angle of the rod tip. The key is to fish a pattern that is heavy enough to anchor itself deeper into the pocket so that it doesn't automatically get pulled to the surface.

Again, to stay in touch with your patterns, jig using the forearm. With a steady lifting and dropping motion from the forearm, you place minimal slack into the system and maintain tension during the entire retrieve. This keeps the rod tip from loading (bending and unbending) and maintains a degree of tension at all times. Using the wrist while jigging loads and unloads the rod, which creates both unwanted slack during the retrieve along with a weak hook set. Because the streamer is not being pulled across the current (i.e., the fly is instead held in a stationary position), you aren't going to feel as much tension during the strike. As a result, the take is almost similar to that of a trout taking a nymph when tight-lining—you may only sense a slight hesitation. This is why using either a long leader or a thin fly line like RIO Euro Nymphing Line provides you with the most sensitivity, which results in more hookups.

Every year I streamline my streamer box. I take out what I no longer use and replace it with an updated version. The Game Changer has become my new confidence fly. It takes time to develop confidence in a pattern, so I make sure I spend part of the year experimenting with new patterns. It took me three separate trips to experiment with, understand, and develop confidence in fishing the Game Changer. Don't give up on a pattern after the first or second trip because you didn't catch a fish.

RIFFLES

Riffles possess a high concentration of trout food, which in turn can attract larger trout during certain periods of time. The oxygen-rich environment attracts bug life, which in turn attracts smaller fish, such as sculpins, minnows, chubs, dace, trout, and other species. For me, streamer fishing the riffles is a hit-or-miss proposition. Because larger fish are light sensitive—at least in many of the pressured waters I fish—my success rate increases when I fish during low-light periods. Dawn and dusk, a rain or snow event, or even a cloudy day can get larger trout feeding in the riffles. Larger trout are attracted to the feeding grounds of larger prey, which also feed on insects during lower-light periods. I have noticed this time and time again when using a flashlight to illuminate a riffle while night-fishing. The riffles come to life with insects feeding on plant matter, smaller fish feeding on the insects, and larger trout feeding on the small fish.

Riffles are prime feeding grounds for larger trout when the right conditions exist. I find that larger trout positioned in riffles are normally ready to feed and are willing to chase food items. My favorite approach is to cast upstream with a floating line, an 8-foot leader, and a weighted fly. If I want to bottom-bounce a streamer, I choose a heavily weighted pattern that will anchor itself, and I can retrieve the fly back at the desired speed. If I want to swim my pattern higher and faster in the water column, I'll cast more across-stream with the floating line and 8-foot leader but switch to a lighter-weight streamer. Casting across a riffle with a floating line creates additional drag, which increases the speed your flies travel downstream. If a downstream belly occurs in your fly line, the fly will move faster as a result of drag. Because of this, you only need to strip line fast enough to manage the slack as the line drifts downstream.

Some anglers prefer to make an upstream mend to eliminate the downstream bow in the line, but I prefer to keep the bow when fishing riffled water. I believe the downstream bow is useful for two reasons: First, it helps maintain control of your drift, as the floating line literally drags your streamers downstream. Drag is often a desired result, especially when fishing streamers, because the floating line acts like a bobber on the surface. The floating line lying on the faster currents creates tension on the streamer and pulls the pattern downstream. Second, the drag created by the downstream belly (tension loop) helps create more tension during the hook set. Often, the tension created by the tension loop is all the pressure needed to set the hook. You can manipulate the size of the loop to increase or decrease the speed of your streamer retrieve. The larger the

Brian Wilt waits for the first push of water on the Little Red River in Arkansas. Some of best times to catch larger fish in the daytime are during rising or dropping water levels. Tailwater rivers such as the Little Red may offer daily opportunities to catch the water on the rise or on the drop.

Colorado's South Platte River is known for difficult trout and for midge patterns. However, periods when water levels are slightly up and off-color create an opportunity for the streamer angler. Be ready to make the switch.

loop, the larger the increase in the speed of your retrieve. A smaller loop (created by an upstream mend) creates less surface tension and will slow down the speed of your streamer retrieve. Again, this is assuming we're dealing with a floating line, not a sinking-tip or full-sinking line. Remember, faster currents lie on the surface, and a sinking fly line will sink below those currents, which will result in less tension. A tension loop will also form when fishing a sinking tip or a full-sinker, but the degree of tension is less when compared to a floating line because the sunken section is positioned in the slower currents below the surface.

Another thing to consider when fishing upstream in a riffle is controlling your drift. Fishing streamers in a down-and-across position is easier because of the immediate tension that is created by placing the fly downstream of your position. Upstream streamer fishing, on the other hand, is similar to tight-line nymphing—you need to retrieve line fast enough to stay in touch with your drift. For a dead drift, you need to retrieve the line at approximately the same speed as the fly is drifting toward you. If you want to move your fly faster than the current, then you need to retrieve faster than the speed of the drift. This is where shooting through an O-ring is an absolute must.

Shooting through an O-ring allows you to maintain control of the fly line. I learned this important lesson in line control while listening to a Lefty Kreh lecture in my early twenties. Lefty said that too often when shooting line during the presentation cast, anglers have a tendency to let go of the line. As a result, there's a delay in line control as you attempt to regain control of the line. In my case, this is because I'm often looking to where my fly landed, so I might completely miss grabbing onto the fly line to begin the retrieve. When fishing upstream in a riffle section, immediate line control is essential, because both the fly and line move downstream at a fast rate. If, for some reason, you let go of the line and cannot grab back onto it after the presentation, it's difficult to regain control.

Remember that riffles run at a faster rate than most other lies. When casting upstream, you must retrieve the line at least as fast as the fly is drifting back to you. If you can't retrieve the fly fast enough and slack accumulates in the line, a trout strike will go unnoticed. For this reason, a floating line offers the advantage of lying on the surface and creating greater tension on the fly, moving it through the riffles.

Sinking line and sinking tips can be fished upstream, but I rarely fish them with an unweighted pattern in a riffled section, because of the stratified current speeds in the riffle. Often, faster currents occur near the surface and slower currents occur at the bottom. Think about the stream in cross section: If you

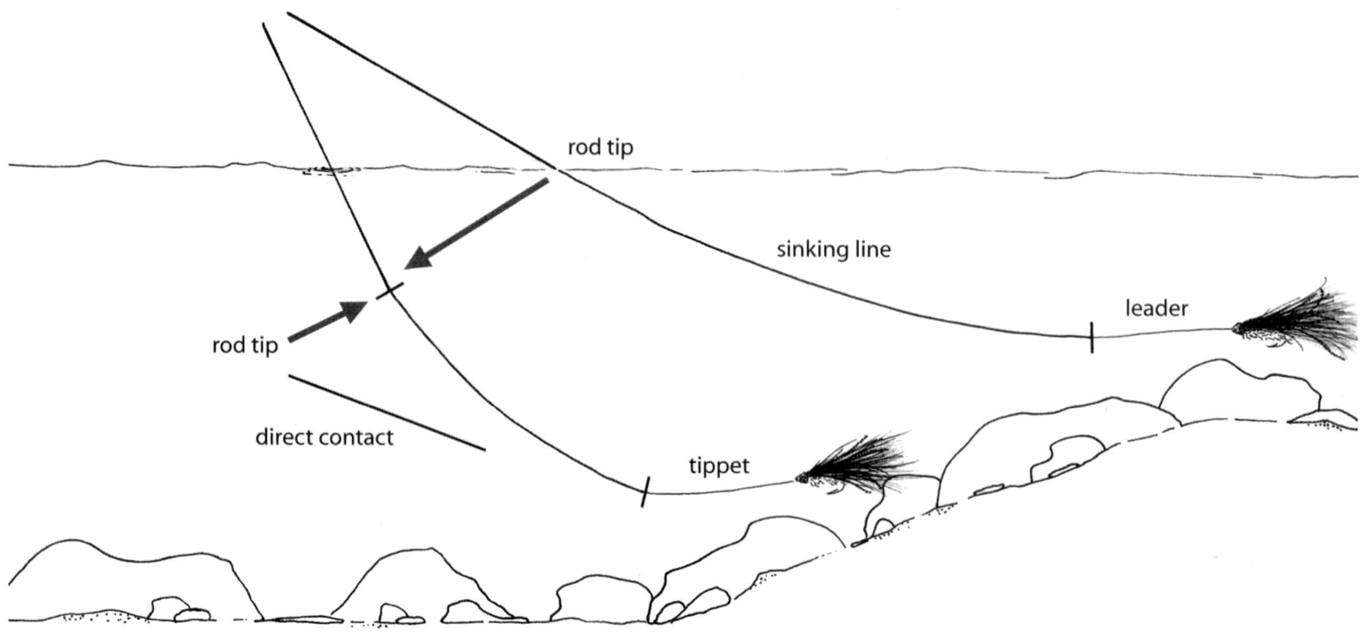

When fishing a drop-off with a sinking line along the bank, keep your rod tip close to the water. As the fly moves into the drop-off, begin to submerge the rod tip deep into the water to allow the fly to follow the contour of the drop-off. This is a quick method for getting your flies to ride the edge and is my go-to approach when fishing from a boat in fast water.

were to place two colors of dye (blue in the top currents and red in the bottom currents) in the water, you would notice the blue moving faster downstream than the red. The same happens with your line if you fish upstream with a full-sinking line and an unweighted streamer in water containing fast surface currents and a slow bottom, especially when fishing a longer leader. The sinking line would begin sinking to the stream bottom, pulling the leader down, and it would eventually settle close to the stream bottom. However, it's likely the buoyant streamer would remain in the faster current, never dropping in the slower currents with the sinking line, and eventually move downstream of the sinking fly line. This alignment between buoyant fly and sinking line creates slack when presenting streamers, causing you to lose control of the rig.

If you decide to fish a sinking line upstream, you can do a few things to reduce slack. First, use a weighted streamer in combination with a sinking line. It doesn't have to be heavily weighted, but it does need less buoyancy so that it can drop faster in the water column. This is why I would not use hanging flies when fishing upstream—their buoyancy would keep them suspended in the faster currents at the top of the water column. I stay away from deer hair head patterns or any streamer pattern with buoyancy, instead opting for weighted patterns with thinner profiles. To maintain control of the fly when fishing upstream, you need to position the fly line downstream of the fly. This creates contact and control between you and the fly.

There's another option if you're forced to fish upstream with a buoyant fly and sinking line: Shorten the leader length between line and fly. When fishing upstream in water with stratified currents, it's best to fish the pattern and fly line at the same level in the current. Shortening the length between the sinking line and the buoyant fly forces the fly to ride deeper. This is no different from using split shot with a nymph. If you want your fly to ride higher in the water column, increase the distance between fly and shot; if want the nymph to ride deeper in the water column, decrease the distance. The point is to stay in control of your rig. Trout don't attack a streamer with full aggression all the time; sometimes they gently inhale it. If you do decide to fish a buoyant streamer upstream with either a sinking line or split shot, make sure to keep the anchor (the weighted line or shot) as close as possible to the streamer. While experimenting with upstream tactics, I noticed when fishing upstream in faster water while using a buoyant streamer, a full-sinking fly line, and a 4- to 5-foot leader, the fly would often ride 3 feet downstream of the fly line tip. In other words, that's 3 feet of slack—too much to register a take from a trout.

On the other hand, you can fish the same rig (buoyant streamer and full-sinking line) either across- or downstream because the faster surface currents will keep the buoyant streamer under tension as the fly line and fly are downstream of you. Remember, casting your fly downstream places immediate tension on your rig—your fly is going away from you rather than coming toward you. Maintaining line control is easier when fishing either directly across or down-and-across because the rig is placed under constant tension.

There are always exceptions, of course, to these guidelines. An upstream presentation *is* possible with the rig described above when fishing slow-moving water or where current

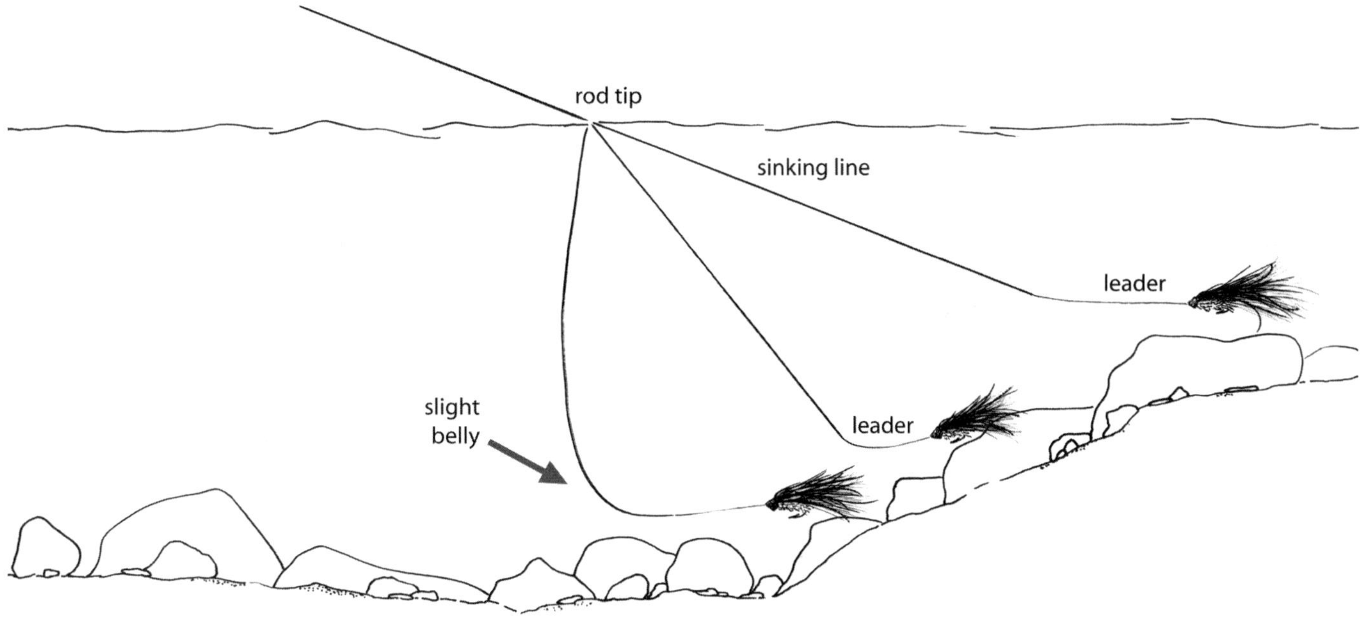

Another option when fishing a drop-off with a sinking line is to keep the rod tip close to water's surface but pause to allow the line to sink along the contour of the drop-off and begin the retrieve. One issue is that the line will form a slight belly during this movement. Also, this set-up takes time, as the line needs to drop along the edge to begin the retrieve.

speeds are uniform throughout the water column. You can fish upstream with a sinking line and buoyant streamer, so long as the surface currents are not moving faster than the bottom. What we don't want is for the streamer to be moving downstream faster than the line, which creates slack when casting upstream and retrieving your flies downward. However, if I'm fishing a flat, a pool, or any river section where there are uniform currents, an upstream approach is possible when fishing a sinking line and buoyant streamer. The surface currents will not drag the streamer downstream past the sinking line during a downstream retrieve.

When fishing a shallow riffle with streamers, you may find yourself continually snagging the bottom. In this case, begin casting directly across-stream or directly downstream—the line will sink slower due to the increased tension. Placing the fly downstream of you creates immediate tension and results in a slower sink rate. On the other hand, if you need to get your flies deeper in the column, you should begin casting directly upstream. Switching from upstream to across-stream will completely change your presentation, but only if you're carrying one line type—it may be your only chance to adapt to the speed and depth of the water. Trout feeding in a riffle are often more willing to move for a streamer than for a small nymph.

When fishing streamers, targeting a specific depth isn't as critical as when nymph fishing, but there are situations in which you need to work the depths. Streamer tactics will trigger a trout's aggressive nature, but we anglers still need to place the fly within a trout's strike zone. We don't necessarily have to bounce bottom, but if we're not moving fish, we need to switch speed or depth. Streamers offer a larger meal for trout, which results in a greater effort from the trout to move toward your fly. For example, fishing a medium-weighted streamer and floating line will produce strikes when fishing riffled water up to approximately 3 feet deep. Even if my streamer rides halfway down the water column, a trout lying on the stream bottom is still likely to move 18 inches upward to grab the streamer. Streamers offer trout more calories than small nymphs, so trout will expend more energy to hunt larger patterns. However, if I'm fishing a 5-foot-deep riffle with a strong current and my floating-line, medium-weighted fly rig presents the fly 1 foot under the surface, a trout resting on the bottom may not be motivated to move 4 feet through the faster currents. As a result, I'd need to change to either a heavier fly, a faster-sinking line, or both.

When fishing upstream in a riffle with a floating line, the fly is often under constant tension, as the floating line is being pulled downstream by the surface currents. Consequently, I prefer to stay away from excessively large patterns; I find trout have difficulty trying to inhale large patterns that are under constant tension. Again, I don't think you need to fish big flies exclusively to catch big fish. Some of my biggest trout have come at daylight when nymphing the transitions between a riffle and a run with a small, rubber-legged Bugger. The transition between a riffle and a run is a prime lie (one that offers a place of protection, a location to eat, and a spot to rest) and the best fish take up these prime lies during low-light periods. This is more true of brown trout; rainbows, on the other hand, can become active during the bright periods of light.

If I had to fish one section of a riffle, it would be at the transition between the riffle and the run, where the drop-off occurs.

When fishing streamers upstream in a heavy riffle, I prefer to use a floating line. The floating line will not sink at my feet like a sinking line.
CHRIS DANIEL

I've found this to be the case during all hours of the day, as sizable trout will hold in prime lies throughout the day. The best fish often hold in such prime lies, and more importantly, they are actively hunting.

When fishing the transition between a riffle and a run, I'll switch from fishing more upstream to directly across-stream. I prefer to fish each individual seam as I would with nymphing, by laying the fly, line, and leader all in the current. This is still a great tactic for fishing a riffle drop-off, but I've experienced greater success when casting and retrieving the streamer parallel to the drop-off. I find that retrieving my flies parallel to the drop-off (often directly across-stream) keeps the flies in the trout's feeding zones. Fishing upstream and retrieving downstream will obviously work, but it takes more casts to cover the water. The key to streamer fishing is covering water fast, but doing so in a controlled manner. Fishing upstream, especially along the edges of banks where the drop-offs occur, covers the areas where trout are likely to hunt—the transitions between the edges and the main current. The same is true when fishing across-stream between a transition of a riffle and a run. I want to move my fly parallel to the drop, as that is the likely holding area of a decent trout.

The same idea holds true if drifting from a boat. In that scenario, you often have one or two casts to cover the water before drifting past the spot. Usually, I want my streamer to move parallel to the drop-off, slightly upstream, as actively feeding trout will likely be positioned in these areas and ready to ambush prey. It's easy to cast straight toward the bank and retrieve the fly back to the bank without actually taking a moment to read the stream bottom before making a cast. While casting from a moving boat, you only have limited chances to make the cast count. So during your next float, don't just get into the rhythm of casting and stripping. Instead, make fewer casts, but properly read the stream bottom before making a cast; this will allow your fly to drift past more aggressive fish. This may mean making a special cast (such as a curve cast; see page 198) or manipulating the line to keep the fly moving through prime zones longer.

Remember that some riffles may be too fast to fish upstream. The speed of the current will move your line and fly so quickly downstream that you won't have the ability to strip the line fast enough to maintain control. In those situations, you'll need to find another angle to fish, most likely down and across. My ideal riffle is at least 18 to 20 inches in depth with a medium-speed surface current and a slow bottom where trout can rest in between meals. The medium-speed currents are slow enough to allow me to cast upstream and control my downstream retrieve, while the 18-inch depth provides enough overhead cover to hide a large trout. The depth also provides a cushion of slower water for the trout to rest near the bottom. Bigger trout will grab these prime lies, and I've had excellent success fishing riffles that meet these conditions.

The availability of slower water is key. A sizable trout is not likely to hold in a riffle where there's no resting area. If the riffle is too shallow, a slower cushion may not occur because there's not enough depth for the water currents to stratify. I've had limited success at catching good-size trout during the daylight hours in riffles that are 10 inches or less. Two possible reasons for my lack of success are lack of overhead protection (shallow water) for the trout, along with the trout having to fight the strong current. Nighttime is a different story. At night, big trout will be found hunting the shallow riffles.

POOLS

A trout holding in the dead center of a pool is often a resting trout, not a feeding one, and therefore, it needs more coaxing to come chase a streamer. In this scenario, I look for tactics that allow me to hold a streamer in front of resting trout long enough to evoke an aggressive strike. When fishing the middle section of a pool for resting trout, I prefer to cast across-stream and hold my streamers downstream at the end of the swing, similar to how steelhead anglers present flies to resting steelhead. I want to keep the flies directly in front of the fish as long as possible, to the point of aggravating the fish so much that the presentation either frightens the trout or triggers a strike from it. I may hold the pattern in an area for up to a minute.

During the swing, you can either mend downstream to create more tension to speed up the drift or mend upstream to reduce tension and slow down the speed of the swing. Because a fish holding in the deep center of a pool is more focused on resting rather than chasing food, I do everything I can to slow down the speed of the swinging fly and hold it in front of the fish as long as I can. If possible, I wade into a position that allows me to point the rod tip at the very center of the pool's deepest section while I am looking downstream. On smaller streams, all I need to do is extend my hand so the rod tip is pointing downward toward the pool's deepest section. The key is to get yourself into a position that allows you to keep the rod tip pointed at where you're holding your flies. This creates a more direct connection between you and your flies and allows you to create greater energy during the hook set. What you don't want is to point the rod tip directly across the stream to the bank while the line is at a 90-degree angle being pulled downstream. This angle creates a disconnect between you and your streamer during the retrieve; it makes it more difficult to feel or register a strike because the bend in the rod tip absorbs much of the energy. While it's advantageous to have a small degree of slack during the strike, too great of an angle between rod tip and line will make you lose connection with your streamer.

When you are fishing with little slack in your line and are completely in touch with your fly, you can actually feel it moving through the water, even sensing the changing tension as the streamer moves through the microcurrents. In this instant, you're feeling the fly move through the water, not feeling the line drag across the stream. This direct contact is created by minimizing line belly and keeping the rod tip pointed toward the fly. If too much slack occurs during the retrieve and a huge belly develops in the line, then you'll feel the line dragging through the water rather than your fly. I know this is common sense, but there have been so many occasions where I've seen a trout casually move over to eat my streamer but I didn't feel an ounce of tension on the line. This was the result of either too great of an angle between the rod tip and the line or too much belly in the line. I firmly believe that a decent percentage of streamer takes go unnoticed by beginning streamer fly fishers due to the lack of contact with their streamer. Trout don't always hook themselves; you are responsible for setting the hook once you feel resistance during the retrieve. Maintaining contact with your fly will allow you to register the take the moment a trout eats your streamer, which allows you to react faster with a hook set.

This grayling was taken on a glacial runoff river in the Italian Alps using a slow give-and-take retrieve. Cold water temps and off-color water forced us to fish our streamers at a slower speed.

This approach really is a great year-round tactic for any deeper pool where trout are resting. In the colder winter season, trout are likely to seek deeper pools because their metabolisms are slowed down by the colder water. Trout in such winter holding lies are sluggish to begin with and not as likely to chase down a streamer. There have been many times in the winter when I would fish upstream (my preferred tactic) and retrieve my flies back to me without a single strike. However, when I would position myself upstream and allow my flies to swing downstream and hold them over a likely holding area, a trout would often move toward my fly. It was not always a committed take, but at least the trout showed some sign of life toward the fly and gave me a reason to switch tactics.

Another section of the pool where I find more active fish is along the banks, particularly along drop-offs where the shallow water meets the deeper water. Trout holding along the edges are often hunting for food and are more likely to chase down a streamer than are resting trout holding near the bottom of a deep pool.

CHUTES

In areas where stream channels tighten and create a narrow but strong-moving body of water, the current can be so strong and fast that an upstream or across-stream tactic fails to get the flies down to the fish quickly enough. Although it appears the water is moving too fast for a trout to hold, it's likely there's a soft pocket on the stream bottom where the trout can hold without having to fight the current. In fact, I think the bottom of a chute is a prime lie—it's where I've taken some of my best trout.

While there may be several ways to approach a chute, one of my favorite methods is to string up a full-sinking line with a short leader. The approach I find most effective is to cast directly downstream parallel to the seam. I focus on a primary target where I believe a trout is likely to be holding. Then I develop a secondary target where I need to place the cast in order to give the streamer time to drop deep enough in the water column before I begin the retrieve upstream. Once the fly lands downstream of my position, drag immediately sets in. This will likely keep the streamer near the surface, even with a fast-sinking line.

The next step after I make the cast to the secondary target is to place the rod tip below the surface. The deeper the trout are holding, the deeper the rod tip must be positioned. If I quickly shove the rod tip down, the sinking line will begin moving deeper in the water column. The shorter leader keeps the streamer closer to the level of the sunken fly line. If the leader is too long as the line settles on the bottom, the longer leader may allow the fly to remain suspended in the faster currents. The key here is patience. If I think a larger trout is holding below the strong current, I'll position the rod tip below that current and pause long enough to allow the sinking fly line to drop to the same level as the rod tip. I prefer to fish weighted flies when fishing chutes, as I feel the additional weight helps anchor the streamer into the softer currents.

Once the line and leader are holding at the correct level, it's time to begin the retrieve. The first thing I do is choke higher on the grip, which allows me to lay the reel seat against my forearm. When fishing with a rod tip pushed toward the stream bottom, an angler has to fight against the current that's trying to push it back toward the surface. This position allows me to use my larger forearm muscle when fighting against the current instead of trying to use my wrist, which is the case if I hold the rod handle too low. The key is to keep the rod tip level and below the stronger current throughout the entire retrieve. What often happens is the current begins to push the rod tip

When fishing a fast chute (fast-moving water concentrated in a narrow area with depth), I prefer to fish directly downstream. I use the tension of the current to maintain line control while I retrieve the fly at the desired speed. In this case, I'm shoving the rod tip a foot under the water to achieve greater depth and implement a give-and-take approach designed to keep the fly in front of a fish and induce an aggressive strike. JAY NICHOLS

upward toward the surface during the retrieve, which pulls my fly out of the kill zone.

This is another reason I prefer fast-action fly rods for streamer fishing, as softer rods will buckle from the tension on the rod tip as it moves past the faster currents. A fast-action rod will bend to some degree, but the effects are minimal. A fully bent rod also creates a disconnect between angler and fly, as the fly line is no longer moving straight through the guides. Instead, the line follows the bend of the rod, and as a result, I will feel the additional tension of the line rubbing the guides during the retrieve.

Another way to decrease the rod bend is to change the angle at which you push the rod tip toward the stream bottom. A rod tip that is shoved vertically toward the water (whether from a boat or while wading) will flex more underwater. Although currents near the stream bottom are slower, there's still enough force to flex the rod tip, similar to how a rod flexes when playing a trout. Instead, I prefer to lay the rod tip at more of an angle. This distributes the tension of the current over a longer surface of the rod, creating a slight bend instead of a short drastic one. The result is a more direct feel for the fly when retrieving streamers with a submerged rod tip.

TAILOUTS

Tailouts can occur when a pool or run transitions into a riffle. The stream channel narrows, which focuses the currents, which in turn focuses the food supply into a smaller but more defined area where trout will take up position and feed. Active trout will normally hold where the riffle transitions into the run or pool, along the edges of a pool, and where the pool transitions into the next riffle.

Tailouts are prime spots for the streamer angler, but due to extreme differences in hydraulics, the presentations are more limited. To make an upstream presentation to a trout holding at the very tail end of the pool, just above the riffled section, you would have to place line and leader on the fast-moving currents directly downstream of where the fish are likely to hold. Such a presentation would quickly rip the fly away from a trout's holding lie, as the top end of the riffle would drag the fly line downstream. While trout holding in tailouts are often active feeders, a fly moving that fast will rarely be followed. The key is keeping the fly in the strike zone long enough to gain the trout's attention, but at the same time not giving the trout too much time to think about it.

Fishing a tailout directly across-stream can be just as tricky. You need to continuously mend upstream if currents grab any part of the fly line and begin to drag it downstream. If possible, I prefer to wade upstream of the target, so I can cast down and

Develop a game plan before making your first cast. Trout will hold in shallow water during low light, so make sure you place a cast in these areas before moving into the water. Think about the presentation in two parts: primary and secondary targets. Primary is where you expect a fish to hold; secondary is where you need to place the cast.

A good way to cover water is to increase casting length and present down-and-across. This a great tool when fishing large or nondescript sections of water. JAY NICHOLS

After the fly has swung directly downstream of you, continue by throwing a mend off to the side, which will move the fly sideways. I find this to be a useful tool when I see a fish following my fly up to me, and suddenly I mend to reposition the direction of the retrieve. This change of direction may trigger a strike. JAY NICHOLS

across and retrieve the streamer across the tailout. I don't feel the need to hold the streamer directly downstream, as I do when fishing deeper pools, because trout in tailouts are generally active feeders and need less coaxing.

This down-and-across approach can be done with any line, but my preference is either a floating or sinking-tip line. Tailouts typically shallow out, and I prefer not to have my sinking line damaged from rubbing on a rocky or hard stream bottom. Floating or sinking-tip lines can also be mended anytime during the retrieve. Remember, the streamer will follow the path of the line on the water, and continuously mending line toward either side of the streamer when fishing down-and-across will keep the fly moving across-stream instead of being pulled directly back upstream. This allows you to cover the entire tailout with fewer casts.

SLACK WATER

This water type often occurs immediately off the bank and is also the water most anglers walk through before casting their line. Some may refer to this as "frog water," a reference to the static or foamy water where a frog would live. While slack water isn't the water type that holds the most fish, it will harbor trout during the right conditions—typically low light, dirty water, and high-water events. Slack water is also an attractor to smaller fish, including chubs, minnows, and smaller trout, as the slower water offers protection from stronger currents. For example, once trout fingerlings are released into the stream, these young trout tend to take up position in the slack water. Some slack water may be considered a primary lie, as it offers large trout slower currents for resting lies, bubbles or foam to provide overhead protection from predators, and a food source. I say "larger trout" because smaller trout may need a continuous source of drifting insects to satisfy their caloric requirements, and a section of slack water may offer little in the form of such prey.

My favorite slack water occurs above the intersection of two separate currents, such as at the tip of an island where two currents join. All the water from the very tip of the island to where the currents join is a potential hotbed of trout. This is also a favorite spot when fishing a flooded river system, as both adult and juvenile fish will seek this slack water as a refuge from fighting the stronger currents. I've seen this scenario play out time and time again while fishing tailwaters during full generation. At these times the river appears to be swollen, as strong currents sweep through the stream channel, and all fish seek refuge in the slower sections.

Shallow slack water (less than 2 feet deep) may hold larger trout during low-light periods, but I find slack water often needs to be 2 feet deep or more to hold resting fish during daylight

Slack water with depth is a prime spot to place a cast, even during midday. Trophy-size trout will often rest in slack water during the daytime.

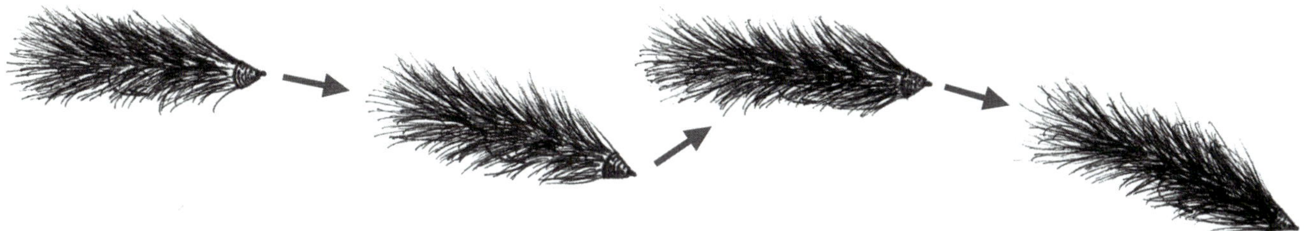

While I do prefer to fish with tungsten, there are conditions where tungsten is too heavy or I may not want my fly to erratically jig up and down. As a result, I sometimes use brass heads, even though they provide less motion than tungsten.

hours. Remember, a prime lie is one that offers protection, and 2 feet is a good depth for overhead protection from predators. If slack water reaches this depth, it often holds resting fish. These trout need to be enticed to strike your fly. Holding your flies in a down-and-across manner directly in front of a likely holding spot is a good choice when fishing midday on a section of slack water. There's a high probability trout holding in slack water during this time are resting, not hunting, and quickly swimming your fly past a resting trout will draw little notice. Instead, you need to keep the fly moving directly in front of the trout, holding it in the trout's killing zone. Even though the trout may be resting, it will likely attack if you keep the fly in the zone long enough. All we're doing is continually dangling a piece of meat in front of the fish. Similar to how we humans can't resist leftover pizza on the counter, even though we may have already had our fill, most trout will eventually break from their resting pattern and attack.

Kelly Galloup, in *Streamer Fishing for Trophy Trout with Kelly Galloup*, provides a great tip concerning the small substrate found on stream bottoms and how it provides resting spots for larger trout. Fine substrate is continually moved through the river system by stronger currents, but Kelly points out that as substrate passes through a soft spot (one with no current), the material drops to the bottom. So an accumulation of fine substrate may indicate a potential slack-water resting spot for a fish. We may need to coax the fish holding in these locations by using a dangling effect, rather than quickly swimming the fly past their position.

As I mentioned earlier, smaller or younger fish are found in shallow slack water and larger trout will hunt these grounds, especially during low light. So often I've been standing still in slack water while night-fishing, and then I suddenly hear the water erupt a couple yards away—very likely a larger trout hunting prey. This is also the same water I've fished during the daylight hours countless of times without touching a fish.

FISHING HIGH WATER

Some trout seek the banks during high water, but not all of them. Midstream boulders, drop-offs, and other structure offer hydraulic cushions where trout can rest and feed in higher flows. The issue becomes one of how to reach them. The stronger currents above will likely rip your flies out of the trout's feeding zone. The only solution I've found for reaching these fish is to use either a long leader or a level fly line with a heavily weighted streamer, just as I would when fishing streamers in pocketwater. I don't like to use fast-sinking lines because I want to focus my weights into a smaller area and reduce the overall diameter of the line and leader that touches the faster surface currents. Instead, I use a heavily weighted streamer in combination with a long leader/nymphing line. My current rig has the RIO Euro Nymph Line created by my friend Steve Parrott in combination with a level tippet tied straight to the weighted streamer. This line has a bright tip that acts as a strike indicator, and the tippet is slightly longer than the water depth I'm fishing. This allows me to keep the line's fluorescent tip close to water's surface and look for any clues of a strike. A section of 0X (approximately 15-pound) fluorocarbon tippet is attached using a loop-to-loop knot. The 15-pound test is strong enough to pull my streamers out of most snags, but thin

Greg Bricker and I pose with a Yellowstone River brown trout taken midstream behind a boulder in a heavy rapid. Wherever there's soft water, a good trout is likely resting and waiting for its next meal. Guides like Bricker will work hard to row you toward these spots, even on the Yellowstone's white-water sections.

A backeddy is a welcome sight, as these slow-moving bodies of water are holding grounds for trophy trout. LANCE WILT

Doug Ouellette is known for catching big fish near his home in Reno, Nevada. Doug catches big trout where most anglers won't even make a cast during the daylight hours—the deep slack water.

enough to allow the streamer to drop to the bottom. Also, the pattern of choice is a jigging-style streamer, where the hook point rides upside-down. This is important when bouncing bottom in heavy water. I want my fly to bounce bottom, but I also want to reduce the number of hang-ups. I'll use weighted streamers when fishing streams that have little or no wood anchored on the bottom. Like with European nymphing, the weighted fly creates a direct connection between rod tip and nymph—there's no slack, and I'm in touch with my streamer while dredging bottom.

However, when fishing stream bottoms laced with woody debris that can eat flies faster than a Venus flytrap, I use a buoyant streamer combined with a heavy split shot. I employ a slinky-style modification commonly used for steelhead and salmon in the Great Lakes: The split shot is tied off a dropper (a piece of tippet weaker in diameter than what the streamer is tied to) instead of the main line. With this rig, the buoyant streamer is suspended immediately above the stream bottom and away from most potential snags. Second, when the split shot hangs up and you can't retrieve your fly, you can just break off the weaker tag and save your streamer.

FLIP AND RETRIEVE

The flip and retrieve technique is a useful tactic for streamer fishing in confined areas. It especially helpful when you're forced to present the fly downstream to the trout. This is a variation of a small stream dry-fly presentation I learned from Joe Humphreys.

1. Grabbing the tippet 6 inches above the fly, I prepare to cast out my streamer pattern. Distance is not critical, as I plan to let the current pull my streamer downstream to its destination.

2. Bow-and-arrow the streamer across-stream. The goal is to place the line belly in a faster current, which creates drag and pulls the streamer downstream.

3. Keep the rod tip angled up to keep additional tension on the rig, so your streamer doesn't snag bottom as the current pulls the rig downstream.

4. As the current pulls your streamer closer to the target, begin to lower the rod tip in preparation for the retrieve. Point the rod tip to the seam you want to hold and fish your streamer in. In this case, I want to retrieve the streamer tight to the bank, so I point the rod tip close to the bank. If I wanted to fish farther out, I'd hold my rid tip farther away until my streamer swung directly below my rod tip.

5. Wait until the streamer is located directly downstream (in line) with your rod tip. Point the rod tip toward the streamer to achieve a direct connection during the retrieve. Pinch the line between your rod hand and the rod cork. In the event a trout strikes during the swing, pull your elbow back to set the hook.

6. Continuing to keep the line pinched, move your line hand toward the stripping guide to begin the retrieve. Do not let go of the line until the line hand has control.

7. Now you can retrieve the fly tight to the bank at the desired speed. You can also use this approach when streams are blown out and fish are forced to move tight to the bank.

UNDERCUT BANKS

Fishing around undercut banks has yielded some of the best trout from my home waters. These lies offer a good trout everything it could want: a resting spot, shelter, and a food source. However, it is important to realize that not all undercuts provide a resting place for a fish. An ideal undercut bank is one that pulls a slow current underneath the bank, but not one so strong that the trout has to fight the currents to hold its position. Remember, prime lies offer protection, a food source, and a place to rest.

Undercut banks occur in a number of situations including outside bends, exposed root systems, and man-made undercut banks created for fish structure. While trout will leave the comforts of an undercut bank to chase down food items, success occurs more frequently when you can extend the drift of their streamer across an undercut bank. I know what you're thinking—that's common sense, right? Then why do we see so many anglers casting directly across the current to an undercut section, which creates drag and will likely pull the streamer away from the bank? Granted, for reasons unknown to me, there are times when trout key in on a streamer that moves away from the bank. This evading maneuver will at times trigger the trout to chase down the fleeing prey. However, there are days (such as bright sunny days) when a trout hold tight to cover and will not likely move too far away from its prime lie to chase a streamer.

Casting directly across-stream and beginning a retrieve (without any mending) allows the streamer to drift several feet before drag sets in and pulls the fly from the bank. I prefer to keep my fly swimming close to the bank for as long as possible. This means either casting directly upstream or downstream (parallel) to the bank, or mending the line belly so the fly runs parallel to the undercut, even when casting from across-stream.

When working undercut banks, I prefer to use a full-floating line, a leader length that allows me to keep my fly down at a trout's eye level, and a weighted streamer, presented with an upstream approach. While any line type can be effective when fishing undercuts, I like the freedom of a floating line—I know that at any time I can reposition the line on the water. On many occasions, I work the belly of the fly line just as a nymph fisher would work a nymph under a suspension device. I often use a shorter, less active, or slower retrieve to maintain action in the fly but not so much that I pull it away from the fish's zone. Remember, trout are not always keyed into eating frantically moving prey. Sometimes an unsuspecting prey casually swims in front of a larger trout positioned in a dark undercut bank.

LOGS

When fishing any type of structure, you need to be able to read how the current is moving off the object. Larger trout take up prime lies, which offer food, protection, and a spot to rest. The last one is important: Larger trout are the kings of the water and are not often found in lies where they have to continuously fight the current, unless there's a good reason. When examining any exposed fish structure, I first look for a hydraulic cushion where there's little current. Often, larger trout will be found holding in this soft cushion. This soft spot becomes my primary target, but I also must develop a secondary target—the place where I need to place my cast in order to allow my fly to drift past the fish. In the case of a fallen log, check which direction the current is moving off the object. A log that falls from the bank into the river at an upstream angle will usually push water away from the bank. This means the inside of the fallen log is likely a holding area for a trout. On the other hand, a tree that falls from the bank into the river with its butt section on the bank and the trunk angled downward toward the water will likely push the strongest current toward the bank. As a result, a larger trout is likely to hold on the outside edge.

In my earlier days, I would just fire cast after cast toward any structure without thinking about where my primary target was. While trout are likely to move farther to chase down a streamer, there are times when you almost have to put it in the trout's mouth. Next time you're working streamers, have a plan on where you expect to move a fish. Look for those soft depressions around structure, and you will likely find a trout waiting for a meal.

When fishing from a drifting boat, you have only one casting opportunity. You must decide what side of the log to cast to. Larger trout often hold in slower-moving water, which often means the downstream side. However, pay attention to the upstream current moving toward the log. If the current is fast, it's less likely a trophy trout will be holding upstream of the log (i.e., lying directly in the fast current). In this situation my first cast would be toward the upstream side—the current is slower and the lie has depth and shade, making it a prime spot for a larger trout.

Even in dirty water, look for dark edges that may represent submerged boulders. Trout will use similar structure both for protection and as a potential ambush area. Find submerged boulders, and you'll likely find a trout on the hunt for food.

BOULDER FIELDS

I define a boulder field as a run or pool that contains a high concentration of submerged boulders. When using the word "boulder," I'm referring to any large substrate that can act as habitat for an adult trout. On my home water, Fishing Creek, you rarely see fish holding in the open unless they are feeding on dry flies. Instead, they are very habitat orientated. They stick tight to structure and will often wedge themselves underneath rocks, even if the rock is about the same length as the fish itself.

Boulder fields are hotbeds for ambushing trout. While the boulders provide ample cover for the trout, the issue is that trout often become glued to the spot, and it's hard to pull them away from the boulder fields. Insects are attached to submerged boulders, and smaller trout, minnows, sculpins, and crayfish will feed on the insects. Trout don't need to move far from the boulders because the food will often come directly to them. As a result, you need to coax the trout out of its lair.

Dredging your streamer along the face of a single boulder is easier than retrieving your pattern in between a cluster of boulders. If I'm working around a single boulder or boulders that are spaced far enough apart, I'll use a rig that allows me to creep my streamer right along stream bottom, depending on the speed and depth of the water. I'll retrieve the pattern at the same level I suspect a fish to be holding. Most likely, I'll be using a jig-style fly to keep the fly tight to the stream bottom. Normally, I use a floating line when fishing water up to 2 feet deep and then switch to either a sinking-tip line or full-sinking line when dealing with water deeper than 2 feet. If I can focus on a single boulder, I first identify the location where a trout is likely to hold. Often, this is the soft spot in the current or any crevasse around the rock where the trout can hold.

The approach is simple. Cast ahead of the boulder to allow your pattern enough time to sink. Once on the bottom, casually retrieve the fly until it passes the potential ambush site. At this point, you should begin to erratically retrieve the fly to mimic a fleeing baitfish, which is usually what triggers the strike. This is why they tell you never to run if you come upon a grizzly bear: Running away may trigger an aggressive response from the bear.

However, if I'm fishing a group of closely positioned boulders, I'll switch tactics, because I'm likely to snag one of the boulders if I use a heavily weighted streamer. Instead, I switch to a full-sinking line with a buoyant hanger-style streamer. I'll shorten the leader to 2 to 3 feet to enable me to pull the streamer as tight as possible to the stream bottom without sliding my line over the boulders' sharp edges. I'll try to position the line directly in between the boulders, but this isn't always possible; microcurrents coming off boulders can quickly move a sunken line into another position. The retrieves are usually short and powerful to create an up-and-down motion as the fly dives toward the boulder during the line strip and then quickly pulls away from a potential trout during the pause.

NERVOUS WATER

When talking about nervous water, most anglers automatically think of saltwater fish either moving through shallow water or busting baitfish near the surface. Although it doesn't occur frequently, trout anglers can also observe nervous water. My most memorable occasion with trout occurred while floating a section of the Au Sable River with Todd Zwetzig and Josh Greenburg. While I was on the bow and focused on fishing directly across to the bank, Josh noticed movement in a flat 100 yards downstream and asked Todd to anchor for a moment. Once the boat came to a halt, Josh showed us the area where he noticed some nervous water. Within a minute, a large wake moved across the flat. It was a large trout hunting prey. Todd asked me to take off the heavier streamer pattern I was using for the swift currents above and switch to a buoyant hanging fly (Tommy Lynch's Double D) to work the shallow flat (6-inch-deep water). As Todd continued to position the boat as we approached the flat, we could occasionally see small baitfish breaking the surface with a large wake circling the area. Just as we approached the kill zone, Todd told me where to place the cast. Once the cast was made and the line sank to the bottom of the shallow flat, Todd instructed me to make a fast retrieve because he didn't want to give the aggressive trout too much time to look at the fly. With the water being only a few inches deep and my using a longer 7-foot leader with the full-sinking line, the buoyant burnt orange Double D barely broke the surface. It began to kick and dart immediately below the surface. Within 10 seconds of the retrieve, a large shadow shot out from the bank and fully committed itself to taking the streamer. While I've only witnessed a few nervous-water events while trout fishing, it pays to keep a lookout at your surroundings as Josh did that afternoon. This allowed us to stop the boat, change our rig, and develop a plan. And once in a while, a plan will come together.

While it happens more frequently in the salt, freshwater trout anglers will also occasionally see nervous water. During a float with Josh Greenburg and Todd Zwetzig on Michigan's Au Sable River, Josh noticed nervous water 100 yards downstream along a back channel while fishing the opposite bank. We repositioned the drift boat to the opposite side and caught this 2-foot fish two minutes later. The moral of the story: Use your peripheral vision. Josh's keen awareness of the overall surroundings was the only reason we caught this beauty.

Joe Goodspeed is one of the top big-fish hunters I know. One of his favorite approaches is to use large streamers to locate and move big fish. Then he comes back at a later time and dead-drifts small crayfish patterns with great results. JOE GOODSPEED

OTHER VARIABLES

While you should always be on the lookout for prime trout habitat, you also need to think about where concentrations of baitfish are holding. While baitfish and other larger prey can be found in any likely trout habitat, there are always a few anomalies that encourage trout to hunt in particular areas. For example, Pennsylvania has a number of transitional streams, where stream temperatures are cold enough to support trout during the spring and fall but become too warm during the summer. The result is a stream system that supports not only trout but also a healthy population of chubs, minnows, and other larger trout food. Many of these minnows spawn during the spring, and provide a concentration of large food to the trout.

Another example would be smaller warmwater tributaries that dump into trout waters. It's important to remember that prior to the dams, many Southern tailwaters were historically warmwater streams. This means many of the tributaries that dump into these tailwaters harbor warmwater minnow species, making them a target for the streamer angler. While fishing the North Fork River in Arkansas with my father-in-law, Walt, we asked the locals where we could buy minnows at the campground. To our surprise, we found out the creek mouth on the property had a good minnow population, allowing Walt to capture live bait. As we were walking down the bank toward the creek mouth, I could see a large school of minnows holding close to the transition where the warm water meets the cold, dam-released water. It was midday, and I wasn't able to see any larger trout—but that changed later that night when I hit the water with a flashlight after coming back from night-fishing. I saw several quality trout (17 to 19 inches) positioned close to the school of minnows.

Other potential hunting grounds may include spawning grounds of both trout and salmon, where fry hatch. I witnessed this several times when fishing the Feather River in California during mid-December when steelhead were focused on eating salmon fry. While I had strikes throughout the river, the majority of them occurred near the salmon's spawning beds. I was told the salmon fry had just begun hatching and had not yet moved far from the spawning beds.

Transitional tributaries (those cold in spring and warm in summer) are hotbeds for minnow populations. While floating the South Holston River in Tennessee, Lance Wilt switched from a nymphing rig to a streamer rig the moment he noticed a creek mouth entering the river. He immediately moved this brown trout on a Game Changer.

Patterns

4

Conditions change for the streamer angler, just as they would for the nymph or dry-fly angler. One minute you're fishing shallow riffles at daybreak and quickly stripping swimming streamers. Later the same day, you're dredging deep runs under a high sun. Carrying a variety of streamer types and pattern designs will allow you to deal with changing stream conditions. Our job as anglers is to find the "flavor of the day" for trout. There are times when a trout's hunger is triggered by a swinging pattern, while other days they're looking for a jigging action. The amount of weight in your fly, or lack thereof, is also an important consideration. Whether you're fishing a weighted fly with a floating line or an unweighted fly with a sinking line (or a combination of all the above), the first step to success is getting the fly to the trout's

I don't pretend to be a fly designer. I let talented folks like Tommy Lynch develop killer streamer patterns for my pleasure. A great pattern is not born overnight in the vise. It takes hours of refinement to develop one. Guys like Russ Madden, Kelly Galloup, Rich Strolis, and Mike Schmidt have put hundreds of hours into their patterns before calling them finished products.

Simplify your gear. Mike Schmidt looks through his streamer box. This is a guy who commercially ties thousands of patterns each year, yet he carries only a couple dozen streamers streamside. While pattern can be critical to success, it is important to remember that a streamer is only as effective as the angler fishing it.

feeding level. Whatever the trout's preference, having a range of streamer designs should allow you to eventually find the pattern that matches both stream conditions and trout behavior.

In an attempt to organize my patterns by the means I fish them, I've created six classifications of streamers—swimming, jigging, swinging, dead-drifting, floating, and hanging. I carry at least two flies from each of my six streamer categories in my fly wallet. This way, I feel I can handle just about any stream condition I face. This classification system organizes my own boxes and makes sense to me; you may find another classification system that works better for you.

Keep in mind that some patterns can fit into more than one category (for instance, I dead-drift a Clouser Minnow under an indicator, but the pattern works best when being jigged.) Also, don't worry about having to carry hundreds (or sometimes thousands) of flies like many dry-fly and nymph fishers. The thing I enjoy most about streamer patterns is that I lose very few of them—not because I don't make bad casts, but because I use heavy tippet. Rarely do I use less than 3X tippet when streamer fishing. Instead, I'm fishing tippet that ranges from 10 to 15 pounds, so I lose very few flies on fish or on hang-ups. With heavier tippet material, I feel confident making casts near structure and being more aggressive with my cast.

This South Holston River rainbow fell to Schmidt's Meal Ticket.

Swimming flies are patterns that can be pulled quickly through the water with little resistance. You need synthetics and natural materials that wick water, as you don't want to retrieve a fly that feels like you are pulling a wet sock. This modified Deceiver is a favorite for when trout are on the hunt and are triggered by a faster-moving fly. LANCE WILT

SWIMMING STREAMERS

A swimming pattern is designed to be fished exactly as it sounds—in a swimming motion. The swimming motion can be erratic, continuous, fast, slow, or any other manner that represents prey swimming though the water. While any streamer pattern can be made to swim, I feel the best swimming patterns have several features. First, I prefer a slender design, which reduces drag as you retrieve the pattern through the water. A quick look at most forage fish will reveal a long, slender appearance that permits them to move through the water with very little surface drag. A thin taper also allows you to pull the fly faster than you'd be able to pull bulky patterns thanks to the smaller diameter. Some of my favorite swimmers include both Single and Double Deceivers, the Murdich Minnow, the Sparkle Minnow, and the Ice Pick.

I use swimming patterns when I want to actively move my pattern, imitating anything from a causal swimming motion all the way to a frightened minnow trying to escape a predator. I prefer to tie my swimming patterns with materials that don't absorb too much water such as synthetics, bucktail, and marabou. When tied correctly, these materials can create great-looking baitfish patterns that can move swiftly through the water with very little resistance. I also prefer to use no or very little weight with this type of pattern because too much weight in the design detracts from the fly's natural swimming action. The only weight I normally use with swimming flies is when building a keel on the fly. Keels are welcome additions to any swimming pattern (especially articulated ones), as they will cause the rear end to kick during the retrieve, similar to a natural minnow's tail.

I look at swimming patterns as prospecting tools for covering a lot of water. Instead of slowly working these patterns in certain pockets or seams, I'll make longer casts and then swim these patterns over a larger area of water. The patterns' thin diameter and water-wicking design also make it easier to cast these flies over longer distances as compared to heavier or bulkier patterns. (You also don't have to worry about hitting your rod or yourself with a heavily weighted fly.) Also, trying to quickly pull a streamer that feels like a wet sock puts tremendous strain on your stripping fingers. Bulkier flies create more resistance on your hand, which in turn places additional strain on your fingers—sometimes to the point of swelling. I used bulkier streamers with jigging and slower retrieves (your stripping hand isn't under as much tension this way), but I try my best to avoid bulk when pulling faster retrieves.

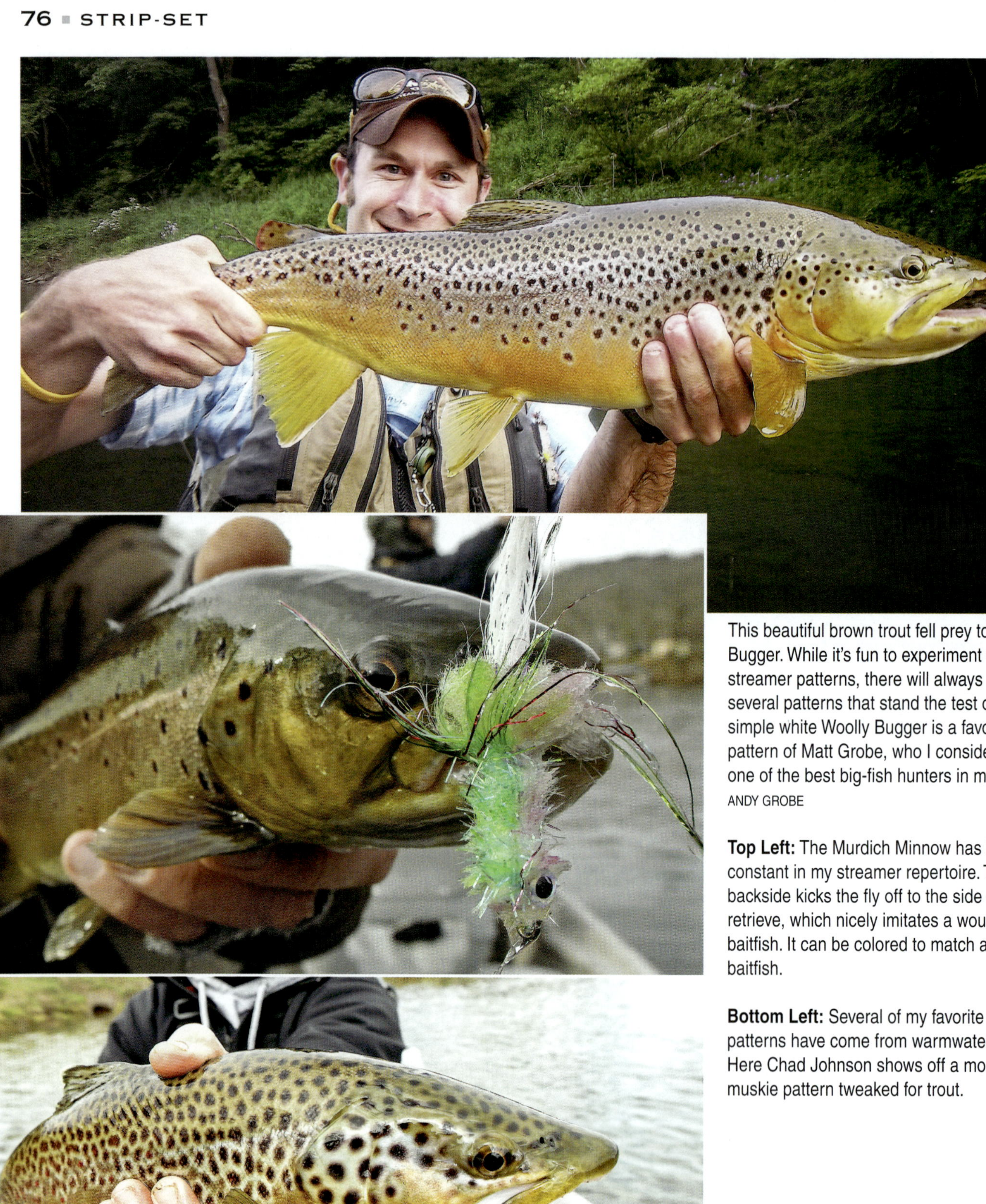

This beautiful brown trout fell prey to a Woolly Bugger. While it's fun to experiment with new streamer patterns, there will always be several patterns that stand the test of time. A simple white Woolly Bugger is a favorite pattern of Matt Grobe, who I consider to be one of the best big-fish hunters in my area. ANDY GROBE

Top Left: The Murdich Minnow has become a constant in my streamer repertoire. The bulky backside kicks the fly off to the side during the retrieve, which nicely imitates a wounded baitfish. It can be colored to match any baitfish.

Bottom Left: Several of my favorite streamer patterns have come from warmwater fly tiers. Here Chad Johnson shows off a modified muskie pattern tweaked for trout.

JIGGING STREAMERS

Jigging-style streamers are by far my favorite type, especially when imitating sculpins near my home water. Jigging streamers are basically any pattern with the bulk of their weight distributed near the front end of the hook. During the actual retrieve, the line and leader put tension on the fly and cause the pattern to move toward the direction of the line and leader. However, during the pause in the retrieve, gravity sets in, and the hook's front weight begins to drop toward the bottom until you strip in the line, creating a continuous up-and-down movement during the retrieve. The Clouser Minnow is without a doubt the world's most recognizable jigging streamer, and for good reason—it catches fish everywhere.

I think the reason I enjoy fishing jigging-style flies is because they imitate the natural movements of the sculpin so well. Remember, sculpins are not continuous swimmers. They move in short spurts and drop back down toward the stream bottom, and a jigging fly behaves in a similar manner. However, any baitfish can be converted to a jig style. And jigging flies don't have to be fished near the stream bottom; they can be fished at all levels. The key to the pattern is the continuous up-and-down motion.

The one challenge with fishing jigs is controlling their sink rate. If you allow too much slack in your presentation, the fly will quickly grab the bottom. You can lose control if you're not able to retrieve line at the pattern's drop rate. This is why floating lines are best for anglers who are starting out—the floating line is positioned above the surface, and the faster surface currents keep the line moving downstream and help maintain greater tension on the rig.

Jigging-style streamers don't have to be tied on jig hooks. Instead, weight placed near the front end of the hook is the key to giving the streamer its deadly quick tip-dropping motion. This is why, when tying lead wire onto the hook shank behind a conehead, you should only make enough wraps so that the wire sits inside the cone and doesn't extend farther down toward the shank. Remember, the farther down the shank the weight is distributed, the flatter the movement of the streamer during the retrieve.

While jig patterns can be constructed from numerous materials and designs, I find myself using tungsten. A tungsten cone sinks twice as fast as a brass one, for example, so the head of a fly tied with tungsten will drop more dramatically than the head of a fly tied with a lighter material, and that quick drop accentuates the jigging action. Other materials, including remolded lead heads and preformed heads like Flymen's Sculpin Helmets, provide a similar up-and-down motion.

When casting heavily weighted streamers (like the Headbanger), I prefer to cast off to the side, as this keeps the fly farther away from my body and the rod tip. Some of my most painful experiences have come from a large tungsten conehead (not the hook point) smashing against the back of my skull. We all make casting mistakes, so when we do, this position reduces the chances of a fly colliding with either your head or the rod tip.

The Headbanger by Rich Strolis incorporates a Sculpin Helmet, which not only anchors the fly deep in the water column, but creates a commotion when landing on the water—an essential for fishing dirty water.

When tied properly, jigs will invert the hook so the hook rides up and away from stream bottom. This will allow you to bounce bottom with fewer hang-ups. It also allows this style of pattern to cross over to the dead-drift category, due to the pattern's ability to get deep and reduce hang-ups.

I use jigs to bottom-bounce my streamers or hold my fly in a pocket for a longer period of time. When the trout aren't active, such as in the winter, I fish patterns slower and closer to the bottom. This slow-and-deep approach is no different than how the minnow fishermen fish their live bait during the dead of winter. While jigs can be fished in all water types, I feel they excel when targeting soft water during high-water events when trout are forced to move to soft water where they don't have to fight strong currents.

Tungsten weighs twice as much as brass. This means the head of a tungsten conehead will drop twice as fast as a brass conehead streamer. When possible, I prefer to fish tungsten heads, as they increase the up-and-down motion of the jig-style streamer.

SWINGING STREAMERS

Swinging streamer patterns are similar to wet-fly patterns—they're lighter in weight, they have little bulk in comparison to other streamer patterns, and they're smaller in overall size. By lighter in weight, I'm referring to patterns that aren't too heavy for you to cast long distances. Again, I look at swinging patterns as tools for covering a large body of water. The first step in having the ability to cover a range of water is casting longer distances when necessary.

The smaller overall size of swinging patterns does a great job of imitating both trout and salmon fry or any small prey item. Remember, big trout eat smaller meals, and there are periods when they are keyed on smaller prey. One such time is from late February through early April, when trout fry hatch from their eggs and adult trout begin to focus on this small but protein-rich food source.

While swinging patterns can imitate a wide range of forage, I like to swing patterns that look and swim like tiny baitfish, baby trout, salmon fry, or even large nymphs such as Eastern Green Drakes or Hex nymphs. These patterns are normally smaller (3/4-inch to 2-inch) and lighter in weight, and I'll swing them higher in the water column or hold them in slow pockets. A thin-profiled pattern will slice its way through the water column. I want the fly to move through the water with as little resistance as possible, so I stay away from bulkier patterns. You can weight patterns, but I stay away from dumbbell-style weights or any materials that create too much bulk, which results in unwanted resistance during the swing. I also want the fly to be small enough that the trout can inhale the entire pattern rather than starting with a small bite, as may be the case when swinging larger articulated streamers.

DEAD-DRIFTING STREAMERS

Large trout meals such as crayfish crawl along the bottom, or sometimes baits will float in the currents if they are stunned or dead, and dead-drifting is an appropriate representation for imitating this prey. A good pattern for dead-drifting moves naturally in the water without my having to impart motion with the line hand or rod tip. Often, these patterns are tied with wool or another material that absorbs water, which helps keep the larger fly deeper in the water column. Patterns like Mike Mercer's Rag Sculpin are very effective for dead-drifting. Several of the jig patterns can also be used for dead-drifting, as the hook rides upside-down and allows you to bottom-bounce your streamers with fewer hang-ups. Another good option is tying on a buoyant streamer like a Bow River Bugger or a Shenk Sculpin and dropping a heavy split shot a few inches off the nose.

Dead-drifting is also effective for those times when trout are not chasing food or when fishing dirty water. In these cases you need to slow down the drift of the pattern. The few times I dead-drift normally coincide with dirty water, and so the few dead-drifting patterns I use are dark-colored with flash. These cut a better silhouette and provide an easier target for trout to see.

Sometimes when trout are not actively chasing down food, you need to place the streamer right in their faces and try to elicit an aggression strike. When two guys trash-talk one another from opposite ends of the bar, it's often just talk until one guy walks over and gets right in the other's face. Even a finger poke can start the fight. That's what I'm trying to do when the trout are not chasing food—I'm trying to present a fly directly in their face and pick a fight with them. I want to set off their aggressive trigger.

Jon Hooper poses with a beautiful Watauga River brown trout that fell prey to a Mike's Meal Ticket. Yellow dumbbell eyes are one of my favorite colors for streamer patterns.

FLOATING FISH AND MOUSE PATTERNS

Fishing topwater streamers is my favorite approach. Anglers who fish locations such as Alaska and Kamchatka will tell you about their successes with floating patterns during the daylight hours. Unfortunately, where I fish in central Pennsylvania, there are only a few occasions where a floating streamer pattern will yield good results during the daytime. One time is when our state agency decides to stock juvenile trout into a stream. For whatever reason, a small percentage of the young trout die on the way from the hatchery to the stream, which results in the fish floating on the surface after being dumped into the stream. From time to time, I've seen several fish greater than 15 inches take a dead juvenile trout off the surface. Other daytime topwater opportunities will take place on tailwaters when a shad kill occurs and the trout start sucking down the floating flesh pieces.

By far, the most opportunities occur at dusk or dawn when trout begin looking up toward the bright sky to search for silhouettes of their prey floating overhead. Fishing a pair of buoyant wet flies or small streamers on the surface at dusk or dawn will catch fish. I fish most of my floating streamer patterns, especially mouse patterns, during low light and throughout the darkness. Mice become active during these periods, and this is also when trout will be more likely to chase a swimming mouse. Although the mouse is considered a mammal, I've listed the pattern as a floating streamer since it's a larger prey item. Given the choice, swimming a floating mouse during the darkness is my favorite type of streamer fishing. Personally, there's nothing more exciting than seeing your floating streamer create a wake on the water before a trout sucks down the pattern—creating a vacuum effect, along with a loud gulping sound.

There's lots of crossover between pattern types. Many of the hanging patterns I fish (such as Lynch's Double D and Galloup's Zoo Cougar) can be fished with a floating or short slow-sinking line. Since there's less opportunity for floating streamers during the daylight for the waters I fish, I only carry a handful of floating patterns, including Todd's Wiggle Minnow and a Gartside Gurgler Minnow. I'm sure I would stock more floating streamers if I lived in a region where trout were more willing to eat them.

Although those in the terminal tackle world are known to toss floating crankbait or similar lures to represent a floating minnow, you hear very little about surface streamer patterns in fly fishing. Steve Dally of Mountain Home, Arkansas, shows off a trout he caught while using his Pole Dancer pattern, which is a floating articulated streamer. This pattern tends to work immediately after a fresh stocking, when the injured fish flop around near the surface.

HANGERS/SUSPENDERS

Hanging flies are a category of buoyant streamer patterns I look at for fishing right off the bottom or higher in the water column, even while using a heavy sinking line. Often I'll use a sinking line or sinking tip in combination with hanging flies to fish a desired water depth. Because of their buoyant features, many hanging flies will begin to rise to the surface when no longer under tension from the sinking line. The pattern will dive toward the bottom again when placed under tension. This up-and-down motion is sometimes the movement a trout needs to trigger a response. Deer hair heads and patterns tied with foam are two popular materials for tying hanging patterns.

My favorite hanging pattern is the Drunk and Disorderly (aka Double D) from my good friend Tommy Lynch. The Double D is the closest thing fly fishers have to fishing a double-jointed Rapala. The fly has a wedged head formed from deer hair and Clear Cure Goo Hydro, which not only creates a slight water seal but also makes the deer hair head extremely durable. The tightly trimmed wedge cuts deep into the water and provides a more dramatic dive, especially if you swipe the rod downward during the retrieve.

I prefer to fish hanging patterns on stream bottoms that are full of woody debris or vegetation where a pattern that bounces on the bottom or that rides too close would often either hang up or collect vegetation. Hanging patterns are also great for pulling fish out of structure. Several of the Michigan rivers I fish are perfect for hanging flies because the stream bottoms are lined with fallen timber, and trout lie within this woody labyrinth. The Double D and similar patterns can hang immediately above structure and then dive inward toward the trout's holding spot as if to tease the fish. It can then dash away from the trout's ambush zone. Because of the erratic up-and-down motion of the Double D, I've found trout really have to be actively chasing food or protecting their turf for it to be effective. While Tommy likes to throw a double- and sometimes triple-articulated Drunk and Disorderly when targeting many of Michigan's larger predatory trout, I find a 3- to 5-inch single is ideal for my home waters in central Pennsylvania.

Another thing to consider when tying a hanging fly is the buoyancy of the fly versus the grain or line weight of the sinking line. Tommy Lynch taught me during our fishing adventures

Lance Wilt shows off a late-evening brown caught on Blane Chocklett's Game Changer. It's important to remember that every pattern fishes differently. Some patterns move best on the retrieve, while other move after the retrieve is done. The Game Changer is a pattern that really comes to life after the pause; you need to learn these details so you can maximize a pattern's effectiveness. LANCE WILT

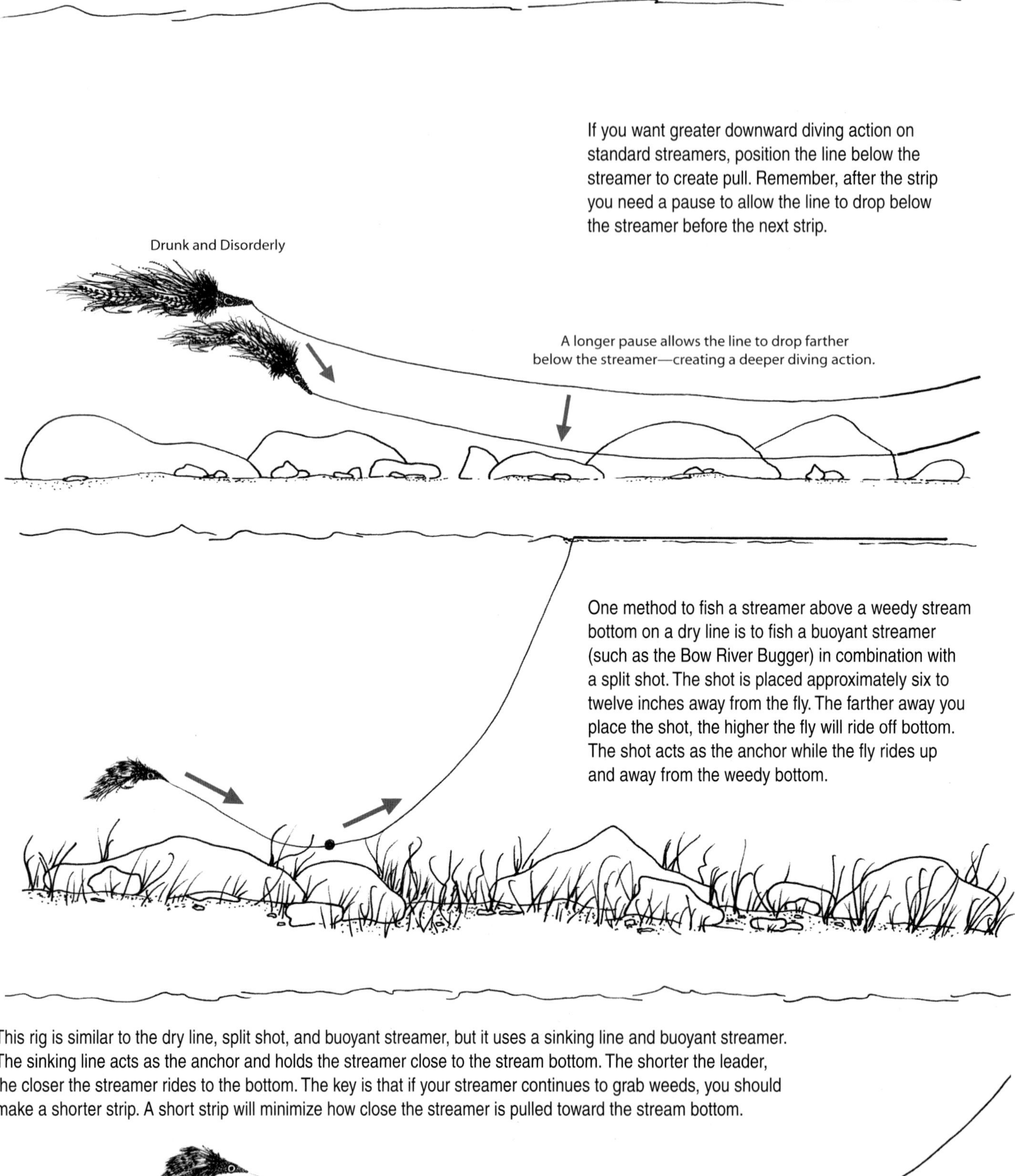

If you want greater downward diving action on standard streamers, position the line below the streamer to create pull. Remember, after the strip you need a pause to allow the line to drop below the streamer before the next strip.

One method to fish a streamer above a weedy stream bottom on a dry line is to fish a buoyant streamer (such as the Bow River Bugger) in combination with a split shot. The shot is placed approximately six to twelve inches away from the fly. The farther away you place the shot, the higher the fly will ride off bottom. The shot acts as the anchor while the fly rides up and away from the weedy bottom.

This rig is similar to the dry line, split shot, and buoyant streamer, but it uses a sinking line and buoyant streamer. The sinking line acts as the anchor and holds the streamer close to the stream bottom. The shorter the leader, the closer the streamer rides to the bottom. The key is that if your streamer continues to grab weeds, you should make a shorter strip. A short strip will minimize how close the streamer is pulled toward the stream bottom.

Tommy Lynch changes a Drunk and Disorderly to an orange color scheme. Fly color is a personal preference, and Tommy has developed a liking for the color orange. He calls orange "the new yellow."

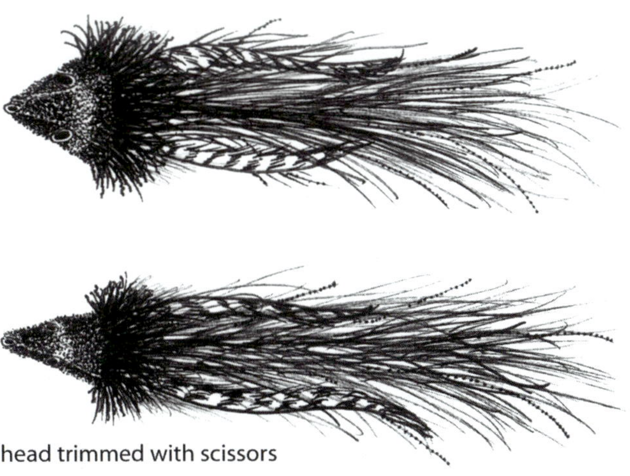

The size of a deer hair head should match the grain of the sinking line to provide ultimate movement. You don't want the line to overpower the fly or the fly to overpower the line. This means you don't want a line that's too heavy and a deer hair head streamer that lacks the buoyancy to move vertical after the pause in the retrieve. Or you don't want too buoyant of a streamer, where the line lacks the weight and sink rate to keep the fly underwater. If you find yourself fishing a variety of grain weights for sinking lines, you may need to trim the heads of the fly to match the grain and sink weight of the line.

to match the buoyancy of the Double D's head with the grain or line weight of the sinking line. You want to make sure the line doesn't overpower the fly or vice versa. Too heavy of a sinking line may drag the fly to the bottom and limit its action. Too light of a sinking line, and you don't have enough weight to pull and manipulate the fly during the retrieve. I most often use a 250-grain Orvis Depth Charge on a 7-weight for this type of fishing.

THOUGHTS ON HOOKS

Gamakatsu's B10S has become my favorite streamer hook for several reasons. First, I prefer a slightly wider hook gap compared to traditional streamer hooks. This is especially helpful when tying bulkier streamers, as it's important to keep a wide enough gap open for hooking trout. Too often, while using traditional streamer hooks, many bulky streamer patterns cover up most of the hook gap, almost to the point of creating a weed guard. I still use traditional streamer-style hooks, but only with slim patterns. Second, it has a relatively thin wire that penetrates well and is very durable. Rarely have I bent out or dulled this hook design when bouncing streamers along the bottom.

Check your streamer after any snag. Here's a Murdich Minnow I fished for an hour before realizing the hook point was broken. It took me six lost fish to realize that I needed to tie on another fly. It should only take one.

While it's important to have a strong wired hook, I think that many anglers sometimes fish too heavy of a wire, and some of the saltwater hooks currently being used for streamers are too thick for good penetration. I feel heavier wire saltwater hooks are fine for freshwater patterns that are designed to be fished with faster and longer pulls on the line. However, I find flies that are jigged on thicker saltwater hooks tend not to cinch deep enough to create a secure hook set. Instead, when tying jig-style patterns or any pattern where I fish with slower or less powerful retrieves, I look for a thinner wire hook, which doesn't need as much energy during the retrieve to get a secure hook set. Streamer hooks like TMC's 8089, Gamakatsu's B10S, and Mustad's C52S BLN all have thinner hook points that allow for more secure hook sets. I understand that I sacrifice durability when fishing thinner points, but it's a compromise I'm willing to make. This is especially true when fishing dumbbell jig eyes (when eyes are tied on top of shank), which invert the hook upside-down and keep the hook point riding up. This decreases the chances of your jig fly's hook point becoming dull.

Hook Points

I not only look for a sharp, yet strong hook point when purchasing hooks, but I also look for a design that allows me to

If you choose to hold on to your streamer while walking to another location, please do not grab the fly. On too many occasions, I've impaled my line hand with the streamer while snagging a nearby obstacle. Instead, pinch the leader 8 to 12 inches above the fly, and create an angle between your index finger and thumb so the leader can't easily slide through your fingers and allow the streamer to impale your finger. JAY NICHOLS continually sharpen the hook. There are a number of great hook designs (such as a circle hook) that incorporate an upward curve for a more secure hookup, but the curve makes it hard to sharpen the hook. Because streamers often take more time and money to tie, I do everything I can to keep fishing a pattern before it loses its effectiveness as a fish-catching tool, and that means repeated sharpenings. I look for a straight hook point with a decent gap that allows me to sharpen all sides of the hook point.

De-Barbing Your Fly

Once a fish is securely hooked, a barbed fly holds a fish better than a de-barbed hook. However, I find that my hooking percentages greatly increase when I completely or partially debarb the fly. While the barb makes it difficult for the fish to slip off the hook, it also creates a substantial barrier (i.e., surface area) for the fish's flesh to slide past during the hook set. Although you may lose a few additional fish with a barbless fly, the increased hook-up rate offsets the number of lost fish.

Add to that my safety and that of the people I fish with. Getting a small nymph hook stuck in your finger is a minor inconvenience. Getting impaled with a size 2/0 barbed streamer hook is a serious problem. And don't forget the trout that we fish for. Large hooks can do a number on a trout's mouth. So, at least consider partially crimping your barbs.

Hook Position

One of my favorite aspects of fishing from a boat is the high vantage point that allows you to observe a trout's hunting behavior from start to finish. From watching fish eat flies, I've come to the realization that trout eat streamer patterns from all angles, not just from one, and this means that there is no clearcut answer—at least for me—about the best position for the hook in a fly.

Advocates for placing the hook close to the eye tend to believe that trout hit their prey headfirst. I've read about how trout are programmed to eat a minnow headfirst. This is because forage fish and other small fish that could be considered potential trout meals have the ability to flare their fins as a defense mechanism. This prohibits some predatory trout from completely inhaling the baitfish while it eats it from behind.

However, as with any animal population, there's always a few that refuse to follow the rules. Several times a year, I find a dead trout in the 14- to 18-inch range with a perch lodged tailfirst in its mouth. Obviously some trout never get the "eat your prey headfirst" memo. One study by a Canadian researcher (T. E. Reimchen, "Evolutionary attributes of headfirst prey manipulation and swallowing in piscivores," 1991) found that headfirst orientation was influenced by the gape of the predator's mouth and the overall size of the prey. Reimchen found that feeding orientation (tailfirst versus headfirst) was random when the prey size was less than half of the predator's gape. However, headfirst orientation greatly increased as the size of prey increased. In other words, as fly size increases, this should correlate with more strikes occurring headfirst.

The result of a long, frustrating day of trying to find the right streamer pattern. Instead of placing the wet streamers back into the box, where they will likely cause other streamers to rust, stick them on a piece of black foam and place it on your dashboard. (This is a tip I got from Rich Strolis.) The black attracts heat and allows you to dry out your patterns before placing them back in your box.

Ultimately, I think the position of the hook point really depends on how you fish the pattern. While it's impossible to predict the angle at which trout will chase your streamer, understanding where you present the fly in relation to a likely holding area may have some bearing on the angle at which trout strikes the streamer. While it makes sense why a trout would eat prey headfirst, I believe there's either an aggressive or hunger mechanism that triggers a trout to strike regardless of how the prey is positioned to the fish's mouth. For example, whether it's an aggression strike or a hunger strike, swinging and holding your pattern downstream often provokes a tailfirst strike, regardless of fly size.

While fishing the Feather River in California with good friend Hutch Hutchinson and our guide, Toby Uppinhouse, I found myself swinging for steelhead for the first time from a parked drift boat. Because of the high vantage point, I was able to watch the few steelhead I landed come from off the bottom and inhale the fly. Toby had us swinging our flies through likely holding areas directly downstream from our position and then had us hold our flies in those areas for up to thirty seconds. I watched three out of the four steelhead I landed approach the fly from behind and inhale the smaller salmon parr. I believe the steelhead ate tailfirst because the salmon parr pattern was positioned upstream from the steelhead. Trout can act like sharks, meaning they'll sneak up from behind and attack the rear position. So when you are presenting flies from a down-and-across position, it may prove more successful to place the hook in the rear. I've found this to be the case for not only small fry patterns, but for any size streamer that is presented upstream of the fish.

On the other hand, when fishing streamer patterns and retrieving them downstream—in other words, moving the fly toward the fish—many of the takes have been headfirst. This is even true when using 4- to 5-inch articulated patterns. Because trout spend so much time facing upstream, when you retrieve a fly downstream, you are pulling the fly headfirst toward the trout, and the trout strikes while facing upstream.

I've also noticed the tailfirst strike when fishing for brown trout around spawning season. Though they can do this throughout the year, in the fall, it almost appears as if trout are striking the pattern more out of aggression than hunger, like the fish is trying to protect its territory. Instead of trying to eat the streamer, they often follow the pattern for long distances and nip at it from behind, so I tend to fish patterns with hooks in the rear.

I noticed this behavior while drifting the South Holston River Tennessee in early December with my wife and our excellent guide, Blake Boyd. While there are several river

The trout ate this pattern headfirst while it was being dead-drifted downstream. I saw this fish come off the bottom to eat the streamer.

This trout took an articulated pattern tailfirst while it was swinging in front of a holding lie. Taking note of the position of the fly in the trout's mouth can give you some direction as to how trout are eating your streamer pattern.

sections closed during the spawn, there's still plenty of water to fish. During our five days of floating, we had numerous short strikes. Even with an articulated pattern with hooks on both the front and rear, I was connecting with only about a third of the trout striking my pattern. The patterns' tails weren't more than 3 inches away from the hook point, but I continued to get short strikes. Halfway through the drift, my wife decided to shorten her pattern's tail so the tip was flush with the bend. She did this without telling me. Within an hour she had landed four fish to my one. She only had five strikes but she connected on four of them, compared to my one-for-ten performance. Eventually she shared her little secret with me and showed me the fly. In my opinion, the once-beautiful streamer pattern I had tied now looked awful, with the tail cut back to the bend. But it caught more fish than the original, longer-tailed version I continued to fish. So don't be afraid to cut back the tail of a beautifully tied streamer if you're finding the trout are short-striking your pattern.

Articulated Patterns

Articulated patterns provide several advantages over single-shank patterns. When tied correctly, the jointed section will flex or bend when placed under tension from either the angler or a current seam. This bending and twisting action imitates a wounded minnow swimming in the water, which can trigger a strike from a predator. Also, if you keep both hooks on the pattern, it provides better hooking opportunities regardless of where the trout strikes the pattern—whether it's headfirst, tailfirst, or from the side. If regulations allow, I'll fish two hook points on flies longer than 5 inches.

While articulated patterns increase the fly's movement through the water, the pattern by itself doesn't flex and bend too much—that's your job while retrieving the fly. As we'll discuss, additional movement with the rod tip is needed to create motion in the fly.

FLY COLOR AND FLASH

I know some anglers have a system for using certain colors for certain conditions, but my opinion is that when trout are on the feed, any number of color combinations may work. There are spikes in trout activity with dry-fly fishing and nymphing, and the same is true with streamer fishing. I've fished with several different anglers using several different-colored flies, and all worked when the bite was on, and all performed poorly when the bite was off. However, as with dry-fly fishing, there are times when the streamer bite is totally turned off. Unlike nymphing, where there's a good chance to catch fish throughout the day, I find the streamer bite can be more limited throughout the day, so I tend to fish a single pattern for a longer period on the theory that it is better to keep my fly in the water than waste my time changing colors or patterns. Through my informal experiments, I did come to the conclusion that the depth at which the fly was fished, along with the retrieve, was more important than color.

While color isn't as critical as depth and the retrieve you use, there are some fisheries where excessive flash can be detrimental, so I like to carry both drab and gaudier patterns. I've found trout inhabiting the limestone and spring creeks near my home in central Pennsylvania prefer drab colors with little flash. This is in comparison to the freestone waters I grew up fishing in the northern part of the state, where bright colors like yellow and chartreuse were effective. I've found this to typically be the case when comparing fertile and sterile streams. Trout in sterile streams are likely to chase gaudier or flashier patterns while trout living in fertile streams are more prone to chase drab colors with little flash. Perhaps piscivores living in fertile waters can be choosy compared to those living in sterile streams.

Though trout in fertile waters may prefer less flashy patterns, there are always exceptions to the rules. At times, trout need a trigger—something to set off either the hunger or aggressive strike. Trout are cold-blooded and their metabolism slows during the colder winter months. I've witnessed trout holding motionless to the bottom during the coldest periods of the year. At these times, I feel the right amount of flash tied into a streamer can trigger some type of movement toward the fly.

Before a recent cold snap near my home waters, a drab-colored Strolis Headbanger Sculpin was a winning fly. We had

A small but flashy jig streamer was used to catch this Italian marble trout in the pocketwaters of a glacial runoff stream. The larger marble trout took refuge into the slow, deep pools while smaller marbles like this one held in the faster pocketwater.

Yellow is one of my favorite fly colors for dirty-water conditions, as it is more visible to both angler and trout. The ability to see how the pattern is moving and its direction of travel in dirty water gives me confidence.

Right: Even when a river may not possess a healthy baitfish population, think about other large protein sources for trout, such as fingerling and adult trout stockings in wild trout rivers. Although large fish in many tailwater fisheries do rely on bugs as a steady part of their diet, most will not turn down an opportunity to eat a large piece of protein.

a steady weather pattern and ideal water conditions for streamer fishing. For four straight days, the local trout population showed a preference for the drab-colored Headbanger. However, a cold front moved in and slowed down the fishing. As a result, the same drab-colored streamer moved the occasional fish, but it was clear that the trout were either not into chasing streamers or that they were looking for another trigger point. I switched to a gaudy gold-and-white Sparkle Minnow. Even though the stream I was fishing has way more sculpins than minnows, the trout chased down the Sparkle Minnow. Thinking maybe I had hit a bite window (a period when trout are chasing streamers regardless of color), I switched back over to the drab Headbanger. The number of trout chasing the streamer dried up. So I immediately switched back to a Sparkle Minnow, and the action once again picked right up where I left it. Whether the trout were motivated by hunger or aggression—or both—I don't know. What I do know is that while this gaudy approach to cold-weather fishing doesn't always work, it has saved countless streamer days for me during cold snaps.

Patterns for Off-Color Water

Dirty or off-color water offers prime streamer conditions. Trout have excellent vision and the ability to pick up small food items in dirty water, but it may help to better expose your pattern to trout during these times. While I'm not a huge proponent of continually changing colors throughout the day, I do prefer to use bright colors (chartreuse, yellow, and white) when fishing dirty water. While the gaudy colors fail to replicate a natural food, they do provide a more visible target in dirty water. This is the reason I carry a variety of brightly colored dead-drifting, hanging, jigging, and swimming patterns for dirty water conditions. Another reason I prefer colors such as chartreuse and yellow is that I can see the pattern during the retrieve and know the depth at which the fly is being fished. If I'm fishing a chartreuse Zoo Cougar (hanging style) and feel my pattern is riding too high in the water column, I can switch to a chartreuse Clouser Minnow (jigging style) to achieve a deeper drift. Essentially, I'm fishing patterns that trout can find more easily but that also allow me to track the direction and depth of my pattern like a tracer bullet.

Fall fishing in the East is a great time to be on the water, as color change occurs both in the leaves and the trout. During fall foliage season, when there are lots of orange, brown, and yellow leaves in the water, I prefer to fish a bright, white streamer to create a distinct contrast between my presentation and Mother Nature. It also helps me track where my streamer is moving during the retrieve, whereas other colors may get lost in the foliage.

Mike Schmidt's Cotton Candy Double Deceiver is one of my favorite rainbow patterns. It has a great profile in the water, yet the bucktail body sheds water and allows you to retrieve and cast the pattern with ease. Blane Chocklett suggests incorporating pink into your winter streamer patterns, as many of the baitfish take on a pink hue during the colder winter months. LANCE WILT

While floating the Allegheny River with Lance Wilt, we encountered ice melt and dirty water. My drab-colored patterns disappeared into the depths of this water. After three hours without any success, Lance suggested I fish a 1/0 chartreuse Half-and-Half (half Clouser, half Deceiver) streamer. Immediately I could see the chartreuse pattern swimming deep in the water, and knowing both the location and depth of the pattern gave me confidence. Twenty minutes after the switch, a trout found the chartreuse streamer and several more followed shortly after. Wanting to see if our limited success was due to a color change or simply fishing during a bite period, we switched back to drab colors but failed to move a fish over the next forty minutes. So we switched again to another brightly colored pattern—a fluorescent yellow and brown traditional Deceiver—and soon another fish was brought to the net.

CARRYING A VARIETY OF WEIGHTED STREAMERS

I look at my streamer selection in the same manner as I look at nymphs. I normally carry a small selection of streamer patterns in a variety of weights and styles of weights. Fine-tuning the weight on your streamer rig isn't as critical as with nymphing, as trout are more willing to move an extra foot for a larger food source. However, there have been several periods when a streamer tied with a tungsten head outfished an identical streamer tied with a brass cone. Why? Because the water temps dropped several degrees, which kept the trout's noise closer to the stream bottom. The tungsten-cone streamer kept the fly nearer to the stream bottom than the brass cone, which was suspended a foot off the bottom.

Again, the beauty of streamer fishing is that you shouldn't lose many flies. Because of this, I only need to carry three or four streamer patterns in a small variety of weights. If the pattern calls for a dumbbell eye, some patterns will have a brass dumbbell eye while others contain a tungsten one. You can also use different-size dumbbell eyes for the same-size hooks. For example, on a size 4 Gamakatsu B10S hook, I can use both large and medium brass and tungsten dumbbell eyes. With the two weight types (tungsten and brass) and the two sizes (large and medium), I have up to four weighted categories for the size 4 pattern. I'm not suggesting you must have a variety of weights for each pattern, but I do suggest you carry several weight categories among all your patterns. This is especially important if you don't carry several sink rates of lines or poly leaders, as you'll need the weight of the pattern to obtain the depth.

Small Streamer Box

I organized my streamers into three categories: small, medium, and large. Pictured below is my small boatbox, containing flies from 1 to 3 inches long. While it's personal preference, you'll notice a large number of my flies possess a conehead or dumbbell eyes, especially in the smaller sizes. This is the box I pull from more frequently when fishing my home waters. As you'll notice, I carry maybe a dozen varieties of streamers, but I vary the weight type, color, and size of each.

Left Side: A variety of root beer variations of the Sparkle Minnow, all tied with a black tungsten conehead. The second row down is the speckled gold variation of the Sparkle Minnow, also tied with a black tungsten conehead. The third row contains a few micro versions of the speckled gold and root beer Sparkle Minnow along with several chartreuse Buggers, mostly tied with a tungsten conehead. The bottom row has a few Sparkle Minnow stragglers along with white Clouser Minnows and several Bunker Busters.

Right Side: The top row contains a few Todd's Wiggle Minnows along with Sculpin Bunny and Headbanger Sculpins, all tied with a Sculpin Helmet. The second row down contains GD's Sculp Snack Buggers, all tied with a tungsten conehead. The third row has a few experimental patterns including a Gummy Bugger and several hanger-style patterns. The rest of the flies in the row are UV black GD's Sculp Snacks for dealing with off-color water or when fishing at night—all tied with a black tungsten conehead. The next two rows contain several micro Buggers and a large number of Slump Busters, tied with both brass and tungsten coneheads. The bottom row contains several Hot Bead Buggers, GD's Sculp Snack variations, and several Autumn Splendors tied with both brass and tungsten coneheads.

Medium Streamer Box

Here's my medium-size box, containing flies from 3 to 4 inches long. This is about the maximum length I use for my home waters in central Pennsylvania. This streamer size class has caught more large fish than the other two size categories combined. With this box, I attempt to place the heaviest flies on the top side, while the lighter flies are located on the bottom side. An overwhelming majority of my patterns are olives and browns to represent sculpins, which are prevalent near my home waters in central Pennsylvania. If I fished waters with a more prominent population of minnows, I would fish more whites and grays.

Left Side: The top two rows are a combination of Home Invaders, Ice Picks, and Headbanger Sculpins. The bottom contains a variety of synthetic and natural Clouser Minnows, medium-size Sparkle Minnows, and a few more Home Invaders, tied with a combination of brass and tungsten dumbbell eyes.

Right Side: The top row contains several Ice Pick variations, along with Mike's Meal Tickets. The second row down contains double- and single-head Banger Sculpins. The third row contains single-head Banger Sculpins with single-head Mike's Meal Tickets. The bottom row has several experimental medium-size patterns, along with Mike's Meal Ticket, tied with a tungsten conehead (normally tied with dumbbell eyes).

Large Streamer Box

Pictured below is my large-size streamer box, containing flies 4 inches and larger. This box only comes out when I'm fishing waters containing a healthy population of trophy-size trout. Note that I don't carry many weighed flies in this category. Casting flies of this size that are heavily weighted are downright difficult and dangerous to cast. When casting larger streamers, I prefer unweighted patterns with weighted fly lines. My two favorite patterns in this category are Mike Schmidt's Double Deceiver and Lynch's Drunk and Disorderly.

This box is dominated by Lynch's Drunk and Disorderly, tied in a variety of color schemes. However, if you take a close look at the color scheme, you'll notice the head sizes change to match the varying grain weights of lines I throw. Again, it's important to remember you don't want a line that is too heavy or aggressive where it slows down the pattern's action. On the other hand, you don't want a streamer head that is too buoyant and will not allow the grain weight of the line to pull it down to the appropriate feeding level of the trout. Also pictured are several triple-articulated Juggernauts tied by Rich Strolis. Rarely do I use triple-articulated patterns, but I keep several on hand just in case I need a large pattern to entice a trout.

Night Streamer Box

A night fisher doesn't need to carry a large number of flies. I carry this box with a small assortment of mice, heavily weighted Bugger-style streamers, and wet flies. Cliff's Bugger Beast is my favorite fly box for carrying patterns like the Lynch White Belly Mouse, Wilt's UV Night Wet, and several light-weighted Conehead Zuddlers.

FLY SIZE

I've already touched on this topic a bit, but I want to circle back and address the current rage of fishing very large streamers—the "go big or go home" mentality. I, too, used to believe this. My streamer addiction began while fishing Michigan's Manistee River in 2002 with Russ Madden. Russ was the first to introduce me to articulated streamers, including his original Circus Peanut. After two boat rides and fishing large 6- to 7-inch articulated patterns, I landed a handful of browns pushing 17 inches. It was the first time I'd fished flies longer than 4 inches, and I thought I'd discovered how to catch big fish everywhere.

Trying for similar results on my home waters, I threw the same large 6- to 7-inch streamers but failed to land many fish. Time after time my local trout population performed a short strike on the pattern and few ever committed to eating the fly. With the incredible results I had in Michigan, I couldn't believe I wasn't able to recreate the same numbers in central Pennsylvania. After fishing in Michigan with Russ, I was beginning to believe that if you build exceptionally large streamers, exceptionally large fish will come no matter where you fished. Over the next two weeks, I realized how wrong my thinking was. I found myself pushing the big-fly theory too far on my home waters and had to step back and reevaluate the situation. Mother Nature, not the fly fisherman, creates big trout. I was trying to create a large-trout fishery by throwing large patterns in smaller trout waters. Several mid- to upper-teen fish attacked the large streamer, but only a few were hooked, and more often than not, I talked more about the large trout I moved on a streamer instead of the ones I landed. I would make excuses like, "trout weren't committed" or "fish were just playing with their food today." I'm all for pushing the limits and seeing how big a streamer I can fish, but there comes a point when excessive length becomes less effective for some trout waters, and I've come to believe that in many instances, when a streamer reaches a certain length (depending on a river's population of big fish), I believe trout strike out of aggression rather than hunger.

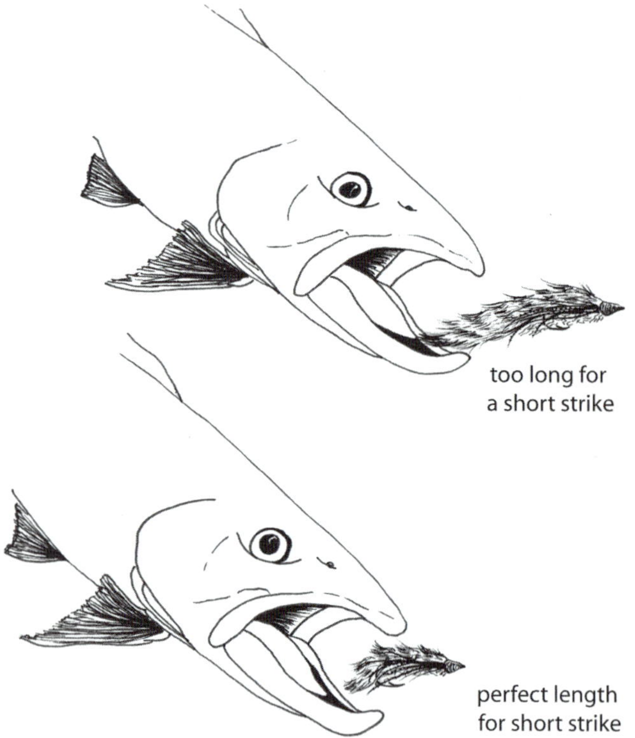

Reduce the length of your fly's tail during periods when trout are short-striking your pattern. I've found that in the fall (i.e., around spawn), trout short-strike more than any other time of the year. Whether it's a territorial or aggression strike, I prefer to fish patterns with shorter tails.

Sometimes you need to downsize your pattern. On this day, my wife, Amidea, downsized her pattern (as suggested by our guide, Jon Hooper) after a number of fish made short strikes on our larger articulated patterns. I stayed with the larger pattern and continued to get short strikes while my wife proceeded to land fish, including the biggest fish of the day. Listen to your guide.

For example, can you recall playing a smaller trout when all of a sudden a large trout comes from the depths and begins chasing down the hooked fish? Only on a handful of occasions did I see the larger trout try to eat the hooked fish. Most often, the larger trout would follow or nip at the tail in an attempt to move the smaller fish away from its daytime holding area. The smaller fish was creating a ruckus, and the larger trout was more interested in chasing the fish away than eating it. For me, the same phenomenon occurs when fishing large streamers. I find most trout chase away large streamers rather committing to eat. Trout are excellent hunters, and when they're hunting for food, they don't miss too many opportunities.

It's mesmerizing to watch a large streamer 7 inches or longer swim through the water. Seeing a trout chase down a large streamer is one of biggest draws to streamer fishing. However, I believe that in many situations, fishing larger patterns induces more follows and short strikes than actual takes. It's so easy to get locked into repeatedly watching trout chase down and short-strike a large streamer instead of switching to a smaller pattern the trout will actually eat. On several occasions, it's taken me a half-day of floating and over a dozen aggressive follows before making the switch to a smaller fly.

With that said, even if I know that smaller streamers may be more effective at hooking fish, when I am floating a large body of water and trying to locate a larger trout, I'll fish larger streamers to try and move aggressive trout from their daytime holding areas. Most large brown trout feed at night or during low-light periods and will often hold in deeper or slower currents during the daytime. Rarely during low light can I actually see the trout chasing my fly. Sometimes the trout will commit to a large streamer, but more frequently it will only give away its location so that I can then come back later to catch it with a smaller fly.

Big Fish Do Eat Tiny Fish

On a recent trip to Northern California, I had the opportunity to swing for steelhead on the Feather River. I had heard the resident steelhead were eager to chase smaller streamer patterns. My initial thought was to swing a smaller size 8 Sparkle Minnow. I had caught a small number of steelhead on size 8 Sparkle Minnows on other steelhead waters, so I had confidence this fly would work for California steel. Although my guide quietly suggested using smaller patterns (a size 12 salmon fry), I wanted to test out my larger streamer first.

After several hours of no fish activity, my guide again suggested switching to a smaller pattern. Point taken. I tied on a size 12 salmon fry pattern. Within fifteen minutes of changing patterns, I had hooked my first California steelhead on the swing—not with a medium-size streamer but with a short size 12 fry. Why? As I later found out, salmon fry had just started hatching, and the resident steelhead were focusing on the fry as a food source. These large 4- to 8-pound steelhead focused on these small 3/4-inch fry patterns and passed over a 4-inch Sparkle Minnow pattern. Also, because of the small fly size, my hooking percentage was 80 percent (4 out of 5), which I feel is excellent when streamer fishing. (When throwing larger patterns, I consider 50 percent to be a good number.)

Just look at how previous world-record trout were caught. For example, Rip Collins caught a 40-pound world-record brown trout on the Little Red River in Arkansas in 1992. He

Rich Strolis's Brown Trout Ice Pick is a simple yet effective imitation of a young brown trout.

used a tiny olive 3/32-ounce jig on 4-pound test. This monster brown trout ate a tiny jig, not a 12-inch baby rainbow pattern. In 2009, Tom Healy landed a 41-pound, 7-ounce world-record brown trout on Michigan's Manistee River throwing a 3 1/8-inch-long size 8 Rapala Shad Rap. In 2013, a new world-record brown trout (42 pounds, 1 ounce) was caught by Otwin Kandolf on New Zealand's South Island using a small red spinner.

So the last three world-record brown trout were caught using small fish imitations. It's interesting to me that while we know how the last three world records were caught, some streamer anglers still prefer to toss 8- to 10-inch streamers to trout. There's no doubt that a world-record trout is capable of inhaling a 12-inch trout, but what's the chance you are going to cross paths with world-record trout that is hungry enough to eat a 12-inch baitfish? I look at smaller baitfish patterns as sizable snacks that almost any trout is capable of eating; a 12-inch pattern represents a meal only a few freaks of nature are able to eat (similar to a human taking on the 72-ounce steak challenge). I prefer to fish a streamer size that is a snack for leviathans and a meal for the average-size fish. It appeals to both sizes of fish. Trophy hunting is fun, but I prefer a little action thrown in from time to time. This is the reason why I throw smaller streamers on trophy-trout waters, including Arkansas's famous White River, and I have had decent success doing so.

PREPARING YOUR FLIES

The first streamer video I watched was Dave Whitlock's *Tying and Fishing Dave Whitlock's Matuka Sculpin*. Before he fished the pattern, Dave talked about a trout's sense of smell and the amount of human scent we put on flies. Dave would store his flies in a Ziploc bag with water and vegetation from the stream to mask any unnatural scent. While anglers continue to catch trout on flies without masking any unnatural scents, you might be able to slightly improve your hook-up rate if you try to cover or mask some of the unnatural odors. Think about all the head cements and glues used to construct streamers. For example, I use a combination of Sally Hansen's Hard as Nails for head cement, Krazy Glue to secure dumbbell eyes, and Clear Cure Goo for creating epoxy-style heads. In fact, my streamer boxes reek of glues and head cement when opened. If I can smell my streamers from a distance, it's safe to say trout can too. By taking simple measures, like rubbing my flies on aquatic vegetation or a rock, I've noticed a small improvement in trout committing to streamers after a long chase. Fish that have continued to follow the fly or continued to short-strike are more likely to commit to eating the fly rather than turning away. While this strategy is nothing new to the fly-fishing community, it's amazing to see how few anglers try masking their scent.

There's another reason for soaking your flies, and it concerns the actual presentation. As Ed Shenk would advise, you need to ensure that the fly sinks to the correct level on the first cast. As with any fly-fishing approach, the first cast with streamer tactics is often the only chance you'll get to fool a trout—there are few second chances with streamer fishing. A number of streamer types (such as deer hair heads) need time to saturate in water, or they'll float on the surface. Ed would preach about making that first cast count, and this was the reason his streamer was wetted before making the cast. So unless your pattern is heavily weighted, it may be useful to keep the pattern moist before presenting the first cast.

A tip I got from my mentor, Joe Humphreys, was to "rough up" subsurface patterns before fishing. It can't hurt, as I can smell the superglues and UV resin scents the moment I open my streamer box. While all of us have caught fish with new patterns that smell like glue, it can't hurt to put a more natural scent on your flies. JAY NICHOLS

MY STREAMER BOX

There are so many great tiers creating incredible streamer patterns that I feel my time is better spent learning how to fish their patterns. I guess my rationale is that I surround myself with such great fly designers that I let them do all the design work while I reap the rewards of a great pattern. Fly designers like Kelly Galloup, Michael Schmidt, Richard Strolis, Tommy Lynch, Nick Granato, Blane Chocklett, Russ Madden, Brent Dawson, and countless others have created patterns to deal with just about any streamer scenario.

So while no one will ever accuse me of being a great streamer designer, one of my favorite hobbies is experimenting with other designers' patterns. I think one of the few good ideas I've ever had was to purchase flies from a number of designers to first look at how to build the patterns. To really see how a pattern works in the water, I would take it and build a duplicate in bright yellow, chartreuse, or bright white, so I could easily see the pattern move in the water. The problem with fishing natural-looking streamers in deeper water is that you can rarely see what the fly is truly doing every time you pause, strip, or twitch the rod tip. By building brightly colored duplicates, I can see every minute detail of the pattern's movement during the retrieve. This has allowed me to tweak some of my favorite patterns to achieve a desired movement. For example, by switching from a tungsten conehead to a tungsten dumbbell eye, I may notice a slight increase in the jig action. This testing allows all movement to become transparent to the angler—making it easier to decide what you like or dislike about the pattern's movement. As a result, we can continue to tweak patterns until they're almost perfect. This is why some patterns fish so much better than others—they've been tweaked and developed to produce the best results.

The following are some of my "go-to" patterns that I've fished over the years. Obviously, I don't carry all these patterns streamside, but my thought is to provide you with a list of patterns for you to fish and experiment with. Hopefully you'll find a few patterns that work for you and the waters you fish.

I prefer to buy flies or tie streamers where the glass beads have enough slack to slide a bit on the articulation. This allows the beads to slide back and forth and slap one another, which creates an effect similar to a glass rattle.

A beautiful rainbow fell prey to an articulated streamer.

FLY PATTERN RECIPES

Jigs

GD SCULP SNACK

George Daniel

Hook: #4 Partridge Predator
Thread: Black 140-denier UTC
Tail: Olive marabou over tan marabou
Legs: Chrome copper pumpkin Sili Legs
Bead/Eyes: Black tungsten cone (medium)
Body: Olive UV Polar Chenille

KRAKEN

Russ Madden

BACK HOOK

Hook: #4 Daiichi D1750
Thread: White 140-denier UTC
Tail: Tan marabou
Flash: Speckled copper Flashabou
Legs: Chrome gold/black Sili Legs
Body: White crosscut rabbit with olive schlappen collar
Connection: 25-pound Maxima Chameleon

FRONT HOOK

Hook: #4 Daiichi D1750
Flash: Speckled copper Flashabou
Body: White crosscut rabbit with olive schlappen collar
Bead/Eyes: Nickel yellow Hareline Tungsten Predator Eyes (medium)

CIRCUS PEANUT

Russ Madden

BACK HOOK

Hook: #2 Daichi 2461
Thread: Brown 140-denier UTC
Tail: Brown/olive grizzly marabou
Legs: Dark olive Hareline Barred and Speckled Crazy Legs
Body: Tan Pearl Chenille (medium), collared with brown schlappen and UV Gold Polar Chenille
Connection: 25-pound Maxima Chameleon

FRONT HOOK

Hook: #1 Daichi 2461
Thread: Brown 140-denier UTC
Tail: Brown/olive grizzly marabou
Legs: Dark olive Hareline Barred and Speckled Crazy Legs
Body: Tan Pearl Chenille (medium), collared with brown schlappen and UV gold Polar Chenille
Bead/Eyes: Lead dumbbell (large), painted black with white pupil
Front Collar: Gold EP Sparkle Brush

CIRCUS PEANUT (VARIATION)

Russ Madden

FRONT HOOK

Hook: #2 Daichi 2461
Thread: Brown 140-denier UTC
Tail: Yellow/brown grizzly marabou
Legs: Amber/gold flake Sili Legs
Body: Gold tinsel chenille (medium), collared with brown and olive schlappen along with wood duck or mallard flank
Connection: 25-pound Maxima Chameleon

BACK HOOK

Hook: #2 Daichi 2461
Thread: Brown 140-denier UTC
Tail: Yellow/brown grizzly marabou
Legs: Amber/gold flake Sili Legs
Body: Gold tinsel chenille (medium), collared with brown and olive schlappen along with wood duck or mallard flank
Bead/Eyes: Yellow dumbbell eyes (large)
Front Collar: Gold EP Sparkle Brush

MIKE'S GRUMPY MUPPET

Mike Schmidt

BACK HOOK

Hook: #2 Gamakatsu SL11-3H
Thread: Tan 140-denier UTC
Tail: Tan Craft Fur banded with brown permanent marker
Legs: Chrome copper pumpkin Sili Legs
Body: Olive copper UV Polar Chenille
Connection: 19-strand Beadalon with orange craft bead

FRONT HOOK

Hook: #1 Gamakatsu SL11-3H
Thread: Tan 140-denier UTC
Body: Olive copper UV Polar Chenille, banded tan Craft Fur, amber mallard flank for pectoral fin
Bead/Eyes: Red dumbbell eyes (large)
Head: Rusty brown and tan Senyo's Laser Dub

MIKE'S MEAL TICKET

Mike Schmidt

BACK HOOK

Hook: #4 Gamakatsu SL11-3H
Thread: Brown 140-denier UTC
Legs: Pumpkin Perfectly Barred Sili Legs
Body: Gold EP Sparkle Brush and tan rabbit strip
Connection: 19-strand Beadalon with orange craft bead

FRONT HOOK

Hook: #2 Gamakatsu SL11-3H
Thread: Brown 140-denier UTC
Legs: Pumpkin Perfectly Barred Sili Legs
Body: Gold EP Sparkle Brush with tan rabbit strip laid on top
Bead/Eyes: White dumbbell eyes (large)
Head: Brown and tan sculpin wool

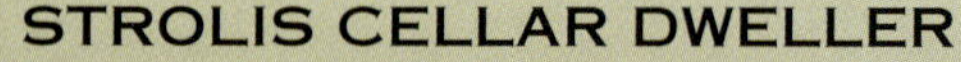

STROLIS CELLAR DWELLER

Rich Strolis

Hook: #2/0 Gamakatsu 60-degree jig hook
Thread: Tan 140-denier UTC
Tail/Overwing: Tan rabbit strip barred brown over white marabou
Bead/Eyes: Chartreuse Tungsten Predator Eyes (medium)
Body: White pearl braid
Collar: White, red, and dark tan Senyo's Laser Dub (stacked)

HEADBANGER SCULPIN

Rich Strolis

Hook: #4 Gamakatsu SL11-3H
Thread: Black 140-denier UTC
Tail: Black and olive marabou
Legs: Olive black flake Sili Legs
Bead/Eyes: Olive Sculpin Helmet (medium)
Body: Olive Pearl Chenille, palmered with black hackle
Overwing: Olive fox fur
Collar: Olive Senyo's Laser Dub

ARTICULATED HEADBANGER SCULPIN

Rich Strolis

BACK HOOK

Hook: #4 Gamakatsu B10S
Thread: Black 140-denier UTC
Tail: Brown and olive marabou
Legs: Olive black flake Sili Legs
Body: Brown Pearl Chenille, palmered with brown hackle and brown fox fur for overwing
Connection: 19-strand Beadalon with orange craft bead

FRONT HOOK

Hook: #4 Gamakatsu B10S
Thread: Black 140-denier UTC
Legs: Olive black flake Sili Legs
Body: Brown Pearl Chenille, palmered with brown hackle and brown fox fur for overwing
Bead/Eyes: Olive Sculpin Helmet (large)
Collar: Brown Senyo's Laser Dub

WHITE/SILVER TROPHY WIFE

Thomas Harvey

Hook: #1 Gamakatsu B10S
Eyes: Nickel tungsten hourglass (large) with earth Fish Skull Living Eyes (6 mm)
Thread: White 140-denier UTC
Tail/Wing: White rabbit over pearl and silver Ice Wing
Body: Silver UV Polar Chenille
Head: White Senyo's Laser Dub

BROWN TROUT TROPHY WIFE

Thomas Harvey

Hook: #1 Gamakatsu B10S
Eyes: Nickel tungsten hourglass (large) with earth Fish Skull Living Eyes (6 mm)
Thread: Tan 140-denier UTC
Tail/Wing: Gold variant rabbit over gold Ice Wing and tan Craft Fur
Body: Olive UV Polar Chenille
Head: Dark tan over tan Senyo's Laser Dub

RAINBOW TROUT TROPHY WIFE

Thomas Harvey

Hook: #1 Gamakatsu B10S
Eyes: Nickel tungsten hourglass (large) with earth Fish Skull Living Eyes (6 mm)
Thread: White 140-denier UTC
Tail/Wing: Olive rabbit strip barred brown over pearl Ice Wing and pink Craft Fur
Body: Pearl UV Polar Chenille
Head: Olive over white Senyo's Laser Dub
Cheek: Pink Senyo's Laser Dub

SCULPIN TROPHY WIFE

Thomas Harvey

Hook: #1 Gamakatsu B10S
Eyes: Nickel tungsten hourglass (large) with earth Fish Skull Living Eyes (6 mm)
Thread: Olive 140-denier UTC
Tail/Wing: Olive rabbit strip over olive Ice Wing and olive Craft Fur
Body: Olive UV Polar Chenille
Head: Sculpin olive over light olive Senyo's Laser Dub

LEGS FOR DAYS

Thomas Harvey

BACK HOOK

Hook: #1/0 Gamakatsu SP11-3L3H
Thread: Olive 140-denier UTC
Tail: Olive marabou
Legs: Olive Sili Legs with orange tip
Body: EP Tarantula Hairy Legs Brush (1")
Wing: Olive rabbit Zonker
Flash: Chartreuse Holographic Flashabou
Connection: 19-strand Beadalon with red craft bead

FRONT HOOK

Hook: 35 mm Fish Skull Articulated Shank
Tail: Olive marabou
Legs: Olive Sili Legs with orange tip
Body: EP Tarantula Hairy Legs Brush (1")
Wing: Olive rabbit Zonker
Flash: Chartreuse Holographic Flashabou
Eyes: Tungsten hourglass (large) with wind Fish Skull Living Eyes (15 mm)

MAXIMUM COWBELL

Nick Granato

BACK HOOK

Hook: #2 Gamakatsu B10A
Thread: Tan 140-denier UTC
Tail: Red grizzly hackle feathers
Tail/Wing: Natural Magnum Rabbit Strips
Body: Copper UV Polar Chenille with glass rattles (4 mm)
Connection: 19-strand Beadalon with orange craft bead

FRONT HOOK

Hook: 1/0 Gamakatsu 60-degree bend jig hook
Thread: Tan 140-denier UTC
Tail: Red grizzly hackle feathers
Tail/Wing: Natural Magnum Rabbit Strips
Body: Copper UV Polar Chenille with glass rattles (4 mm)
Head: Brown over white sculpin wool
Eyes: Red Tungsten Predator Dumbbell Eyes (medium)

CHUBBY MUFFIN

Nick Granato

Hook: #2 Gamakatsu B10S
Thread: Brown 140-denier UTC
Flash: Chartreuse and red Holographic Flashabou
Tail/Wing: Dark olive rabbit strip
Body: Orange hen hackle, palmered
Pectoral Fins: Speckled brown soft hen hackle
Head: Brown over olive sculpin wool with black permanent marker on top
Eyes: Red Tungsten Predator Dumbbell Eyes (medium)

CHUBBY MUFFIN (VARIATION)

Nick Granato

Hook: #2 Gamakatsu B10S
Thread: Brown 140-denier UTC
Flash: Gold Holographic Flashabou
Tail/Wing: Olive rabbit strip
Body: Orange hen hackle, palmered
Pectoral Fin: Speckled brown soft hen hackle
Head: White sculpin wool with dark olive permanent marker on top
Eyes: Chartreuse Tungsten Predator Dumbbell Eyes (medium)

JC SCULPIN

John Collins

Hook:	#4 TMC 5263
Thread:	Tan 140-denier UTC
Tail:	Ginger rabbit strips barred brown
Body:	Ginger/white variegated chenille, tapered
Pectoral Fins:	Ginger rabbit strips barred brown
Head:	Sculpin Helmet, painted ginger with olive dots (medium)

RED-EYE LEECH

Mike Schultz

Hook:	#4 TMC 800S
Thread:	Black 140-denier UTC
Flash:	Gold Flashabou
Tail:	Black rabbit strip
Body:	Black rabbit strip, palmered
Veil:	Natural mallard flank, palmered
Head:	Black rabbit strip, palmered
Eyes:	Red metallic eyes (medium)

SINGLE FLY CRAY

Mike Schultz

Stinger Hook:	#4 Daiichi 2557 looped with 30-pound FireLine
Thread:	Burnt orange 140-denier UTC
Legs:	Olive Sili Legs with orange tip
Flash:	Speckled copper Flashabou
Pinchers:	Natural brown rabbit strips
Body:	Olive rabbit and gold variant rabbit, both palmered
Eyes:	Red Tungsten Predator Eyes (medium)

S3 SCULPIN

Mike Schultz

Trailer Hook:	#4 Daiichi 2557 looped with 30-pound FireLine
Bead:	Copper brass bead (5/64")
Front Hook:	#4 Tiemco 800S
Thread:	Burnt orange 140-denier UTC
Flash:	Gold Flashabou
Tail/Wing:	Natural rabbit strip barred black
Body:	Olive schlappen, olive mallard flank, and gold variant rabbit, palmered
Cheek:	Tan grizzly hackle tied off on both sides
Feather Wing:	Brown grizzly hackle fibers
Eyes:	Yellow Tungsten Predator Eyes (medium)

MIKE'S MEAL TICKET (VARIATION)

Mike Schmidt

Hook: #4 Gamakatsu B10S
Thread: Tan 140-denier UTC
Tail/Wing: Yellow rabbit strips barred brown
Body: Copper EP Sparkle Brush
Head: Tan Senyo's Laser Dub
Eyes: Yellow dumbbell eyes (medium)

BROWN TROUT HOG HUNTER

Ben Furimsky

Trailer Hook: #6 Daiichi 2557 looped with 30-pound FireLine
Thread: Tan 140-denier UTC
Front Hook: 35 mm Fish Skull Articulated Shank
Tail/Wing: Ginger rabbit Zonker over white marabou
Underbelly: Yellow Ice Fur
Top Wing: Yellow marabou barred brown
Eyes: Chartreuse Tungsten Predator Eyes (medium)

BUNKER BUSTER JIG

George Daniel

Hook: Wapsi 1/8-ounce premolded jig hook
Thread: Black 140-denier UTC
Tail/Wing: Black Magnum Rabbit Strip
Body: Purple EP Sparkle Brush
Legs: Black round rubber legs (medium)
Head: Black Senyo's Laser Dub

RAINBOW TROUT HOG HUNTER

Ben Furimsky

Trailer Hook: #6 Daiichi 2557 looped with 30-pound FireLine
Thread: Tan 140-denier UTC
Front Hook: 35 mm Fish Skull Articulated Shank
Tail/Wing: Light olive rabbit Zonker barred brown
Underbelly: White and red Ice Fur
Top Wing: Light olive marabou barred brown
Eyes: Chartreuse Tungsten Predator Eyes (medium)

VEGAS STRIP

Shawn Combs

BACK HOOK

Hook: #4 Gamakatsu B10S
Thread: Brown 140-denier UTC
Tail/Wing: Dark green rabbit strips
Flash: Copper Flashabou
Body: White rabbit, palmered
Throat: Tuft of orange rabbit

FRONT HOOK

Hook: 35 mm Fish Skull Articulated Shank
Tail: Sculpin olive marabou
Body: Copper UV Polar Chenille
Wing: Dark green rabbit strip
Head: Copper UV Polar Chenille
Eyes: Dumbbell eyes with pearl eyes (medium)

DOUBLE-WIDE CHEECH LEECH

Clark "Cheech" Pierce

BACK HOOK

Hook: #4 Allen S402
Thread: Brown 140-denier UTC
Body: Brown Arizona Mega Simi Seal
Flash: Copper Flashabou
Rib: Root beer Palmer Chenille
Connection: 19-strand Beadalon with olive Fly Fish Food Articulation Bead

FRONT HOOK

Hook: #4 Allen S402
Body: Brown Arizona Mega Simi Seal and olive schlappen, palmered
Legs: Olive Sili Legs
Eyes: Allen Barbell Eyes
Head: Brown Arizona Mega Simi Seal

MONGREL MEAT

Clark "Cheech" Pierce

BACK HOOK

Hook: #8 Allen B200
Thread: Brown olive 140-denier UTC
Tail: Olive marabou
Body: Olive Holographic Cactus Chenille
Hackle: Olive schlappen
Collar: Olive marabou wrapped soft-hackle style
Connection: 19-strand Beadalon and two Electric Lizard Fly Fish Food Articulation Beads

FRONT HOOK

Hook: #4 Allen B200
Weight: Lead barbell eyes and .035 lead wraps
Tail: Olive marabou
Body: Olive Holographic Cactus Chenille
Hackle: Olive schlappen
Flash: Chartreuse holographic Flashabou
Collar: Olive arctic fox tail fibers
Head: Sculpin olive Senyo's Laser Dub, striped with sepia-colored Prismacolor marker
Eyes: Yellow Tungsten Predator Dumbbell Eyes (medium)

BUG-EYED BOODLE

Clark "Cheech" Pierce

Hook: #2 Allen E601
Eyes: Allen Barbell Eyes
Thread: Olive 140-denier UTC
Body: Olive Holographic Cactus Chenille
Collar: Olive Spirit River UV2 schlappen
Overwing/Body: Olive arctic fox tail hair

LUNCH LADY

Clark "Cheech" Pierce

BACK HOOK

Hook: #6 2X Allen B200
Thread: Olive 3/0 MFC Premium Tying Thread
Eyes: Allen brass dumbbell eyes (6.3 mm)
Tail: Brown dyed olive Magnum Barred Zonker Strip
Body: Gold UV Montana Fly Company Lucent Chenille (large)
Hackle: Olive schlappen
Connection: Purple Fly Fish Food Articulation Bead

FRONT HOOK

Hook: #6 2X Allen B200
Tail: Brown dyed olive Magnum Barred Zonker Strip
Body: Gold UV Montana Fly Company Lucent Chenille (large)
Head: Olive over yellow Fly Fish Food Bruiser Blend Dubbing (tied in clumps)

HOME INVADER

Doug McKnight

Hook: #4 Gamakatsu B10S
Thread: White 140-denier UTC
Flash: Silver Flashabou
Tail: White marabou
Body: White EP Foxy Brush (3")
Wing: Pair of grizzly hackles
Eyes: Yellow Tungsten Predator Eyes (medium)

TUNGSTEN JIG BUGGER

George Daniel

Hook: #8 Orvis Tactical Jig Hook
Thread: Olive 70-denier UTC
Tail: Olive grizzly marabou
Body: Olive rabbit dubbing
Rib: Red Ultra Wire (medium)
Collar: Olive hen hackle
Bead: Slotted tungsten black bead ($^{1}/_{8}$")

WEDDING CRASHER

Randy Hanner

Hook: #8 Tiemco 5262
Tail: Tuft of tan marabou
Body: Brown Arizona Simi Seal dubbing
Hackle: Brown soft hen hackle
Legs: Pumpkin Perfectly Barred Sili Legs
Collar: Natural hare's ear dubbing
Eyes: Yellow Tungsten Predator Dumbbell Eyes (small)

WARPATH WHAMMY

Brent Dawson

BACK HOOK

Hook: #4 Gamakatsu B10S
Thread: Olive 6/0 Uni-Thread
Tail: Olive chenille
Body: Olive barred marabou
Flash: Chartreuse Flashabou
Legs: Hareline Barred Olive Black Rubber Legs
Connection: 19-strand Beadalon with red craft beads

FRONT HOOK

Hook: #4 Gamakatsu Jig Hook
Thread: Olive 6/0 Uni-Thread
Tail: Olive chenille
Body: Olive barred marabou
Flash: Chartreuse Flashabou
Legs: Hareline Barred Olive Black Rubber Legs
Wing: Olive rabbit strip
Collar: Olive Warpath Dubbing Brush
Head: Olive Warpath Epoxy

COFFEY'S SPARKLE MINNOW

Greg Coffey

Hook: #4 Gamakatsu B10S
Thread: Black 140-denier UTC
Tail: Sculpin olive over white marabou
Flash: Copper Flashabou
Body: Copper EP Sparkle Brush, colored with black marker
Underbody: White EP Sparkle Brush, pulled under
Cone: Black tungsten conehead (medium)

EL SCULPITO

Clark "Cheech" Pierce

Hook: #4 Tiemco 8089
Thread: Olive 140-denier UTC
Eyes: Red Tungsten Predator Dumbbell Eyes (medium)
Tail/Wing: Olive rabbit strip
Body: Olive Arizona Simi Seal dubbing
Fins: Olive Sili Legs
Head: Congo dubbing with black permanent marker

BLACK SEX DUNGEON

Kelly Galloup

BACK HOOK

Hook: #6 Daiichi 1750
Thread: Black Ultra GSP 100
Tail: Black marabou and red Flashabou
Body: UV Black or Peacock Black Ice Dub
Hackle: Black schlappen
Legs: Black and red flake Crazy Legs
Connection: 19-strand Beadalon with 2 large red glass beads

FRONT HOOK

Hook: Daiichi 1710
Tail: Black marabou and red Flashabou
Body: UV Black or Peacock Black Ice Dub
Hackle: Black schlappen
Eyes: Red lead eyes (large)
Head/Collar: Black deer hair

YELLOW ZOO COUGAR

Kelly Galloup

Hook: #4 Daiichi 2220
Thread: White Ultra GSP 100
Tail: Yellow marabou
Body: Pearl Sparkle Braid
Underwing: White calf tail
Wing: Wood duck gold or yellow mallard flank
Head/Collar: Yellow deer hair

BLANE CHOCKLETT'S GAME CHANGER

Blane Chocklett

Hook: Gamakastu B10S #4
Thread: White 140-denier UTC
Articulations: Fish Skull Articulated Fish Spine
Connectors: Large Senyo Intruder Wire
Tail: Minnow Body Wrap, trimmed with Clear Cure Goo
Body: UV White Minnow Body Wrap

FEATHER SCULPIN GAME CHANGER

Blane Chocklett

Front Hook: #2 Gamakastu B10S
Rear Hook: #4 Gamakastu B10S
Head: Deer body hair, trimmed to shape
Eyes: Black lead
Thread: Olive 140-denier UTC
Articulations: Fish Skull Articulated Fish Spine
Connectors: Large Senyo Intruder Wire
Body (Back Taper): Metz Magnum Hen Saddles
Body (Front Taper): Hareline Schlappen
Fins: Soft-hackle hen feather

FEATHER SCULPIN GAME CHANGER (VARIATION)

Blane Chocklett

Front Hook: #2 Gamakastu B10S
Rear Hook: #4 Gamakastu B10S
Head: Brown Sculpin Helmet (large)
Thread: Olive 140-denier UTC
Articulations: Fish Skull Articulated Fish Spine
Connectors: Large Senyo Intruder Wire
Body (Back Taper): Metz Magnum Hen Saddles
Body (Front Taper): Hareline Schlappen
Fin: Soft-hackle hen feather

Swimmers

SOUTHBOUND TRUCKER

Russ Madden

Hook: #1 Daiichi 2461
Thread: Brown 140-denier UTC
Tail: Pair of brown schlappen feathers
Secondary Tail: Tan bucktail
Legs: Chrome gold/black Sili Legs
Beads/Eyes: Red dumbbell (large)
Rear Body: Olive, white, and brown schlappen, palmered
Front Body: White crosscut rabbit
Overwing: Gold variant Hareline Barred Rabbit Strips
Collar: Olive and brown schlappen

DOUBLE DECEIVER

Mike Schmidt

BACK HOOK

Hook: #2 Gamakatsu B10S
Thread: Brown 140-denier UTC
Body: Tan bucktail bullet head
Tail: Pair of tan schlappen feathers
Connection: 19-strand Beadalon with tan craft beads

FRONT HOOK

Hook: #2 Gamakatsu B10S
Thread: Brown 140-denier UTC
Body: Tan, brown, and yellow bucktail bullet head with yellow schlappen
Bead/Eyes: Earth Fish Skull Living Eyes (8.5 mm)

MIKE'S VOODOO SQUATCH

Mike Schmidt

BACK HOOK

Hook: #1 Gamakatsu B10S
Thread: Brown 140-denier UTC
Tail: Tan marabou
Body: Copper UV Polar Chenille
Collar: Tan marabou and brown Craft Fur
Connection: 19-strand Beadalon with orange craft beads

FRONT HOOK

Hook: #1/0 Gamakatsu B10S
Thread: Brown 140-denier UTC
Body: Copper UV Polar Chenille
Collar: Tan marabou and brown Craft Fur
Bead/Eyes: Ice Fish Skull Living Eyes (8.5 mm)
Head: Silver minnow belly Senyo's Laser Dub, trimmed

MIKE'S RED OCTOBER

Mike Schmidt

BACK HOOK

Hook: #2 Gamakatsu B10S
Thread: Tan 140-denier UTC
Flash: Gold Holographic Flashabou
Tail: Tan rabbit strip
Body: Yellow schlappen, palmered through tan Pearl Chenille
Collar: Tan schlappen
Connection: 19-strand Beadalon with yellow craft bead

FRONT HOOK

Hook: #2 Gamakatsu B10S
Thread: Tan 140-denier UTC
Flash: Gold Holographic Flashabou
Body: Yellow schlappen, palmered through tan Pearl Chenille
Collar: Tan schlappen
Bead/Eyes: Tan Fish Skull Living Eyes (medium)
Head: Rusty brown and dark tan Senyo's Laser Dub

RAINBOW TROUT ICE PICK

Rich Strolis

Stinger Hook: #4 Gamakatsu Octopus looped with 30-pound FireLine
Thread: Tan 140-denier UTC
Body: 35 mm articulated shank
Tail/Overwing: Sculpin olive rabbit strip
Bead/Eyes: Tan Fish Skull Living Eyes (small/medium)
Body: Pearl EP Sparkle Brush
Cheek: Pink Senyo's Laser Dub
Collar: Olive over white Senyo's Laser Dub

BROWN TROUT ICE PICK

Rich Strolis

Stinger Hook: #4 Gamakatsu Octopus looped with 30-pound FireLine
Thread: Tan 140-denier UTC
Body: 35 mm articulated shank
Tail: Hareline Gold Variant Rabbit Strip
Bead/Eyes: Tan Fish Skull Living Eyes (small/medium)
Body: Speckled Gold EP Sparkle Brush
Cheek: Yellow Senyo's Laser Dub
Collar: Dark tan Senyo's Laser Dub

TRIPLE-ARTICULATED HOG SNARE

Rich Strolis

BACK HOOK

Hook: #2 Gamakatsu B10S
Thread: Tan 140-denier UTC
Tail: Yellow marabou
Hackle: Yellow schlappen
Body: Orange Pearl Chenille
Legs: Orange/black flakes Sili Legs
Wing: Tan Craft Fur

MIDDLE HOOK

Hook: 35 mm Fish Skull Articulated Shank
Tail: Yellow marabou
Hackle: Yellow schlappen
Body: Orange Pearl Chenille
Legs: Orange/black flakes Sili Legs
Wing: Tan Craft Fur

FRONT HOOK

Hook: #1 Gamakatsu B10S
Tail: Yellow marabou
Hackle: Yellow schlappen
Body: Orange Pearl Chenille
Legs: Orange/black flakes Sili Legs
Eyes: Yellow dumbbell eyes (large)
Collar: Dark tan Senyo's Laser Dub

AUTOEROTIC ARTICULATION

Mark Millward

BACK HOOK

Hook: #4 Gamakatsu B10A
Thread: Brown 140-denier UTC
Tail: Brown marabou
Wing: Gold variant rabbit strip
Legs: Pumpkin Perfectly Barred Sili Legs
Body: Root beer EP Sparkle Brush
Connection: 19-strand Beadalon with root beer craft beads

FRONT HOOK

Hook: #2 Gamakatsu B10A
Tail: Brown marabou
Wing: Gold variant rabbit strip
Legs: Pumpkin Perfectly Barred Sili Legs
Body: Root beer EP Sparkle Brush
Head: Brown over olive sculpin wool
Eyes: Red dumbbell eyes (large)

DRUNK AND DISORDERLY

Tommy Lynch

BACK HOOK

Hook: #4 Tiemco 811S
Tail: Gold Ice Wing
Body: Gold UV Polar Chenille with tan rabbit, palmered to eye
Wing: Amber mallard flank
Connection: 19-strand Beadalon with orange craft bead

FRONT HOOK

Hook: #4 Tiemco 5263
Tail: Gold Ice Wing
Body: Ginger rabbit, palmered; Gold UV Polar Chenille; and olive schlappen, palmered
Wing: Amber mallard flank
Head: Olive and orange deer body hair, trimmed into a tight wedge
Head Finish: Clear Cure Goo Hydro applied over head
Eyes: Earth Fish Skull Living Eyes (5 mm)

STEVE DALLY'S LAP DANCER

Steve Dally

BACK HOOK

Hook: #1 Gamakatsu B10S
Thread: Olive 210-denier UTC
Flash: Several strands of pearl Flashabou Accent
Tail: Two long natural brown hackles
Body: White Pearl Chenille
Wing: Tan and olive bucktail, tied Deceiver style with two long olive grizzle hackles

MIDDLE HOOK

Hook: 35 mm Fish Skull Articulated Shank
Thread: Olive 210-denier UTC
Flash: Several strands of pearl Flashabou Accent
Tail: Two long natural brown hackles
Body: White Pearl Chenille
Wing: Tan and olive bucktail, tied Deceiver style

FRONT HOOK

Hook: #1 Gamakatsu B10S
Thread: Olive 210-denier UTC
Flash: Several strands of pearl Flashabou Accent
Tail: Two long natural brown hackles
Body: White Pearl Chenille
Wing: Tan and olive bucktail, tied Deceiver style with two long olive grizzle hackles
Head: Olive popper head (large), glued with red eyes (10 mm)

DEER HAIR ZONKER

Variation on traditional pattern

Hook: #4 Gamakatsu B10S
Thread: Olive 140-denier UTC
Tail/Wing: Light olive rabbit strip barred brown
Body: Copper EP Sparkle Brush
Head: Yellow deer body hair, trimmed

BROWN TROUT GAME CHANGER

Blane Chocklett (tied by Todd Johnson)

Rear Hook: #2 Tiemco 600 SP
Front Hook: #1 Tiemco 600 SP
Thread: Clear Uni-Mono (medium)
Articulated Shanks: 20 mm Fish Skull Articulated Shanks
Tail: White EP Fiber, colored to match
Body: White EP Fiber, trimmed and colored to match
Eyes: Earth Fish Skull Living Eyes (6 mm)

RAINBOW TROUT GAME CHANGER

Blane Chocklett (tied by Todd Johnson)

Rear Hook: #2 Tiemco 600 SP
Front Hook: #1 Tiemco 600 SP
Thread: Clear Uni-Mono (medium)
Articulated Shanks: 20 mm Fish Skull Articulated Shanks
Tail: White EP Fiber, colored to match
Body: White EP Fiber, trimmed and colored to match
Eyes: Earth Fish Skull Living Eyes (6 mm)

LONGNOSE DACE ZONKER

Todd Johnson

Hook: #1 Daiichi 2461
Thread: Clear Uni-Mono (medium)
Body: Gold Sparkle Braid
Tail/Wing: Gold variant rabbit strip
Throat: Light yellow and gold Ice Dub
Eyes: Yellow Tungsten Predator Dumbbell Eyes (small)

BLEEDING SHINER

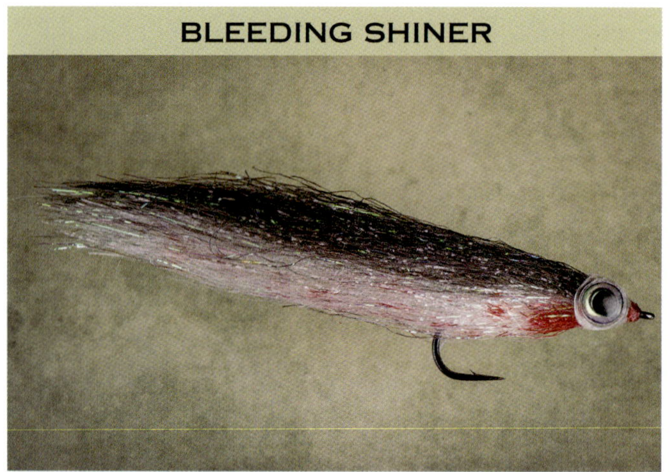

Todd Johnson

Hook: #1 Gamakatsu B10S
Thread: Clear Uni-Mono (medium)
Body: Pearl Baitfish Emulator Flash ($5\frac{1}{2}$")
Head: #10 Fish Mask
Eyes: Earth Fish Skull Living Eyes (8 mm)

Note: Gray and black permanent marker on top with a red throat

MURDICH MINNOW BROWN TROUT

Bill Murdich (tied by Todd Johnson)

Hook: 2/0 Daiichi 2461
Thread: White 140-denier UTC
Tail: Speckled copper Flashabou
Kicker: White EP Fiber
Rattles: Glass rattles tied under Estaz body (4 mm)
Body: Pearl Estaz (grande)
Eyes: Earth Fish Skull Living Eyes (6 mm)

Note: Color with permanent markers to match forage fish

RAINBOW TODD'S WIGGLE MINNOW

Todd Boyer

Hook: #2 Tiemco 8089
Mono Loop: 20-pound Mason Hard
Tail: Olive over white Craft Fur
Flash: Pearl Flashabou
Body: Foam cylinder ($\frac{3}{8}$"), colored
Eyes: Pearl stick-on eyes (6 mm)

MURDICH MINNOW RAINBOW TROUT

Bill Murdich (tied by Todd Johnson)

Hook: 2/0 Daiichi 2461
Thread: White 140-denier UTC
Tail: Pearl Baitfish Emulator Flash ($5\frac{1}{2}$")
Kicker: White EP Fibers
Rattles: Glass rattles tied under Estaz body (4 mm)
Body: Pearl Estaz (grande)
Eyes: Earth Fish Skull Living Eyes (6 mm)

Note: Color with permanent markers to match forage fish

MOTO'S MINNOW

Moto Nakamura

Hook: #8 Tiemco 5263
Thread: White 140-denier UTC
Tail: 6 strands of peacock herl with gray marabou
Body: Dun mallard flank, palmered
Collar: White hen hackle
Cone: Gold conehead (medium)

DIAMONDBACK SCULPIN

Jac Ford

Hook: #4 Tiemco 800S
Thread: Tan 140-denier UTC
Flash: Gold Flashabou
Tail/Wing: Peach rabbit strip barred brown
Head: Olive sculpin Senyo's Laser Dub
Pectoral Fin: Amber mallard flank
Eyes: Earth Fish Skull Living Eyes (4 mm)

JAC'S SIMPLE

Jac Ford

Hook: #2 Tiemco 800S
Thread: White 140-denier UTC
Body: Silver tinsel
Flash: Pearl Flashabou
Tail/Wing/Head: White rabbit strip

SNOW PUPPY

Jac Ford

Hook: #1 Tiemco 800S
Thread: White 140-denier UTC
Body: Silver tinsel
Underwing: White Craft Fur
Overwing: Silver pheasant coated with Clear Cure Goo
Head: White deer hair head, trimmed to shape
Eyes: Red mono

TROPHY TROUTS

Chris Willen

BACK HOOK

Hook: #2 Gamakatsu B10S
Thread: White 140-denier UTC
Tail/Wing: Grizzly hackle dyed yellow
Body: Yellow bucktail, tied Deceiver style
Connection: 19-strand Beadalon with yellow craft beads

FRONT HOOK

Hook: #1 Gamakatsu B10S
Thread: White 140-denier UTC
Wing Accent: Several strands of pearl Flashabou with grizzly hackle dyed red
Body: Yellow bucktail, tied Deceiver style
Collar: Dyed olive grizzly hen hackle
Head: Clear Cure Goo with glitter
Eyes: Earth Fish Skull Living Eyes (10 mm)

LYNCH WHITE BELLY MOUSE

Tommy Lynch

Hook: #2 Gamakatsu B10S
Thread: Tan 140-denier UTC
Tail: Gold variant rabbit strip barred black
Foam Strip: Brown foam (1/8") pulled over with lip
Body: White crosscut followed by gold variant rabbit strip, both palmered
Legs: Natural round rubber legs (medium)

SOFTEX MOUSE

Russ Madden

Hook: #2 Tiemco 8089
Thread: Black 140-denier UTC
Tail: Muskrat strip
Back Legs: Black schlappen
Front Legs: Black schlappen
Body: Pearl E-Z Body (extra large), coated with Softex and covered with muskrat dubbing
Foam Strip: Black foam (1/8") pulled over with lip

Dead-Drifters

STROLIS HEADCASE CRAYFISH

Rich Strolis

BACK HOOK

Hook: #1 Gamakatsu B10S
Thread: Rusty brown 140-denier UTC
Underbody: Two Fly Rattles (4 mm)
Body: Brown Cactus Chenille (medium)
Antenna: Copper Flashabou
Claws: Rusty brown rabbit strips
Legs: Orange/black barred Crazy Legs
Wing: Brown fox fur

FRONT HOOK

Hook: 35 mm Fish Skull Articulated Shank
Hackle: Brown hen hackle
Underbody: Two brown Sculpin Helmets (small)
Wing: Brown fox fur

LOW-WATER CRAWFISH

Mike Schultz

Hook: #10 Tiemco 5262
Thread: Burnt orange 140-denier UTC
Flash: Speckled copper Flashabou
Legs: Olive Sili Legs with orange tip
Body: Olive grizzly marabou, palmered
Collar: Burnt orange grizzly marabou, palmered
Head: Copper brass conehead (medium)

AUTUMN SPLENDOR

Tim Heng

Hook: #4 Tiemco 5263
Thread: Rusty brown 140-denier UTC
Tail: Rusty brown marabou
Flash: Rusty brown Flashabou
Body: Brown rayon chenille
Hackle: Dyed orange grizzly
Legs: Yellow round rubber legs (medium)
Cone: Large copper conehead

Swingers

HOT-HEAD SLUMP BUSTER

John Barr

Hook: #10 Tiemco 200 BL
Thread: Black 70-denier UTC
Tail/Wing: Black micro squirrel strip
Body: UV Black Polar Chenille (micro)
Collar: Black micro squirrel strip, palmered
Head: Fluorescent orange tungsten bead (1/8")

SOUTH HOLSTON SWINGER

Mike Adams

Hook: #18 TMC 5263
Thread: Black 140-denier UTC
Tail: Light olive marabou
Flash: Pearl Flashabou Accent
Body: Olive rayon chenille (medium)
Hackle: Grizzly hackle, palmered
Bead: Fluorescent orange tungsten bead (5/32")

MICHIGAN FRY

Unknown

Hook: #10 Tiemco 200 BL
Thread: Olive dun 8/0 Uni-Thread
Tail: Olive/yellow grizzly marabou
Body: Golden brown Ice Dub
Collar: Olive/yellow grizzly marabou
Bead: Black tungsten bead (1/8")

WILT'S UV NIGHT WET

Brian Wilt

Hook: #4 Partridge Predator
Thread: Black 140-denier UTC
Tail: Black marabou
Body: Black UV Polar Chenille
Wing: Black marabou

A Dynamic Streamer System

5

Trout can be just as moody as humans. Variables including water temperature, angling pressure, amount of light, water clarity, and flow fluctuation can all influence your approach to streamer fishing. All successful streamer anglers need a system that allows them to build a program for any number of stream conditions they may encounter. As conditions change, so must your approach and the tools you use. Variables including water clarity and trout activity all have a profound effect on how I decide to approach a section of water. The traditional method of fishing streamers (remember the old customer I mentioned during the intro) was to cast down-and-across and strip the fly back upstream. While this approach will work in just about any situation, it pays huge dividends to match your approach to both stream conditions and trout behavior.

If you look on the boat of a professional bass fisherman, you may see more than a dozen rods strung up. The bass fisherman's system is built to handle just about any scenario the

An angler dead-drifts his streamer pattern on a cold winter afternoon. While trout will chase during extreme cold, it often pays to slow down the retrieve during cold snaps.

A Chilean guide took this beautiful brown trout using a long rod and a jigging technique off the bank. Notice the weed beds downstream of the angler. Suspended weed beds make it difficult to make longer casts and retrieve your streamer over a longer stretch. It may prove more effective to use a heavily weighted jig-style fly, a longer leader, and long rod so that you can literally drop your streamer in between the beds. LANCE WILT

water presents. I'm not saying you need to carry a dozen rigs at any one time, but I am suggesting you think about various methods for approaching a section of water. Think about what casting angle, line type, pattern type, and retrieve type will best match the water you're fishing. Think about carrying several sinking lines on spare spools. Think about having a variety of streamer types in our six categories (hangers, jiggers, dead drifters, floaters, and swimmers), and think about changing the angles of your presentation.

Most of my experiences have come from fishing central Pennsylvania waters. To diversify my knowledge, I spent countless hours fishing a number of river systems across the Lower 48. This has provided me with an opportunity to learn from a variety of professional guides and observe their approach to the waters they fish. There's absolutely nothing wrong with knowing a particular river system intimately. In fact, this is the reason I would never hire a guide who doesn't live on the water I want him to guide me on. However, the only way I continue to learn and to improve my fly-fishing approach is to travel to new waters and spend time with professionals who have dialed in their respective river systems. Every river system has its nuances, and the guides who repeatedly fish these waters know how to exploit their weaknesses.

There are so many types of retrieves, angles, and depths you can use to present your pattern to the fish, and I believe this "no rules" approach is one main reason why I continue to employ streamer tactics. Keep an open mind, and remember that variety is the spice of life—in other words, if you continue to experiment with approaches and equipment, you will never fall into a rut in which you feel there's no other way to fish streamers. I see this happening to anglers who've fished for more than five years. These anglers find confidence in a couple of approaches and quickly develop tunnel vision, blind to all other strategies. You should always keep your mind open to other approaches. As Albert Einstein once said, "The measure of intelligence is the ability to change."

While there are some anglers who know a waterway so intimately they don't need to spend as much time observing, there are more anglers who rig up their favorite system and already have in their mind what approach they're going to use before seeing the water. Successful anglers look at the current stream conditions and develop a plan of attack before fishing. There are a number of potential variables to consider when approaching the water, and for every water type and every time you enter the water, you need to answer a different set of questions. Once you assess the situation, you need to choose the rig, fly pattern, and tactic to match the current conditions.

For simplicity, I break streamer fishing into three approaches: upstream (directly upstream and up-and-across), across-stream, and downstream. Below, I discuss the conditions that are best suited for each approach, the advantages and disadvantages, and rigging, general presentation, and line control. These tactics are not set in stone, as there are times when you will need to marry two approaches, such as casting up- or across-stream and letting the streamer swing to the end of the drift. The purpose of identifying the three approaches is to provide you with three plans of attack for dealing with both varying stream conditions and trout behavior. It's in no way the final word on breaking down potential streamer approaches, but it's a system that works for me.

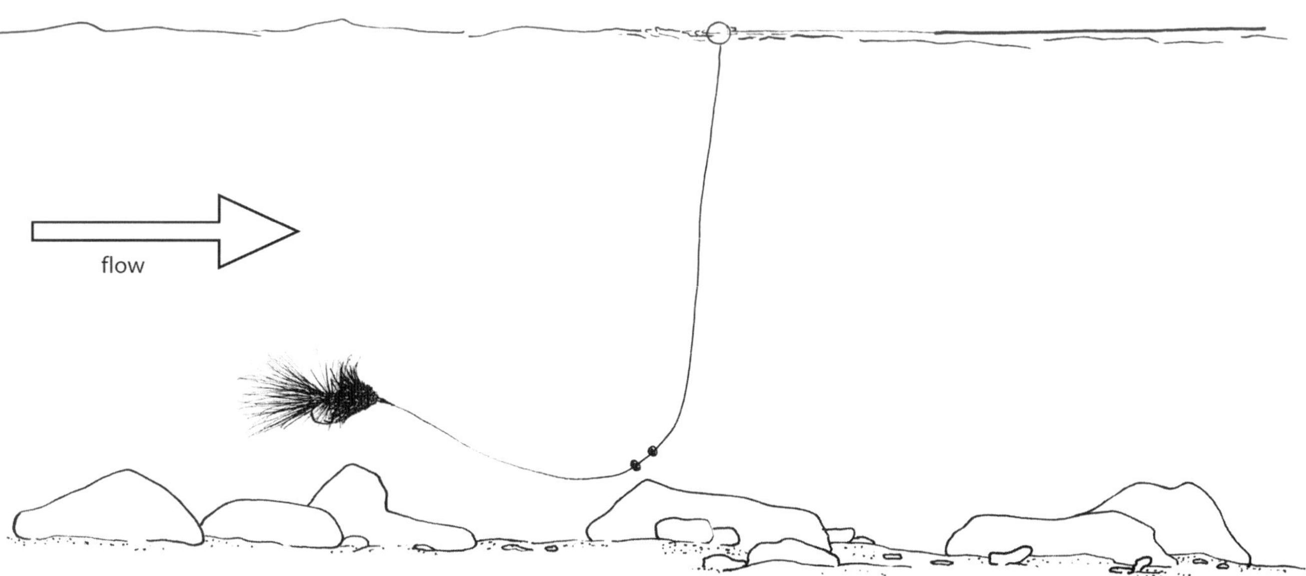

The Greg Bricker Bow River Bugger Rig is a favorite dead-drift rig of Greg Bricker, owner of Freestone Outfitters in Bozeman, Montana. Greg introduced this rig to me while floating the Yellowstone River, when trout weren't active. Greg uses heavy shot (1/0 and B) so the shot will drop vertically below the suspender. This means you should place the suspender at a length equal to the depth of the water you want to fish. For example, if the water is 4 feet deep, then the length from suspender to rig should be about 4 feet. The farther you space the shot from the Bow River Bugger (a buoyant deer hair streamer), the higher the Bugger rides in the water column. I try to keep 6 to 12 inches between shot and streamer.

UPSTREAM TACTICS

My father-in-law, Walt Dickey, is both a live minnow fisherman and a fly fisher, and he first taught the upstream approach to me. I find it fascinating that so few streamer anglers spend time talking with live minnow or spin-tackle anglers. Whether I'm fishing dry flies, nymphs, or streamers, I make it a point to ask these guys, "How's the fishing?" Most of the time, I find these folks to be far more laid-back and willing to share information than many fly fishers. They cover so much more water than fly fishers and often catch more fish. Tommy Lynch says, "These guys have so much more data that it's crazy not to spend time talking with them."

When Walt starts fishing with his live minnows, he usually begins fishing upstream, like most of the other live minnow anglers that I have talked to in Pennsylvania. When asked why they fish upstream rather than across- or downstream, the most common answer is, "Trout like an easy meal." As we know, trout are definitely willing to chase down larger food items, but will also seize the opportunity for an easy meal. Also, the live minnow guys will tell you that they feel they are imitating more of a wounded minnow when fishing upstream, which may initiate a predatory strike. In the wild, predators certainly do chase their food, but many also focus on the young, old, or injured—those who cannot flee or defend themselves as well as the stronger members of the group. A wounded baitfish may not have the energy to fight the current to move upstream or across-stream. Have you ever seen an injured fish in the current? It will move with the current, not against it, and slowly kick and turn as it's pulled downstream.

The upstream approach also caters to ambush predators. I've heard several comments that baitfish don't swim toward a larger trout and that the upstream approach is an unnatural presentation. While it may be true that prey will not willingly swim toward a known trout position, it's important to realize that we're not imitating this scenario. Instead, we are talking about fishing a streamer as a prey item that is casually moving through the water and finds itself passing through an ambush spot.

The upstream approach also allows you to thoroughly cover a section of water. Unlike with across-stream tactics, where you are swinging your pattern through a wide arc and covering water fast, the upstream approach allows you to keep the flies in holding spots for a longer period of time. Just as with nymphing, when fishing streamers upstream, I focus on a particular seam, current, or holding lie. Instead of casting across the seam, I cast directly upstream in line with the current, which places the line, leader, and fly all in the same speed current.

I feel this is a huge advantage, especially when presenting to undercut banks or long sections of structure running parallel to the current. When casting to long undercut banks with an across-stream approach with no mending, the fly may drift to within several feet of the structure, but soon drag sets in and begins pulling your fly away from the bank. If trout are active and willing to move from the protection of an undercut bank to hunt food, then this across-stream tactic isn't a bad concept. However, there are periods when trout are not willing to leave their cover to chase food, and this is when we need to change our tactics to allow the streamer to ride close to cover for a longer period of time. Changing the angle of the presentation from across-stream to a more direct upstream angle will allow us to keep the fly riding parallel to the targeted seam for a longer period of time.

The upstream approach also creates an opportunity for a more secure hook set. Trout face upstream while looking for food to float or drift toward their position. When you are positioned downstream of the fish and retrieve the fly, the fly is being pulled directly downstream toward the fish. This means when you set the hook, the hook is pulled directly toward the fish instead of being pulled away, as is often the case when fishing with the across- or downstream presentation. Note that this is not always the case, as there are times when a trout will first let the streamer drift past it, and then come up from behind the fly and strike. However, it's been my experience that trout will more often eat a streamer headfirst as it floats downstream toward them.

I don't always fish articulated streamers, but when I do, I pay attention to which hook the fish took along with the position of the hook in the trout's mouth. If the front hook is located on the upper jaw and the hook eye is positioned toward the tail, this tells me the trout took the fly headfirst. If the rear hook is located in the lower jaw and is angled away from the trout's mouth, this can indicate the fish took the fly tailfirst. There are

Chad Johnson adjusts his leader lengths (from fly to sinking line) to achieve different actions. One of his favorite approaches is to work the White River's drop-offs with a longer leader (6 to 8 feet). The greater the distance between the sinking line and fly, the deeper the fly will dive during the retrieve. This fish was the result of fishing a longer leader, making a long pause before the retrieve, and using a deep-diving bucktail-style streamer.

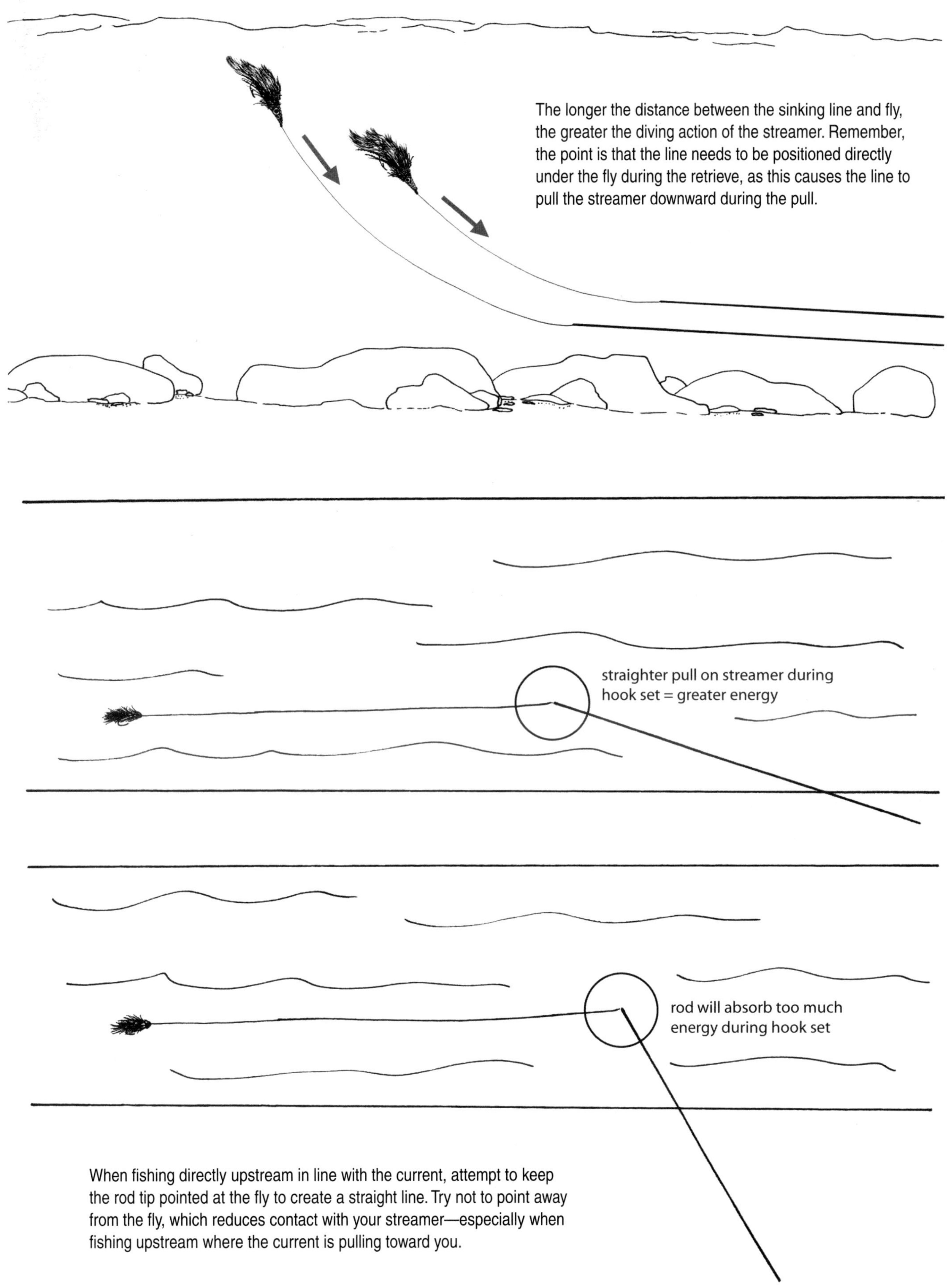

The longer the distance between the sinking line and fly, the greater the diving action of the streamer. Remember, the point is that the line needs to be positioned directly under the fly during the retrieve, as this causes the line to pull the streamer downward during the pull.

When fishing directly upstream in line with the current, attempt to keep the rod tip pointed at the fly to create a straight line. Try not to point away from the fly, which reduces contact with your streamer—especially when fishing upstream where the current is pulling toward you.

When fishing downstream with a floating line, I let the line fall on the water instead of managing line in my hands. The currents will pull the line downstream and away from my feet, reducing the likelihood that the line will snag a part of my body. However, when casting upstream the current will pull the line directly downstream toward my body. This is why, when casting upstream, I manage line in my hand instead of allowing it to fall on the water. JAY NICHOLS

times when fishing the upstream approach where trout will move right up on the streamer and inhale the pattern headfirst. Then there are times when the trout will allow the streamer to pass by, or perhaps it only notices the pattern as it's drifting past, and so it will come up from behind the pattern and eat it tailfirst.

However, more often I find that trout will eat the pattern headfirst when fishing the upstream approach, and I feel that tactic offers you a much higher hooking percentage.

Another hook set advantage is that an upstream approach doesn't keep the fly under continuous tension, as is often the case with the across- and downstream approaches. If the streamer, especially a larger pattern, is under continuous tension, trout don't have as much time to inhale the pattern. This is why some wet-fly anglers prefer to fish softer-action rods and to keep the rod tip at a higher angle to allow the line to sag and to create a slight bowing action in the line and leader. This creates a small degree of slack in the rig and provides a better opportunity for a trout to suck in the pattern. The same effect happens when fishing upstream and when using a strip to retrieve the line. As the currents bring the fly downstream, you strip to achieve both line management and to move the fly. At the end of the strip, you need to pause, let go of the line, and grab higher on the line to start the sequence again. The moment the pause occurs, a small degree of slack forms before the line hand begins to retrieve the line—and this is often when the take occurs. I feel this method offers the trout a better opportunity to inhale a streamer pattern, and I find this to be especially true when fishing larger patterns that offer a mouthful to a trout.

The key to fishing the upstream approach is to isolate ambush spots where a large trout may be waiting for a meal to pass by. An upstream cast is needed to allow the streamer time to reach the ideal level before you begin retrieving the line. This is no different than leading a dry fly to a rising fish. You don't want to cast on top of the fish—just far enough upstream to give the fly time to reach the appropriate level before beginning the retrieve.

Another advantage of the upstream approach is that it gives you the ability to quickly drop the streamer through the water column before beginning the retrieve. Unlike across- and downstream tactics, where the line is under constant tension, the upstream approach allows more slack to occur. The greater the tension, the slower the sink rate of both line and fly. The upstream approach allows anglers to fish deeply submerged boulders and pockets more efficiently because they can drop their streamer deeper and faster near these potential strike zones.

While sinking lines can be used with the upstream approach, I prefer to use either a full floater or a short tip. I want the floating line on the surface to create surface drag, which will maintain a small degree of tension on the rig. Because the faster currents are near the surface and the slower currents are closer to the bottom, a floating line on the surface will move faster than the sunken streamer near the bottom, which I feel creates better control during the retrieve. A full-sinking fly line can be used for upstream tactics, but it requires better line management because both line and flies will be anchored in the slower currents.

Line control is more difficult with the upstream approach because you are stripping in line to achieve line control while you are in the process of retrieving and manipulating the fly. This means you need to retrieve line at least slightly faster than the speed it's traveling toward you, but in a very smooth manner. "Smooth" meaning that it's not erratic, which can cause slack off the rod tip. This is where the full use of the hand, rather than the wrist, comes into play; using your wrist can cause erratic movement in the line, making the retrieve similar to casting. The full use of the hand during the retrieve will create a smoother retrieve.

Next time when you're retrieving line, keep the rod tip an inch off the water, and watch the loops off the rod tip during the process. You are seeking loops that go from a bowed position to a taut position, and do so in a very smooth manner. This smooth movement indicates that you're in direct contact with the streamer, which is especially important with upstream tactics because the take is often softer than with the across- and downstream approaches. Because a small degree of slack occurs and the rig isn't under nearly the amount of tension as it is with the other two methods, the feel of the take is nothing more than a little hesitation during the retrieve. If there's even a small degree of slack in the line, strikes will likely go unnoticed, making the upstream approach similar to nymph fishing.

The upstream approach doesn't always have to be directly upstream. An up-and-across tactic allows for the same presentation but with a little more tension during the drift. When casting directly upstream, my object is to place line, leader, and fly all in the same-speed current. The floating line lying on the surface creates a small degree of tension as it pulls the submerged streamer downstream. However, there may be situations where you cannot get into position to cast directly upstream, or maybe you want to swing the streamer toward your position.

One key to the upstream approach is using drag or tension on the line to help control the drift. This is also known as a tension loop. The bigger the loop, the more tension is created on the rig. When casting up-and-across, the line (whether it's floating or sinking) needs to be in either the same-speed current as the fly or in a faster current. When the fly line is downstream of the fly, this creates tension, or control, between line and fly. What we don't want to happen with the upstream approach is for the fly to be downstream of the line, which creates slack.

This slack can occur when you cast up-and-across stream and the line lands in a slower current while the fly lands in fast

When fishing from an upstream angle with faster surface currents, the line has a tendency to belly and create slack. Sinking line bellies when fishing upstream aren't ideal, especially with faster currents near the surface. They're not detrimental in slow-moving water, though.

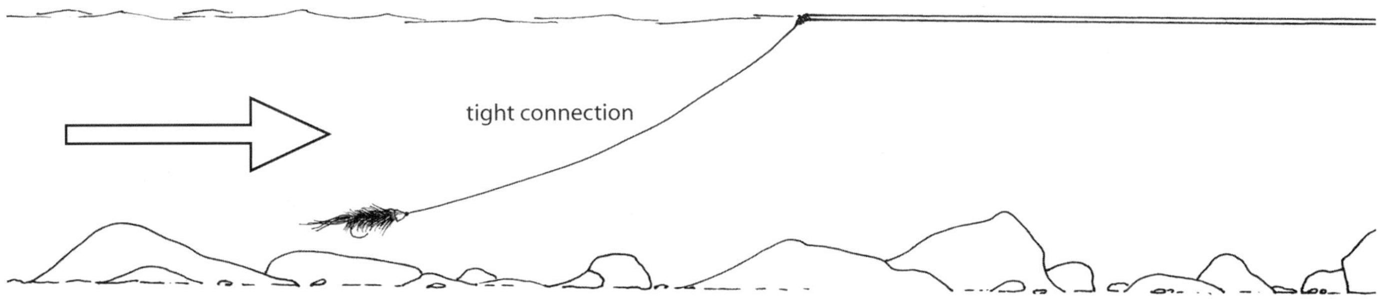

I find an upstream approach is best done with a floating line. The floating line lying on the faster surface currents creates surface tension and helps keep the rig tight as the streamer travels downstream toward the angler.

water. When fishing the upstream approach, we need to think about the line in the same manner as we do when nymphing with a suspension device—control is best achieved when the suspension device floats either directly above or is located downstream of the fly. Line control is so critical with the upstream approach because the line is drifting downstream toward you, and strike detection will be lost if you don't position the line directly downstream from the streamer.

On the other hand, a slight up-and-across approach can often place the streamer tight to the bank in slower water while the line is positioned midstream. This approach is similar to the direct upstream approach except for the fact that you're upstream (across the currents) rather than casting directly upstream (in line) in the current. This across-stream angle will immediately create tension on the fly, so long as the fly line is positioned in a faster current. One advantage of the up-and-across tactic is that line management is easy; the line belly will create surface tension, which will pull the streamers downstream. In this case, you are still responsible for retrieving line, but line control is executed by the tension loop. You only need to retrieve line fast enough to keep up with the slack moving downstream, along with enough to move the line faster than the surface current to create a faster retrieve.

Another advantage of the up-and-across tactic is that it gives you the ability to dead-drift your patterns without a suspension device. When I say dead-drift, I mean the pattern will be moving at about the same speed as the surface currents as line tension on the water moves the streamer. The up-and-across tactic can produce a tensioned loop in which the floating line section forms a J-shape and creates tension on the drift. To achieve this, execute an aerial downstream reach mend after casting up-and-across stream. As soon as the line falls on the water, the rod tip swings upstream (allowing several feet of line to slip through the guides) to create a J-shape of line on the water. As the line drifts downstream, the rod continues to point toward the fly during the drift, which maintains the tension loop. Keeping the rod tip pointed toward the fly and allowing the line belly to accumulate will maintain the tension loop. You can strip line at the same speed as the current to move the streamer at the same speed as the surface, or short strips and longer retrieves can be placed at intervals to provide additional movement to the fly. You may also need to mend to maintain the tension loop. The up-and-across tactic is useful for both faster retrieves and for dead-drifting streamers downstream.

An up-and-across technique with a full-floating or short sinking-tip line gives you the ability to choose the direction of

Though you won't always hook up when fishing them, streamers are great tools for locating fish. This fish rolled on a Double Deceiver during a float. We anchored, waded upstream, and caught this fish while sight-fishing with a midge. Streamers bring out the aggressiveness in larger fish, so make sure you mark every large flash you see. There's a good chance that same fish will be around during the next trip.

Tommy Lynch holds a solid Manistee River brown trout that fell to a Drunk and Disorderly. Tommy developed this pattern to mimic Rapala's lures, and it has more movement than any pattern I know. The key to the pattern's success is the dense wedged deer hair head, which cuts and dives in the water during the retrieve and makes a sudden upward lift during the pause.

the drift through line placement on the water. Think about the floating line section lying on the water as you would a suspension device drifting on the surface current. When the line is positioned downstream of the fly, surface currents will pull the line belly downstream, which will pull the streamer in the same direction. This allows you to control the direction of the drift at all times. At any time you can reposition the belly on a different current, which will pull the streamer in a different direction. Changing the direction of your pattern during the drift can trigger a strike from a trout. This line manipulation also permits you to either move the fly parallel to the bank or to pull the streamer away from the bank. Or maybe you're working a section with exposed boulders, and you need to move your line around a boulder to avoid dragging your streamer into the rock. While you can do this repositioning with all line types, the floating line is easiest to control because it is positioned above the surface at all times, which is helpful when mending during the drift. You can also reposition the line with both across- and downstream tactics, as we'll discuss later.

Another point of reference to look at during the retrieve is the line lying on the water. This is another reason I prefer the floating line: It sits above the surface where I can see if the line is under tension or has too much slack. I look for the line to run in a smooth line—it can be straight or curved, but the line needs to lay smooth without any S-curves. If you're just starting to streamer fish with the upstream approach, watching both loops off the rod tip along with the line on the water is a good start in identifying whether or not you're in control of the drift. Eventually, with a little experience, you will be able to feel during each retrieve whether or not you're in control with your fly. Every time you begin to retrieve line, you should feel a small degree of tension during each movement. If you find yourself retrieving the line without feeling any tension, there's a good chance that too much slack has accumulated in the line and leader.

Unlike with the across- or downstream tactics where the line is under constant tension, the upstream approach relies heavily on your ability to maintain tension throughout the drift. During the upstream retrieve, you want to feel that the line is under a small degree of tension, and this also means you need a heavy enough fly to anchor itself near the stream bottom. This is why I carry a variety of weighted flies. For example, when fishing shallow flats near the bank, I will often opt for a brass conehead fly or aluminum dumbbell eyes. When fishing heavier currents, I may need to switch to a tungsten conehead or lead dumbbell eyes. If the flies are properly anchored, you feel a higher degree of tension during the retrieve—very similar to when you're running your line through a cleaning pad and feel increased tension when reeling in the line. I'm looking for a streamer heavy enough to serve as an anchor, which will slow down the drift with a floating line section lying on the faster upper currents to create tension.

An angler fishes dirty water on the South Platte River in Colorado. Although many fish will move to the bank during periods of high and dirty water, others will hold in their normal positions and continue to feed. During higher water, fish hold behind large obstructions, such as boulders, as they provide a resting spot for the smaller fish that are hunted by large trout.

When using weighted flies, I employ a weight system similar to my nymph patterns. For example, an angler could use both a large and a medium tungsten conehead for a size 6 hook. When fishing shallow water, I will often use a brass conehead pattern because tungsten will likely be too heavy. (I can readily tell the difference between brass and tungsten because I build white thread between the hook eye and the tungsten bead and coat it with a UV curing agent.) By using two different-size conehead beads, along with switching between tungsten and brass, I have four weight categories for size 6 streamers. You don't have to go to these extremes, but it is important that your box contains variously weighted streamers to deal with changing water speeds and depths.

Full-sinking lines or long sinking-tip lines can be used with the upstream approach, but I find control is far more difficult. Because the lines are not under the same degree of tension as they are with across- and downstream tactics, they will sink at a faster rate. The more tension the line and rig are under, the slower the sink rate, and vice versa. If I do end up using a full-sinking line, I tend to stay with an intermediate, due to its slower sink rate. At a sink rate of approximately 1 inch per second, the "slime line" (intermediate) will often remain in the upper current seams—supplying additional surface tension and allowing for better line and leader control. One of the few occasions when I switch from a floating line to an intermediate while fishing upstream is during exceptionally windy conditions. When the wind is blowing strong on the water, it can greatly affect a floating line lying on the water's surface. This is like watching the wind blow a suspension device, such as a traditional indicator, across the water's surface; the wind can drag the floating line any direction it is blowing. To counter this, I'll switch to an intermediate line, so the line sits just below the surface. I'll also shove the rod tip several inches under the surface, greatly reducing disruption from the wind.

On too many occasions, I have used a fast-sinking line with an upstream tactic only to have the line quickly sink and scrape the sharp rocks on the stream bottom, eventually shredding the line. For most of the streams I fish in Pennsylvania, a medium- to fast-sinking line drops toward the stream bottom too fast when employing upstream tactics. However, there are streams where the speed and depth will allow for a fast-sinking line to be fished upstream, if you decide to do so.

I look at upstream streamer fishing the same way I look at tight-line nymphing; it's a tactic for dissecting small sections of water. I don't use upstream streamer tactics as a searching tool for covering large areas of water. I'll use the upstream approach when there are defined sections of potential holding water. For example, if I want to keep my streamer riding tight to a 15-foot undercut bank, I will cast the streamer directly upstream, where the line, leader, and fly all land in the same-speed current along the bank. The result is the fly riding parallel to the undercut bank for all 15 feet, instead of swinging away from the bank as it would if the cast was made across-current. Upstream streamer tactics allow me to dissect every inch of water with precision. Instead of swinging through a seam or current, I keep the fly riding within it the entire drift. This is a great approach if you want to pick apart a section of water instead of partially covering it. The upstream approach works when fishing these defined holding waters, where potential holding spots are easily identified. It would not be my first choice when fishing large or featureless bodies of water where defined holding spots can be isolated. If I want to cover a wider range of water, I would make long casts across-stream and swing through a wide radius.

If you are not using a stripping basket with the upstream approach, the currents will push the sunken line sections toward your feet. That, or you need to keep managing the line in your hands instead of letting it fall to the water during the retrieve. This isn't as much of an issue when fishing downstream because the water tension keeps the fly line away from your feet and doesn't allow the line to sink as fast. We'll look at several solutions to this common problem in the chapter on casting and line control.

I find the upstream approach to be most useful when dealing with trout that are structure-oriented and less likely to move away from cover to chase food. My home water, Fishing Creek, is a limestone stream known for its fickle trout, along with a wild brown trout population that maintains positions close to structure. Rarely will you spot a fish holding in the open. Instead, you'll find them hugging tight to one of the midstream boulders. While quickly retrieving your streamers across-stream will move fish from time to time, my favorite approach is working streamer patterns along the edges of the submerged boulders. For reasons unknown to me, Fishing Creek trout do not move too far from cover to chase food, so as anglers, we need to find an approach that keeps our streamer moving tight to cover during the entire drift.

While I still use the strip-set during the upstream approach, I find that hand position in relation to the body is important in creating the maximum amount of tension when setting the hook. This is why I prefer to retrieve with my rod hand extended far away from my body. Remember, when fishing upstream, much of the retrieving is first done to maintain the slack as the line moves downstream. What often happens is the fish will strike at the end of the retrieve, when the fly pauses for a second. If the line hand is fully extended during the take, a strip-set cannot be achieved, as the line hand cannot move any farther. One way to cure this is to extend the rod hand as far from the body as possible. This longer separation between rod hand and line hand will permit a longer range of motion to occur during the hook set. The key is not to fully extend the hand during the retrieve. Instead, we need a long enough pull to maintain line control and to move the fly, but we need to stop short of a full line-hand extension to allow enough room to make a strip-set when a fish strikes. I understand there may be situations when you need to use your full range of motion during the retrieve, but when possible, leaving a foot of leverage for the line hand to make a strip-set will create a secure hook set.

The upstream approach isn't for all scenarios. Some rivers have current speeds that move too fast to permit you to both maintain line control and to move the pattern. While fishing the Owens River in California with my friend Marshall Bissett, I discovered several bottlenecked sections where the bank tightened up and increased the current speed. These waters moved too fast downstream to maintain line and leader control. The fast current speeds had the fly back to my feet within seconds of it landing on the water. Even when trout are chasing prey, the drift of this retrieve would be too fast.

GET OFF THE BANK

Trout will hold tight to the bank during high-water periods, especially when tailwaters are generating. Working the banks is a good approach, but only for so long. Regardless of whether you're wading a stream or drifting a boat, there's a period where you have to let go of the notion that you need to fish the bank. Now, if you were one of the first anglers to fish a bank, then I would focus on that area until it the approach is no longer effective. The problem I notice on all rivers is that anglers have a tendency to work tight to the banks, even if they're the tenth boat floating past the same bank within an hour. This is ineffective because banks are often shallow and provide more of a feeding lie than a prime lie, and once fish holding in feeding lies receive pressure, they move out into the depths.

While fishing the South Holston River in Tennessee, we got a late start on our drift boat trip. Six boats had already covered the bank I wanted to fish, but I insisted that we could still move some big fish even after the bank had been bombarded with streamers by a flotilla of boats, some of which I could see downstream. Forty minutes later I was fishless, so I decided to cast off the opposite side. I struck a 17-inch brown trout on my first cast. I immediately asked our guide to pull us off the bank by 40 feet so we could target the transition between the drop-off and the bank. The results were almost immediate, with numerous fish willing to chase our streamers. When trout see that much pressure in a short period, they move into deeper water for security. So if I'm one of the first couple guys to work a river section, I'll focus my efforts toward the bank where trout are in feeding mode. However, I'll quickly move off the bank and focus on the deeper water if I feel the trout have already received sufficient pressure. Sometimes it is good to march to a different beat. ■

DIRECT UPSTREAM APPROACH

1. When fishing streamers upstream, I prefer to keep the rod tip pointed in a direction that creates the highest degree of tension. Because the current is moving the fly toward me, which creates slack, I point the rod tip directly at the fly and make sure the line is lying in a straight line on the water. A straight line indicates you're in contact with the streamer, as compared to a curved line on the water, which indicates slack, along with a loss of control.

2. As the streamer continues to drift downstream, keep the rod pointed at the fly during the retrieve. Keep your hand fully extended, allowing the line hand to move a longer range during the retrieve. Remember to pinch the line between the fingers on your rod hand and the cork before letting go of the line to begin the next retrieve.

3. Keep the rod tip low to the water as your line hand reaches toward the reel to pinch the line and begin another retrieve. Make this movement smoothly—no jerking motions. If you keep missing the line during the pinch, move the focus of your eyes from the rod tip to the line. This allows you to see the line you're grabbing and allows quicker hand/line control. Over time you'll no longer need to look at the line, as this movement will become second nature.

4. Continue the retrieve with another strip of line with your forearm. Notice in this photo how my forearm is stiff during the retrieve and how close the rod tip is to the water's surface. The stiff forearm creates a smooth but powerful movement. By smooth, I mean you should ease the line off the water (not rip it). Also, with the rod tip pointed at the surface, I eliminate lifting line off the water. Instead of pulling the line off the water, I'm pulling line through the water.

5. Again at the end of the retrieve, pinch the line to the cork with your rod hand, and the process continues.

6. As the streamer slowly drifts toward the opposite bank, continue to point the rod tip toward the fly to reduce slack. Keep as straight of a line as possible during the movement. The straighter the line, the more contact you have with the streamer. If you see continuous S-curves in your line when fishing upstream, you need faster or longer strips to maintain contact as the streamer drifts downstream.

UPSTREAM LINE CONTROL

1. When fishing streamers upstream, I prefer to keep the rod tip pointed in the direction that creates the most tension. Because the current is moving the fly toward me, which creates slack, I point the rod tip directly at the fly and make sure the line is lying in a straight line on the water. A straight line will indicate you are in contact with the streamer, as compared to a line with curves on the water, which indicates slack, along with a loss of control.

2. This is what you don't want to see when streamer fishing upstream. Notice the slack in the line. This slack won't let you feel a strike when it occurs. Remember, you need a straight/tight line when casting upstream. This means you need to move the fly the same speed (if dead-drifting) or faster (if retrieving) than the current.

ACROSS-STREAM TACTICS

The across or down-and-across approach involves casting either directly across-stream or down-and-across. This is the most common technique, and for good reason. Line and leader control is easier because the line immediately is placed under tension while the streamers move downstream from you—unlike the upstream approach, where you need to both manage line as it drifts downstream and create enough energy to impart additional movement into the fly. With the across-stream technique, you are responsible for manipulating the pattern's action along with any necessary mending.

Across-stream tactics are by far the most exciting. The strikes are more aggressive, since the line is under the most tension. This is also known as the "tug"—that point when a trout strikes your pattern while the line is under tension. These takes can literally rip the rod out of your hands, and that is the reason why so many streamer addicts will fish all day for the chance to feel the tug.

In this approach, the line is under more tension, and with that additional tension, retrieving line can create a fast-moving presentation. You can implement a mend with the across-stream tactic to both slow down the drift and to increase the speed. To slow down the drift, make an upstream mend to reduce tension on the line. Make a downstream mend to increase the tension on the line and speed up the drift. Trout need to be in chasing mode for you to use this approach. Trout develop moods just as humans do, and when they're not in the mood to chase food, a fast presentation across-stream won't work as well. As a result, I'll likely use this approach during

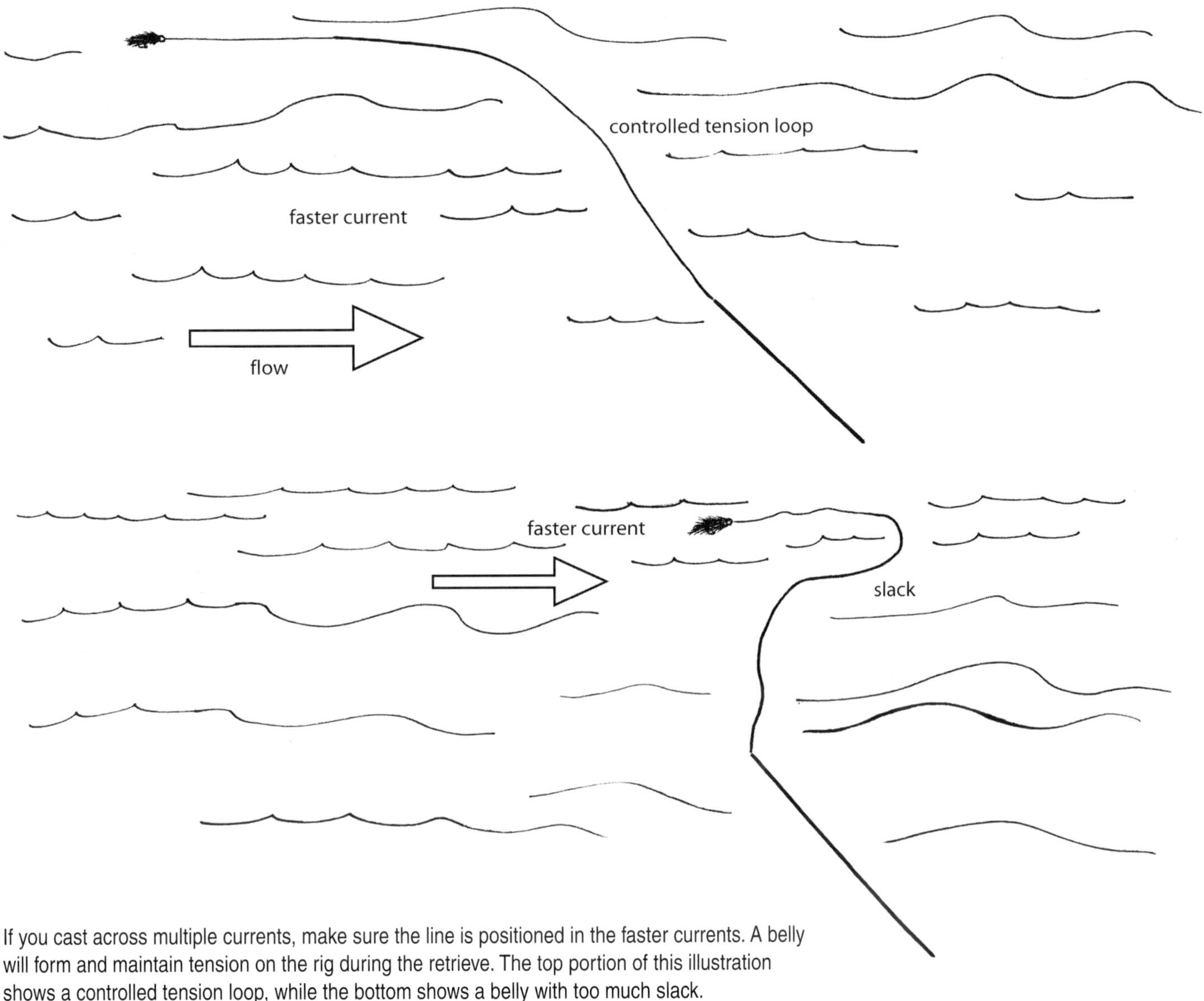

If you cast across multiple currents, make sure the line is positioned in the faster currents. A belly will form and maintain tension on the rig during the retrieve. The top portion of this illustration shows a controlled tension loop, while the bottom shows a belly with too much slack.

low light or during heavy cloud cover when pursuing trout on my home waters.

This isn't always the case when looking at other trout waters across the country. Trout living in states like California are conditioned to longer periods of sunlight. As a result, some of my best streamer action while fishing the Sierra occurred during periods of bright sunlight. Not all bodies of water fish the same, as trout behavior will vary from one system to another. Your job is to experiment with presentation angles and retrieve speeds in order to determine the trout's willingness to move. Just as with dry flies, there are periods throughout the day where trout will not chase down a streamer, no matter what the angle and speed of the presentation. While I try to stay committed to the streamer approach, there are days when I will have both nymphing and dry-fly rigs ready to go. Always be prepared to fish other tactics.

The across-stream approach enables you to cover a wider arc, which is why I use this approach when covering larger rivers with undefined holding spots. This approach enables you to cover more water than any other approach I know, and in doing so, it has the potential to move fish from the stream bottom. A fish doesn't have to strike to give away its location. Instead, all I need to see is a follow or a flash that indicates either interest in feeding or territorial behavior. While the upstream and downstream approaches will also locate fish, this wide-angled approach covers a broader range of water during each presentation. If I'm fishing unfamiliar waters or haven't fished a body of water for some time, I'll go with the across approach to cover more water and help identify the trout's holding patterns.

My friend Joe Goodspeed is one of the fly-fishing industry's brightest R&D guys, and he is also one of the best big-fish hunters I've had the pleasure of fishing with. The one streamer approach Joe has used with great success near his home waters in New York has been swinging oversize streamer patterns. When I say oversize, I'm referring to a streamer pattern that is overkill for 95 percent of the resident trout he's fishing over. However, one thing I have noticed is that a big fly will provoke

Fog rises from the North Fork River in Arkansas during a January morning. Although majestic, I find fog has a negative impact on fishing. When heavy fog sets in, seek out backwaters where fog appears to be less common.

a territorial dispute with the trout kingpin. While large trout will eat an excessively large streamer pattern, I believe many of the strikes or follows we witness when fishing such items are more from aggression than from hunger. Joe uses this approach to his advantage as he locates large trout that are following his patterns. Joe will then remember each fish he moved on the stream and come back later with a smaller streamer pattern. He often covers the water again with a smaller crayfish pattern fished with an approach (either upstream or downstream) that keeps the pattern in the trout's holding area for a longer period of time.

When working the across-stream approach, I prefer to position myself midstream, so I can make casts toward either bank. This isn't always a possibility, as some stream conditions will not permit wading midstream. I'm looking to cover all water types, starting with the bank and moving outward toward the deepest sections midstream. During low-light periods, trout will be hunting the shallow-water sections. A mistake I made for years on bigger water was wading one side and making longer casts to the opposite bank. Nowadays, instead of walking up the bank and spooking trout feeding off the bank on one side of the stream, I'll walk through the deeper sections of water (the typical daytime holding spots). By wading carefully, I can double my chances because now I can target both banks instead of one. This tactic works on medium-size streams during low light. Streams no more than 30 feet wide can be split in half by a carefully wading angler. It never ceases to amaze me how close I can get to trout in low light. During daybreak I've walked up to within 15 feet of a large feeding trout. With a 9-foot rod, all I need to do is to cast 6 feet of line and leader to cover the fish.

The upstream approach allows you to sneak up from behind the trout, allowing you to make a shorter cast. However, with the across- or down-and-across approach, you need to commit to longer casts. There are exceptions to this, as dirty water or low-light periods often allow you to get closer to the fish. However, when fishing throughout the day, I find I need to lengthen my cast, because the across-stream approach puts us in the trout's view. This goes back to early-morning tactics, when trout are feeding in shallow water and are on high alert. When fishing similar low-light conditions and trout are feeding in shallow water, my favorite approach is from behind the fish. Carefully coming in from behind positions you in a trout's blind spot. As long as you're cautious while wading, you can take up a close position (up to 15 feet away) to a large feeding fish.

Early spring is a favorite time for streamer fishing. Trout activity begins to peak before the major hatches and amid the warming water temps. LANCE WILT

Right: Lenny Gliwa from the TCO Fly Shop releases a brown trout taken on the West Branch Delaware River. This fish made three short strikes before committing to the streamer—a good reason to use the strip-set. It's not uncommon for a trout to strike a pattern multiple times before committing.

My preference is to have a downstream loop in the line during the drift. This loop will achieve at least two things: First, it will create additional tension during the drift, which means you are less responsible for line control. Second, the downstream bow will keep the fly moving in a downward direction, so when a trout does strike the fly, the streamer will be moving toward the fish during the hook set instead of away. This is a key point to remember—the idea of keeping the fly moving toward the fish during the hook set. To increase hooking percentages, I believe it's more effective to strike toward the fish's mouth rather than pull the hook away from the fish. Even when you're upstream from the fish and retrieving the pattern across or down-and-across, as long as there's a downstream bow in the line, the fly will first follow the direction of the loop when tension is created during the hook set. This is why I try to stay away from keeping a straight line positioned directly upstream from the fish (unless the tactic calls for it), as the fly will be pulled directly upstream and away from the fish. While this tactic will hook fish, I prefer to keep a downstream loop to allow the fly to move toward the fish during the hook set, which gives the fly an easier target.

Ideal conditions for the downstream loop are slower-moving bodies of water with uniform-speed currents. The downstream loop will create tension and therefore speed up the drift. If you lay the downstream loop on fast-moving water, too much tension may be placed on the rig—speeding up the drift and keeping the fly riding higher in the water column. This may be okay when fishing shallow hunting grounds along the banks and shallow flats, where the fly will ride closer to the stream bottom despite the increased tension. However, too much tension may keep the fly riding too high on waters such as deep runs and pools—potential resting areas where trout are more likely to not chase down food items. When trout are aggressively chasing food, the tension created by the downstream loop may not have any negative effect on the presentation. However, trout may refuse to chase down a streamer if the pattern is moving too high in the water column or too fast. This is when you need to slow down the drift by using an upstream mend, as you would when indicator fishing.

While I prefer the downstream loop, there are times when you need to create upstream mends to slow the drift speed of the streamer. Runs offer faster surface and will create too much drag on a floating line if a downstream belly is created. There is such a thing as a streamer moving too fast. This may not be a concern during the few times each year when trout will go out of their way to chase down a streamer. However, while trout are active hunters, they are efficient and will not chase down a food item moving too fast, because the calories taken in are not worth the calories expended. This is one reason top predators often seek out the young or old members of a herd—they can isolate and attack the easiest meal. Trout will go to great lengths to chase down a meal, but we need to slow down our presentation when they're not moving far for food.

The side from which you present the fly (i.e., your right- or left-hand side) will affect the degree of tension on the rig. If you're a right-handed caster, casting across-stream with the current flowing right to left, casts off to your right side and slightly upstream, the line will be positioned downstream of the fly, likely causing a downstream loop. In turn, this will create additional tension on the rig and speed up the retrieve. On the other hand, if you cast slightly downstream and off your left shoulder, the fly line will land upstream of the fly, similar to an upstream reach cast in dry-fly fishing. This will create less tension and slow down the retrieve. Instead of having to change weighted flies or sinking line types, the first step to slowing down or speeding up the retrieve is to change casting angles.

My preference is to change angles or mend in the air rather than having to mend after the cast is made. Trout will strike a streamer from the moment it lands on the water all the way until the end of the drift. If you mend on the water, you lose control at the moment you place slack in the line—the exact moment a trout may strike your streamer. When mending in the air or changing the casting angle, the line positioning is done in the air instead of on the water, allowing me to stay in touch with the streamer throughout the entire drift.

I believe the across-stream approach allows for an easier (although not the best) hook set, due to the tension created during the retrieve. Unlike the upstream approach, where the line is under a small degree of tension and you have to retrieve line as it drifts downstream, the across-stream approach immediately places line under tension as the fly is being pulled away from you by the current. While you are retrieving and stripping the line and creating additional tension, much of the tension is created by line being pulled. The bigger the loop, the more tension created. As a result of the high degree of tension, all you often need to do is make a short movement with either the rod tip or your line hand to manipulate the pattern on the retrieve.

One method of maintaining control and tension with an across-stream tactic is to keep the rod tip pointing directly at the fly or downstream of the swinging streamer. When combined with a straight, slack-free line and a rod tip pointed directly at the streamer or downstream, this creates a connection with the streamer. Not all streamer takes are aggressive, so you need to stay in contact with the streamer. This is similar to nymphing, as you will not always see a trout attack the streamer, especially when a soft take occurs. As the streamer begins to move downstream, the rod tip needs to be pointed either at the fly or downstream, and that streamer needs to keep moving at the same speed or faster during the retrieve, or a downstream U-shape will occur, leaving you in a bad position for a strong hook set

If you make a downstream mend to increase the speed of the retrieve, the rod tip needs to be pointed at the downstream loop and not at the fly. If the rod tip is pointed at the fly, then a downstream U-shape will occur. If you want to mend upstream to slow down the drift, the mend should position the line in roughly a straight line. An upstream mend, which places the line upstream of the fly, can be used to slow down the drift but will likely create a disconnect between angler and streamer. I will intentionally use such an upstream mend when I need to create enough slack to allow the streamer to drop, but I won't do this during the actual retrieve of the streamer, when I feel a trout is likely to strike. This upstream slack mend is great in deeper waters, where trout are holding close to the stream bottom and not as likely to strike in the upper current.

Another thing I consider is the speed at which I want to move the fly. If I want it moving dead slow or to hold it in an area, I'll present the fly from a downstream angle. If I want to retrieve the streamer at approximately the same speed as the current, I'll present from an upstream position and retrieve the pattern slightly faster than the current. If I want the fly to move at maximum speed, I'll use the tension of the currents to increase current drag and use the fastest possible retrieve. Changing the angle of my presentation is my first move when deciding on whether I want to speed up or slow down the drift; the second would be a fly change, and the third would be switching to a fly line with a different sink rate. The order in which I make the switch is based on time. For example, it takes less time to change the angle of the presentation than to change a fly. And it takes less time for me to change a fly than to change a fly line.

UPSTREAM MEND

You can use an upstream mend for a number of reasons, including to slow down the retrieve speed or to keep your streamer riding closer during a swing. While I prefer to maintain a slight downstream belly in my line to keep tension during the retrieve, at times I need to slow down my fly. I prefer to use the upstream mend only when casting across-stream or down-and-across stream, as the downstream fly placement means that I'll have tension with my fly. I only use the upstream mend when fishing upstream in deeper pools to allow the streamer to drop to correct depth before retrieving. Also, the upstream mend can be used to reposition a fly back toward the bank, after the current has begun pulling the fly and line away from the bank.

1. The current is beginning to pull the streamer and line away from the bank.

2. Lifting with a steady forearm, begin to move the rod in a large, upside-down U-shape. Again, don't use the wrist for this movement, as it will give you too small a movement.

3. Move the rod tip as high off the water as possible. The higher rod tip picks more line off the water, which makes for an easier mend, as you're moving less line off the water. The less line on the water, the less water tension you need to break while implementing the mend.

4. After you've lifted the rod tip high in the air, the next step is to make a mending movement, where the rod tip travels in a wide (downward U) shape toward the stream bank. The rod tip should land on the current where you want to fish your streamer. This is another reason why I prefer 9- to 10-foot rods for fishing streamers, as mending is a huge part of my streamer game, and the long rod allows for easier mending.

5. Place the line on the outside edge of a seam, where you want to hold your streamer pattern.

6. You can hold the streamer in place or retrieve it back. You may hold the streamer in this position for several minutes and then decide to reposition it using another mend—without having to recast the line.

7. This is an example of a mend thrown perpendicular to the current at the end of a swing to change the direction of the retrieve. In this case, the fly will follow the path of the line belly away from the angler and toward the bank.

DOWNSTREAM TACTICS

With the downstream approach, you can either cast directly downstream or allow the pattern to swing to a direct downstream position after executing an across-stream approach. At the very end of the retrieve, where the streamer swings downstream, you can hold the pattern, retrieve the pattern, or mend to either side to move the pattern sideways. While this tactic isn't as active in terms of stripping and retrieving line as the upstream and across-stream tactics, the downstream approach offers something the other tactics cannot—a static presentation. By static, I mean the ability to hold a fly in an area for an extended period of time. It's important to remember that successful streamer tactics do not always mean swinging a large streamer across an undercut bank. Trout are not always in the mood to chase down their food. Variables including water temperature, time of day, and water clarity might force a larger trout to move into a resting area. When resting, trout will still eat but are not likely to use energy to chase food. As a result, a streamer pattern would need to be presented at a slower speed or held in front of a trout. Another application is when a trout's visibility is limited to dirty water. Trout will still feed, but locating food becomes more difficult as clarity decreases. A trout may not see a large streamer ripping through dirty water. However, a streamer held static in an area for an extended period will give the trout a better opportunity to eventually locate the pattern.

I use this approach combined with the across-stream tactic. I'll retrieve the pattern across-stream and allow my streamers to hold in a fixed position for an extended period of time. I'll cast directly downstream in line with the seam I'm fishing only during periods of extremes, and in those situations, I disregard swinging my patterns down-and-across. If the stream is blown out with little visibility, swinging a streamer may not be a good approach, as trout will find it difficult to find a fast-moving pattern in water with little visibility. As visibility decreases, your presentation may need to slow down to provide a trout with

Lance Wilt holds a West Branch Delaware brown trout taken while he was fishing in front of the boat. The Delaware is known for its spooky trout, so casting long distances in front of the boat (instead of across) may be your best approach.

The concept of give-and-take is important for streamer fishing. Hold the pattern in front of a fish for an extended period of time. Keep the fly away from the fish, then allow the streamer to drift closer to the trout, then pull it away. This is my favorite approach when targeting a resting location, where a trout may be more interested in resting than hunting for food.

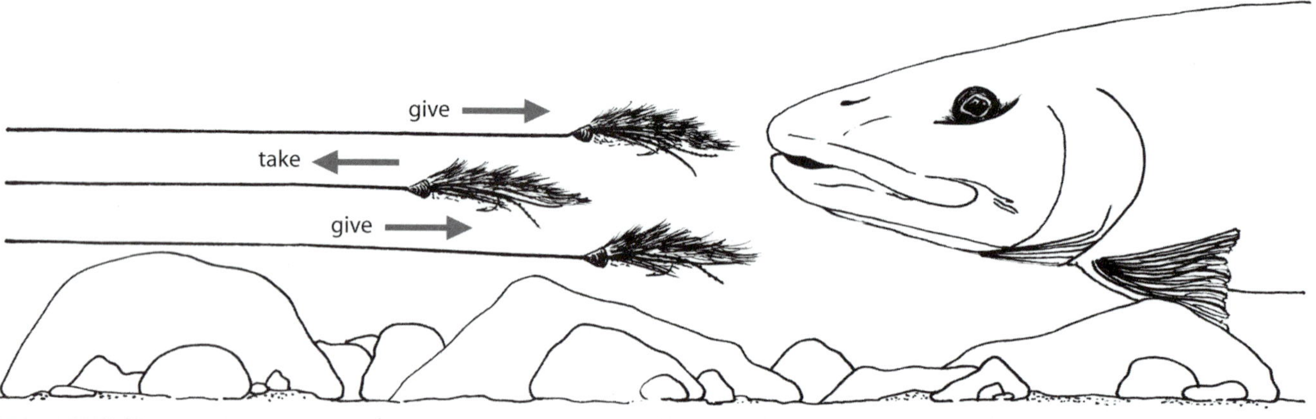

A windy day on a Scotland loch. Even in clear water, a windy day can create chop, which allows a trout to feel comfortable closer to the surface. As a result, fishing a floating line with a medium-weighted streamer in deep water often produces good results, as trout will be feeding closer to the surface.

more time to locate a food item. When fishing water with little to no visibility, I prefer to hold my patterns rather than retrieve them. Instead of trying to cover water, I target specific high-water holding areas. This can include but is not limited to shallow edges along banks, pockets behind boulders, or any area a trout will hold during high water. Instead of swinging my pattern through the holding area, I position the rod tip directly upstream of the targeted location and hold the pattern in the current, so the line, leader, and fly are sitting in the same current. I use the downstream water surface to maintain tension on the streamer. During muddy water I may hold a fly in a pocket for over a minute in the hope that a trout is in the area and will eventually find my fly.

I used this approach in the fall of 2009 when State College hosted the U.S. National Fly-Fishing Championships. A rainstorm struck the night before the event and flooded all the rivers. Entire trees and even a dead cow floated down Penns Creek during one of the sessions, and wading was not possible during the second day of the tournament. During my session on Penns Creek, the entire river was flowing 10 to 15 feet onto the banks. Luckily, I located a large sycamore tree along the bank where the water was flowing around it. Throughout my 200-yard beat, this tree provided the only slack water, and that was where I focused my three hours on the beat.

The pocket was approximately 2 feet deep and was the color of chocolate milk. Positioning myself upstream of the pocket and casting directly downstream, I placed a single size 8 black Slump Buster in the middle of the pocket. The slow surface currents pulled the medium-weighted streamer away from my upstream position and kept tension on the fly, allowing me to hold the fly in the pocket without my streamer dropping to the bottom. I had to make two fly changes to find the correct weight to achieve enough depth so the fly was under tension but didn't sink to the bottom. I would hold the streamer in the middle of the water column for up to a minute, slowly retrieve the fly back with a short strip with the line hand or a jig movement with the rod tip, and then allow the fly to fall back into position. The movements were slow because dirty water dictated a slower-moving pattern.

I'm a big believer in fishing my flies somewhere in the middle to the top of the water column during muddy water. Although the water is muddy, trout will still look toward the surface and use natural light to pick out prey silhouettes—it's more difficult to look down into the dark muddy water to spot food. It was a slow three hours, but I landed two fish with that approach. The holding tactic is a mundane approach, but it can yield fish in muddy water or periods of low fish activity.

THE FOREARM JIG

1. When jigging streamers, I prefer to lift the flies using my forearm rather than my wrist. The forearm lift creates a more powerful lift, which creates a better hook set. The forearm usually starts about stomach level.

2. Lift your forearm upward with a short and powerful movement. This movement doesn't jerk the streamer, which can create slack. Instead, this movement maintains tension between rod tip and streamer and allows you to feel the slightest hesitation anytime during the presentation.

3. Continue to lift your forearm until it is about shoulder height. This motion moves the fly no more than a foot. After raising your rod hand to shoulder level, drop your forearm back down to its original position with a smooth and controlled movement.

The Give-and-Take

The give-and-take is a variation of the downstream approach in which the angler will let a pattern drift into an area and then pull it away and continue the process for up to several minutes. The key to this tactic is making sure there's enough water tension on the rig—along with using a light enough streamer rig—to keep the fly from dropping to the stream bottom. For this approach, I prefer the pattern to hold closer to the trout's feeding level, as I feel this tactic initiates a trout's aggressive instincts. I want the pattern to remain close to the trout's eye level, moving away and then coming right back to its original space. I'm looking to obtain an aggressive strike, not a hunger strike. I also use this approach as a last resort when trout are positioned in resting areas and are not chasing flies fished with the upstream or across-stream tactics.

If given a choice of rigs while implementing the give-and-take, I would opt for an intermediate line in combination with a lightly weighted or even unweighted streamer. A heavy streamer is likely to drop to the stream bottom even when under water tension, while an intermediate line with a lighter-weight streamer will not. I'll use the line and position of the rod tip to hold the streamer at the desired depth. The higher the rod tip, the higher the fly rides and vise versa. If I want a deep-riding streamer, I'll shove the rod tip under the water surface to achieve a deeper ride. Normally, I'll start working midcolumn and then begin to work downward if trout are not moving up to chase the streamer.

Like all the tactics discussed above, this give-and-take can be adapted for drifting in a boat. While I was drifting the Pere Marquette with guide Tommy Lynch, we encountered little action when using the traditional across-stream approach. After two hours, Tommy decided to begin targeting holding pools—deep water where trout were more likely resting than feeding. Tommy began slowing down the drift boat and had me casting more downstream, in line with the deeper pools instead of the banks. Using a fast-sinking tip and his buoyant Double D streamer, he had me conduct a short countdown (allowing the line to sink) and then begin short strips toward me before immediately kicking out line. This allowed the streamer to move downstream back to its original position. After the pattern moved back to its original position, Tommy again had me strip the streamer back to me. The Double D, with its wedge-shaped head, would dig in the water and dart downward toward the trout during the strip. During the pause, the buoyant deer hair head streamer would pull upstream toward the surface. This continuous swooping and darting pulled a good number of trout away from their holding areas and changed the outcome of the day. As anglers, we need to remember that trout are not always in the mood to chase food. At these times, we need to present a pattern that invades the trout's personal space and creates a territorial strike instead of a hunger strike.

Another point worth mentioning with the downstream approach is your ability to use a mend to reposition the fly in a different seam. After you have exhausted an area with your

While I rarely fish lighter than 2X diameter tippet, there are times when lighter tippets are needed to fool fish. For example, clear conditions may require a longer leader (8 to 10 feet) tapered down to 4X. CHRIS DANIEL

presentation, you can use a mend to reposition the fly into a different seam without having to make another cast. For example, if I want to change the position of my downstream presentation without having to reposition my body, I'll reposition the belly of the line so it lays on the next targeted seam.

The one disadvantage of the downstream presentation is the angle of the hook set—a trout is likely to strike tailfirst, and with the angler positioned upstream during the set, the fly will be pulled upstream and away from the trout's mouth. When I'm retrieving my fly, I make sure to know the location of the streamer, and when the strike occurs, I set both upstream and to the side. Which side to set the hook depends on your body position in relation to the flow of water. You need to think about which side movement will create the greatest amount of tension. If I'm facing directly downstream and positioned between a heavy seam and soft edge, I will strike to the side of the soft edge. I do this because pulling directly against the heavy current will cause the pattern to slow down versus the pulling to the soft edge, which will allow me to create more force during the set. This attention to detail will create more secure hook sets and put more fish in the net.

If I decide to focus on downstream presentation, I opt for a pattern with a shorter tail to eliminate short strikes. Again, I feel the downstream presentation invokes more territorial strikes rather than hunger strikes. This means the trout isn't always trying to inhale the pattern; instead it's striking the pattern to chase it away, so it nips at the tail without fully committing to the fly. I believe this is why so many steelhead swinging patterns possess a short tail and stinger hook, as many of the takes occur at the end of the swing as the fish approaches the pattern from behind. This is especially true with larger articulated patterns, which I feel are large enough to generate just as many territorial strikes as hunger strikes. However, if I'm fishing microstreamers (such as trout parr or size 12 microbuggers), I'm not as concerned with using a super-short tail or a stinger because these sizes of flies evoke more hunger strikes.

GIVE-AND-TAKE

1. The give-and-take is a tactic used to elicit a strike by aggravating a trout. It's a downstream presentation where the angler holds the fly directly in a downstream position, pulls the fly away from the trout for several seconds, and then allows it to float back toward the fish. The process can be repeated for minutes. The first step is to identify a potential resting area and present a cast, so it can swing directly downstream of the angler into the holding area. Once the fly has swung into position, keep the rod hand far away from your body. Pinch the line with your line hand (at a 45-degree angle), and hold it away from the rod hand. Holding the line close to the body, you can feel the tension of the current wanting to pull your streamer downstream.

2. When ready to let the line slip downstream, keep the rod tip pointed straight at the target to allow a clear path for the line to travel. When giving line to the target, slide your line hand away from your body toward the stripping guide, as the tension of the water current pulls the fly downstream. Let the degree of tension determine how fast the "give" should be, meaning you can't give line faster than the actual speed of the current. If you do move the line hand faster than the current, you'll accumulate slack. Again, you want the current to pull the fly downstream, so you have a tight connection during the entire give. If a little slack does occur, wait until the line goes under tension. Continue to hold this position for several seconds.

3. To take line back, keep the rod tip pointed toward the target, and strip line back to the original position of the line hand. Keep the line pinched between your fingers so that an aggressive strike won't rip the line from your grasp. Again, don't use the wrist to pull back on the line but keep the hand in a fixed position and pull back with the elbow. Using the elbow to pull creates a smoother and more powerful loading movement. Continue this process until you are satisfied that you have thoroughly covered the area. Note that the elbow will pull the line back to set the hook when a strike occurs.

MAKING A CHANGE

The question of how many casts to make is asked just as many times with streamer fishing as with nymph fishing. The simple answer is, "Let the conditions dictate your approach." If trout are chasing food, then I make one cast and move 5 feet before making the next presentation. If trout are chasing, they are willing to move long distances and the 5-foot rule has worked well for me during peak trout activity. On the other hand, if conditions are slow and I decide to swing a pattern and hold it in front of a potential resting spot, I may present twice to the same area before moving only 2 feet and repeating the setup.

Another consideration is visibility. In dirty water I may make up to five casts into an area before moving several feet. On the other hand, if the water is crystal clear, I may only make one cast before moving. Try to develop an understanding of the trout's mood and then decide how much water you want to cover and the speed you want to fish your patterns.

Phil Croft poses with a steelhead while floating a northern Michigan stream. This steelhead came from the depths of the dark water, where a fast-sinking line, a heavily weighted Sparkle Minnow, and a rod tip shoved deep into the water was the only approach for moving this steelhead, along with several others, from the depths.

Below: Patrick Williams holds a taimen during a recent trip to Mongolia. Patrick explained how he initially tied flies the size of squirrels, but found that smaller, troutlike streamers moved more fish. Most of his taimen were caught on a 4- to 6-inch articulated streamer. Make sure to have a variety of styles and sizes to deal with all streamer conditions. PATRICK WILLIAMS

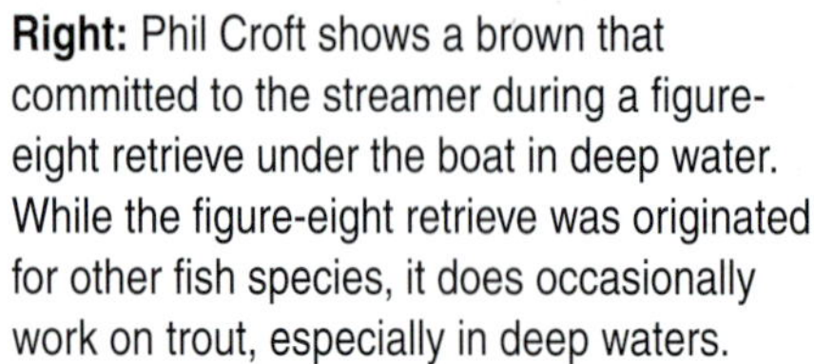

Right: Phil Croft shows a brown that committed to the streamer during a figure-eight retrieve under the boat in deep water. While the figure-eight retrieve was originated for other fish species, it does occasionally work on trout, especially in deep waters.

FISHING FROM A BOAT

Many of the tactics explained in this book can easily be implemented while fishing from a boat. The key to remember is that when you're wade-fishing, you are likely standing in a fixed location as your pattern moves either directly toward you (if you're casting upstream) or away from you (if you're casting down-and-across). If you're fishing from a boat, the actions of the oarsman can determine your streamer presentation. As many who fish from a boat know, success has as much to do with the rower as it does with the fisher. When you want to fish your patterns slower or closer to the stream bottom, the boat needs to move at about the same speed as the current. If the boat and the streamer rig move approximately at the same speed, less tension occurs between the two, allowing the rig to sink faster. If I want my patterns to swing off the bottom faster, I will ask the person behind the oars to back-row harder. With the boat moving slower than the surface currents, tension increases and forces the flies to be lifted off stream bottom faster. ■

The guide staff from Outcast Anglers prepare to launch a boat on Arkansas's North Fork River.

There is no cookie-cutter set of rules you can follow when results are less than desirable. However, I generally do have a standard sequence of approach when I feel I need to make a change.

1. Change the speed of the retrieve. Always think about the conditions you're fishing and how that should relate to the speed of your retrieve. Rate of retrieve plays a huge role in the overall success of the day, and for that reason it's often the first change I make in my presentation when one is needed. The trout's level of feeding activity determines the speed at which you move the fly. There are several things to consider in regards to rate of retrieve: water type fished, time of day, water temperatures, and water clarity. In water with strong or broken currents, trout cannot see as far they can when feeding in a flat pool. As a result, I'll slow down the retrieve when visibility is reduced. The opposite is true when trout have a large window of vision, such as in a clear, flat pool. In those scenarios I'll speed up the retrieve to give the trout less of a chance to investigate the pattern. Also, think about water temperatures and when a trout's metabolism may slow down. During the coldest winter days, a slower retrieve is normally a better option than a faster retrieve.

2. Change the depth of the retrieve. While streamer fishing brings out the aggressive nature of trout, there are periods when predatory feeding trout are not always in the mood to chase food. You must recognize these conditions and develop a strategy that encourages the less active trout to eat your pattern. This is especially important when fishing slow, deep pools. These slower-moving bodies of waters are often resting areas for trout, which means they may not be in the mood to move a far distance to strike. You need to present the fly closer to the zone of the trout. Often all that's required is a couple-second pause to allow the streamer to drop deeper, before beginning the retrieve.

3. Change pattern colors. During the 2014 World Fly-Fishing Championships in the Czech Republic, as captain of our squad, I was asked to observe a bank-fishing session and relay information back to our guys. I witnessed bite windows when it appeared most anglers were either moving fish or hooking fish while pulling smaller streamers. As captain, I was permitted to walk around the lake and observe what pattern, rig, and approach each angler was using. I was interested to see if there was a common fly-color theme with the anglers catching fish. However, what I found was a broad range of streamer colors, with no one particular color being the top fish-catcher. Instead, the common theme with the successful anglers was depth and speed of the retrieve.

   My point is not to say that fly color doesn't matter, because at times it does. However, I believe there are periods when trout are hunting larger prey and when trout are in super hunting mode, and at these times I don't think fly color is as important as the depth and speed of your retrieve. Yet in dirty water, high water, or in deep water, fly color can have a larger role in my success rate.

FISHING THE EXTREMES

We can't dictate the conditions we face along the stream. Since we are forced to work with the hand we're dealt, understanding how to "fish the extremes" is something all anglers need to learn. The streamer angler can catch fish in all extremes, but first, you need to know how trout often (not always) react to certain extremes, as this knowledge will help guide your streamer approach.

If you're going to fish muddy water, try to fish early in the day before the sun comes out or during cloudy conditions. Muddy water contains suspended solids. Bright sunlight will reflect off these particles, creating difficult viewing for trout. Think about driving through a snowstorm with your high beams on; it's a similar effect with dirty water and bright sunlight. When fishing deeper in muddy water, a good approach is to cast down and across and hold your streamer higher in the water column. In muddy water, trout will look up for their food, waiting for any silhouette to appear.

When muddy water occurs, holding your pattern directly downstream offers trout a longer opportunity to locate your streamer.

Dirty Water

Dirty water can occur for any number of reasons—rain, runoff, a tributary dumping dirty water into a larger body of water—even without a high-water event. When targeting trout in dirty water, you should focus on the shade lines where the bright sun and dirty particles make it difficult for trout to see. My friend Mike Schultz explains it best: "Fishing muddy water in bright sunlight is like driving through a snowstorm with the high beams on." What he means is that muddy water likely contains lots of suspended particles drifting through the water, and the sunlight illuminates those particles. The brighter the sun, the more difficult it is to see through the particles. This is similar to a driver using low beams when driving through a snowstorm at night—it allows the driver to see better through the particles. Because of this, when fishing dirty water, I prefer to fish during the periods of lowest light. This may mean fishing early or late in the day when the sun isn't shining directly on the river. If I'm forced to fish during midday, I will seek the shaded sections. While you can catch fish in muddy river sections in sunlit conditions, I've noticed a far higher percentage of fish caught when fishing muddy water during low-light periods or along shaded river sections.

While trout have excellent vision in most dirty water conditions, certain fly colors do help a fish locate your fly easier in such water. If I'm forced to fish deeper or off-colored water, I use brighter colors like chartreuse and yellow, often with ultraviolet material built into the fly. Brighter-colored streamers are more visible at deeper depths and in stained water, where less light is able to reach and illuminate your pattern. A brighter pattern can tell you how deep the pattern is moving in the water, along with indicating the exact path of the retrieve. This is especially helpful for beginning streamer anglers; it provides confidence in knowing exactly where their pattern is drifting in dirty water.

In addition to brighter colors, I prefer to use patterns tied with ultraviolet (UV) materials. UV materials have been used for years by many of the great European stillwater anglers. I didn't consider using the material until a fishing event on Hume Lake near Fresno, California, in 2006. I met my boat controller and was excited to hear that he was from Scotland and an accomplished stillwater angler. We discussed a number of items, including materials for fishing deeper water. It was during the last session of the event, after the fish had been beat on for nine hours, that the trout began to move deeper in the water column. My controller suggested that I switch to a pattern containing UV material since I was now fishing my small streamers deeper in the water column. I told him I had no UV flies. He informed me that I needed to have them—he and many of his colleagues used UV exclusively in the deeper waters in Scotland's lochs. Before UV became readily available in commercial fly-tying materials, he would take a UV light into craft stores and shine it on all potential tying materials until he found

The amount of fishable areas may be limited during high-water events. It's not uncommon to walk several miles during a half-day outing while fishing high water. Hit the spots hard and move on.

materials that would light up. He would use these materials when fishing the darker depths of waters like Loch Leven and similar waters. After getting home, I immediately bought a UV light and began to purchase materials using UV; this allowed me to tackle deep and dirty water conditions with excellent results. I now use UV streamers exclusively when visibility is less than 6 inches.

When fishing muddy flats during a high-water event, I prefer to use a floating line with a lightweight streamer. I often tie on a Muddler-style head with a lightweight conehead. The deer hair head will move water yet is buoyant enough not to snag bottom. The conehead keeps the nose of the pattern anchored below the water's surface. This combination allows me to fish my streamer pattern as slow or as fast as I want without worrying about the fly dropping too fast in the shallow flat. In my opinion, anglers usually fish too heavy of streamer pattern when working shallow flats, which forces them to move the fly too fast to avoid hanging up on bottom. In dirty water, I like short strips followed by longer pauses to give a fish time to locate my pattern in the mud.

Another thing to consider when fishing dirty water is the degree of impact you want to create when presenting your streamer. Trout use their lateral line to sense both predators and prey. When a trout's vision is limited in dirty water, it pays to smack the fly on the water's surface to obtain a trout's attention. The dirtier the water, the harder I smack the fly. To do this during the presentation, sweep the rod tip through a wide arc to create a wide loop, which will force the fly to smack the water in the same manner as a swimmer doing a belly flop off the diving board. The force used during the acceleration can be increased to create a greater impact during the presentation. This approach is also effective when fishing streamers or mouse patterns in total darkness. The opposite approach—using less force during the presentation—should be used in low or clear water when trout are on high alert.

High-Water Events

High water doesn't always mean dirty water conditions. A number of the freestone streams I fish in north-central Pennsylvania can receive heavy rainfall and rise a foot without becoming off-color. In high water, I'll target the soft edges during a high-water event. I prefer to fish these soft or slow-moving sections because they provide both a resting spot and ideal hunting grounds for a trout. As the main current is transporting the suspended sediments (i.e., the dirty water) downstream, the edges likely will possess a few more inches of visibility, making for ideal hunting grounds for a trout. Remember that when dirty water conditions exist, visibility is restricted when looking toward the stream bottom. In my experience, it almost seems as if trout will position themselves lower in the water column and look up toward the brighter sky, where the silhouette of prey can spotted easier.

Another alternative to the jigging approach is to fish a buoyant streamer in combination with heavy anchor point such as a heavy sinking line or split shot. When working the edges, I will opt for a full-floating line along with a buoyant streamer in combination with a split shot placed near the nose. If you're working a long edge (20 feet or more), then you can use a full-sinking/sinking-tip line. The ample sinking line will need to rest in the water in order to pull the buoyant streamer below stream surface. However, if I'm working a soft edge that's 3 feet long, then I will opt for a heavier split shot placed close to the nose. The key to both scenarios is keeping the fly suspended off the bottom, so the trout can locate the pattern's silhouette when looking toward the sky. When using sinking lines or sinking tips, I'll use a short tippet of 3 to 4 feet. The shorter tippet will help keep the buoyant streamer below the surface. This is also the reason I may use a broader pattern such as a Shenk Sculpin or a Zoo Cougar—it provides a larger visual target to the trout.

SHALLOW WATERS

You can break down water types into at least three realms: feeding lies, resting lies, or both. For example, early morning is a favorite time to streamer fish because larger predatory trout often hunt the shallows, feeding on larger prey items that may be feeding on insects or other small prey. This is when the entire food chain is working at the same time. When fishing streamers during these times, I prefer to target shallow reaches that are in close proximity to daytime holding lies for larger trout. A shallow can occur near a head of a riffle, along the banks, or near the tailout of a pool. Larger prey including sculpins, juvenile trout, and crayfish, along with other smaller fish species, can be found hunting these shallows during low-light periods. Larger trout know this and will attack when their prey is focused on feeding. I've found when trout are in hunting mode, they will move fast to the prey. I've seen trout move faster toward my streamer during low-light periods than during times of brighter light. As a result, I prefer to work my streamer faster during low-light periods. I'm not talking about dark of

When fishing low water, I may crouch at the end of the retrieve to reduce the chance of spooking a trout pursuing my streamer. I only crouch when retrieving the flies toward me in low water, where the trout has a good opportunity to see me head on.

Spend time fishing secondary or overflow channels in high water, as trout will quickly move into these areas.

the night, but rather the first thirty minutes of daylight in the morning and the last thirty minutes of light in evening. A faster retrieve provides less time for the trout to think about whether or not to attack the streamer, very much like fishing a nymph in a riffle.

Another thing to consider when fishing shallows during low light is that you must be ready for a strike the moment your fly lands on the water. If wading, I will place my fly right off the bank and immediately begin the retrieve. An active stream bank during low light will likely hold a trout waiting to jump on your fly. Often, no sooner does my fly land and I am about to make the first strip of line when suddenly a trout attacks my streamer. The fish eats the fly within one second of it landing on the water. This is why I prefer a high-trajectory cast, where I can position my rod tip low to the water and have my hand on the line to begin the retrieve before the fly lands. I want my line hand to be in complete control of line management from the very beginning of the presentation. This is also the reason I shoot through the O-ring: It keeps the shooting line within grasp at all times, instead of completely letting go of the line and forcing you to regain control.

Since trout are more on the hunt and willing to chase prey on the flat, I prefer to approach shallows with an up-and-across tactic. I believe this approach allows for a better hook set because you are more likely to be retrieving the fly toward the fish rather than away from it. Also, the rig isn't under as much tension, which I believe allows for the right amount of slack for the trout to inhale your fly.

When fishing a soft edge (not a flat, but a soft section of water with a little depth), I prefer to cast downstream, parallel to the seam, because the water's surface tension will keep the buoyant streamer under tension, which will allow for constant contact during the retrieve. If I was to cast upstream with sinking line and an unweighted streamer, the faster surface currents may push the streamer downstream of the sinking line, which will create immediate slack in the system. Remember, if the streamer is positioned downstream of the sinking line when casting upstream, slack will accumulate and strikes will not be registered.

After the cast you can use a short countdown to allow either the split shot or the sunken line to pull the streamer to the correct depth. Once the shot or line reaches the correct depth, make a slow and smooth strip of several inches, followed by a long pause. The pause may last up to twenty seconds before you make another strip. This combination will keep the fly moving in the water, but not so fast that the trout has little opportunity to locate it. The strip creates movement by pulling the streamer toward the stream bottom, while the pause creates slack that allows the streamer to float toward the surface. The longer the leader between fly and sunken line, the higher the fly will ride. I'll use the sinking line and buoyant streamer when fishing water more than 20 inches in depth. When fishing shallower water, I'll stick with the split shot placed on or near the head of a buoyant streamer.

When fishing shallow water, I don't want the pattern to dive up and down, as that would likely cause a streamer to snag bottom. Instead, I'm looking for the pattern to hover off the bottom. We achieve this by using a buoyant streamer with a lightly weighted head (e.g., conehead, bead, or dumbbell eye) or crimping a split shot up to the eye in combination with a floating line. Stripping a streamer while a sinking line sits on the stream bottom will pull the streamer toward the anchor point (the stream bottom) and likely cause the fly to snag. That's why we want a streamer with buoyant characteristics: It keeps the fly from fouling on the stream bottom and provides just enough weight to keep it floating on the surface.

The floating line will not pull the streamer toward the shallow bottom. Instead, the line will be positioned above the fly so the streamer will be retrieved in the direction of the line. The other difference between the two rigs (sinking line and buoyant streamer versus floating line and weighted streamer) is that the weighted streamer allows me to cast both upstream and downstream. Because the streamer contains weight that is positioned on or near the head, when used in combination with a floating line the surface tension of the floating line will aid in pulling the streamer downstream and therefore maintaining line control. Leader length with the dry-line approach ranges from 4 to 8 feet. The shorter the seam, the shorter my leader becomes—I want to place the line, leader, and fly all in the same current.

I do not cast across-stream because drag will likely occur and pull my streamer off the edge too quickly, instead of keeping it positioned along the edge. The dirtier the water conditions, the longer your fly needs to stay in the strike zone. When water clarity is limited to several inches, I exclusively employ the downstream tactic because it allows me to hold a streamer for as long as I want. When trout are hunting in clearer water during high-water events, the upstream approach allows me to cover more water with speed. I've had great days while fishing upstream when water visibility was around 10 inches. During high-water events, feeding trout will hold tight to the bank, which means your presentation must land right off the bank.

Target the edges of aquatic vegetation. Such vegetation is a magnet for insects, which in turn attract smaller fish. Locate smaller fish, and you'll likely find a predatory trout.

COLD WEATHER

Water temperatures are not always an accurate indicator of trout activity. I've heard countless times that trout will not chase streamers during extreme cold snaps. This is not true. Trout appear to react positively to constants and react negatively to sudden changes in temperature. Some of my best streamer fishing has occurred during the coldest winter months when water temps remained steady at 34 degrees for at least two or three days. It's purely a theory, but not only are aquatic insects less predominate in the winter, but I believe that in the winter, when a trout's metabolism slows down, it becomes willing to move a greater distance for a single large meal instead of having to constantly move up and down in the water column to inhale drifting insects. Talking with live minnow and spin fisherman, there's a consensus that wintertime is their preferred period for imitating baitfish.

An angler fishes the Madison River during the offseason. Some of my best streamer days have come during the winter, a time few anglers experience. CHRIS DANIEL

Night Fishing

Nighttime is the right time. The night game is a world few fly fishers ever experience, which is shame since it can provide the most excitement. Your sense of sound and touch are heightened because your visibility is limited. Every sound is louder in the still of the night. The sudden sound of a deer running in the woods during the daytime will create a slight reactive response; the same sound heard in the still of the night may cause an accident in your waders.

Many of the daytime streamer strategies are transferable to the night game. So many large trout are caught during the low-light periods of dawn and dusk because that's the time when larger trout feed. It's a short window, maybe an hour on either side of sunrise and sunset. However, those who are willing to fish through the nighttime drastically increase their chances of catching a leviathan. It's true that many large trout are taken during the daytime, but on many of the more pressured waters

Red lights are useful tools for night anglers. So often while bringing a fish to the net, a traditional white light would freak out a fish the moment it was turned on. A red light appears to spook fewer fish.

the larger fish will switch over to low-light feeding, even during the wintertime. Michigan's famed Au Sable offers the angler few daytime opportunities to catch large fish, so the large-fish hunters often fish into the nighttime to up their chances.

I don't fish at night solely to catch big fish, since large trout can be caught during the daylight. Instead, I spend thirty to forty nights each year on the stream in order to "relearn" the waters I fish during the daytime. The water conditions—water levels, visibility—may remain the same during the transition from light to dark, but the trout's feeding behaviors can drastically change. The same shallow water where you may never see a trout holding during the daylight may now hold the largest fish in the stretch. The head of a riffle, along a bank, or near a tailout are all potential hunting grounds for nighttime feeders. At nighttime, the river switches to big-boy rules, where the large trout move in and occupy the prime feeding spots. It's like fishing two completely different waters.

It's a misconception that big trout let down their guard during the night—that they move far from the comforts of their daylight resting areas to feed in the unprotected shallows. While this may be true for unpressured nighttime waters, it's not true on waters that receive regular angling pressure. A good example is Michigan's Pere Marquette River (the PM), where Tommy Lynch guides almost every night. The PM is similar to many of the northern Michigan streams in that its bottom is strewn with timber that offers unlimited cover. As Tommy

A cold front moves in and shuts down the Green Drake spinnerfall. Instead of going home, Amidea Daniel ties on a mouse pattern and hooks a respectable brown trout.

Mice work during the day, too. LANDON MAYER

Alex Lafkas holds a trophy brown trout. Alex is known for spending more time on the water. Steven Dally, owner of Dally's Fly Shop in Mountain Home, Arkansas, says, "Alex catches big fish because he spends more time than most." If you want to catch trophy trout, you need to put in the time. This is the reason Alex is a big-fish magnet.

rowed my wife and I down the river under the cloak of darkness during one trip, he was adamant about casting our mouse patterns no more than a few inches off the bank. His reasoning for making tighter casts to structure was the increased night pressure on the PM, which has forced the nighttime feeders to hold closer to wood. In fact, Tommy prefers that his anglers frequently get stuck on the bank—he believes you are not fishing aggressive enough if you aren't occasionally catching the bank. His advice was spot-on. My wife, who frequently got her mouse pattern stuck on the bank, moved three times the number of trout I did while trying to be conservative. This was an eye-opening experience for me, and has led me to fish structure more aggressively on pressured waters. This is why it's so important to know the water (or have a guide who does) when you're fishing at night.

The force of your presentation can also spook fish at night. Smacking your fly line and leader hard on the water in a 4-inch-deep flat is likely to spook every trout holding in that area, even in the dark, as compared to doing so in a head of a riffle where the current muffles the sound of your presentation. You need to know the water you fish before presenting flies at night, and you must adjust your presentation just as you would during the daytime. When fishing mouse patterns on shallow flats, it may be useful to aim high and let your mouse fall softly to the water. The opposite is true in broken water where you want to create a loud presentation so the trout can locate your pattern. You need to approach each condition separately at night, just as you would during the daytime.

NIGHTTIME FISHING GEAR

Red Lights

The first tool a night fisher needs is a red light. Red lights offer several advantages over traditional white lights. First, red light helps you preserve your night vision—after you use the red light to tie on a fly or untangle a rig, your eyes will quickly readjust back to the night. With white light, your eyes will take a longer time to adjust. Second, my experience has shown that red lights don't negatively affect trout at night as much as white lights do.

I do have one tip for restoring night vision after being exposed to white light. Several of my nighttime fishing spots are located near a road, and occasionally I'll be positioned in a location where a vehicle's high beams will be pointed directly at me. Most of the time I hear the car coming from a distance, and I will close my eyes as the car passes. From time to time, the car will sneak up on me, hit me with the high beams, and basically blind me for the next several minutes. If this does happen after being exposed to white light, shut your eyes tight for at least ten seconds, or until you see more black than white. Then open your eyes. Although there haven't been any scientific studies to support this technique, it helps me.

Flies

When I night-fish on waters that I know harbor larger fish, I have a tendency to use a single fly. Although you can often catch smaller trout at night, my target is the larger residents. During those occasions when I hook into a large trout, the last thing I want during the fight is to have the fish run me into a logjam and have the second fly catch the obstruction. This happened to me several times on my first time fishing the woody stream bottoms of northern Michigan. Even when you have 15-pound tippet, you still have to play a fish—you can't just rope it in. If you hook a large fish tight to a submerged log, it doesn't take long before that fish is moving toward the obstruction, even when fishing heavy tippet. Trout instinctually know where to go when being hooked, and having a second fly usually serves as a potential snag. Remember Murphy's Law?

On my home waters I'll fish two wet flies as a means to cover more water. While my home waters do produce fish 20 inches or larger, I find that these big fish are far less frequent than on other well-known waters. As a result, I'm not as concerned with having a fish run me "into the woods" and allow my second fly to get snagged. However, I will stick to a single

Make every effort to rig everything at home or near the car before hitting the water. This eliminates using artificial light along the stream. Such light may spook a trout and also requires your eyes to adjust back to darkness after it.

A black deer hair head–style streamer is a good choice for night fishing. The color contrasts against the night sky, creating a silhouette when viewed from the stream bottom. The deer hair head pushes water, creating commotion, providing a target for a hunting trout. Pictured here is Phil Croft's favorite night fly, the Skunk.

Right: Chad Johnson from Dally's Fly Shop hoists a trophy brown taken from the White River. If you want to catch a world-class brown trout, you need to travel to waters that harbor large fish. CHAD JOHNSON

fly when fishing mouse or large streamer patterns because those patterns create a disturbance. A large trout on the hunt will move for a larger meal, so I don't feel the need to fish multiple flies when throwing the big stuff.

Leaders

Night-fishing leaders are simple and often consist of a two-part leader formula (50/50 butt-to-tippet ratio). They follow the same rules as daytime streamer fishing. The only difference is I never use less than 12-pound test during the night. I often use fluorocarbon or Maxima Chameleon or Ultra Green for its abrasion-resistance, since I do have a tendency to get too aggressive when fishing tight to the bank and often find myself hanging on rocks and tree limbs. Since Maxima's material is easier on the pocketbook than many fluorocarbons, I frequently use it at night. Both Chameleon and Ultra Green are nylon; they have the best abrasion-resistance of all the nylons on the market that have I used. The other reason I like the Chameleon is when tying a dropper (using a blood knot) for a wet fly, the 90-degree dropper and the stiff nylon keeps the wet fly away from the main leader and reduces tangles.

Glow-in-the-Dark Fly Lines

Glow-in-the-dark lines are great tools for line control at night. No matter how well you think you know the water, in the dark of the night it's difficult to remember every current seam you fish. You may forget a strong current exists midstream, which may create enough tension on your rig to pull the flies out of the kill zone too fast. During the daytime, we would be able to see the large downstream bow in the line caused by such a strong current. During the nighttime, we often don't have the ability to see the line on the water. Trout are not always aggressive on streamer and mouse patterns, and having too much slack in your system may not allow you to register a take.

A glow line allows you to focus on the line to see if the rig is under tension. If the line is lying on the water in a series of S-curves, it's likely too much slack is occurring during the drift. At night you go more by feel to determine a strike, and having even the smallest amount of slack may not allow you to feel a trout inhale the fly. When I'm night-fishing, I want as much contact in the system as possible to detect strikes. That means I'm looking to keep the line on the water in either a straight line or a tensioned downstream loop. Of course, most seasoned anglers can feel if the line is under tension during the retrieve.

RIO's Lumalux Fly Line was used to catch this fish. Glow-in-the-dark lines like Lumalux allow you to read the currents based on how the line is shaped or positioned on the water.

If too much slack occurs in the line, you will feel little resistance during the retrieve.

Finally, the glow line allows me to judge distances better. By knowing where the end of my fly line is, along with the length of my leader, I can make more accurate casts. In the dark of the night with a traditional line, the only way I can find out if I'm close to the bank is when I overcast my target and get stuck on the bank. The glow line helps reduce such occurrences.

The line I use is RIO's AquaLux Gold taper. This line can be charged with a regular flashlight, and a fully charged line will stay lit for close to a half-hour before needing a second charge. To charge a line, I first strip out the length of line I plan on fishing and wrap it around my line hand. Then I take my headlamp or flashlight and shine the light on the line for up to thirty seconds. The brighter the bulb you use, the brighter the line glows. At times, I may use a small headlamp with fewer lumens, so the line doesn't glow too bright. If I want my line to look like a lightsaber, I will hold the line in front of my car's high beam light or use my 300-lumen torch.

Black Lights

Anglers in the know have been using black lights for years. A black light and a fluorescent monofilament leader allow you to vividly see the leader at night in order to dead-drift or jig a streamer. The fluorescent leader material is highly visible when hit by the black light, which provides you with enough vision to see a soft take at night. The black light tactic is not a searching tool, where you're trying to cover a lot of water. Instead, it's essentially a nymphing strategy where you're picking apart a specific area. There are those nights when trout feed closer to the stream bottom than near the surface, and this is when night anglers need to fish their streamer patterns slower and closer to stream bottom. You can dead-drift or jig your streamer, and the light gives you the ability to actually see the strike in complete darkness.

Black lights that can mount on a hat can be purchased just about anywhere; my current light is a $12 model from Wal-Mart. The leader I use is a modification of Dave Rothrock's Hi-Vis leader, constructed of 5 to 9 feet of 17-pound fluorescent blue Stren followed by 2 feet of 14-pound gold Stren. I then attach a level section of 12- to 14-pound fluorocarbon tippet to my streamer. Since I nymph my streamers up-close at night, the tippet length should always exceed the depth of the water I'm fishing, as this will allow my colored sighter to remain above the surface.

Wherever the black light is mounted on your body, it's important to keep the light focused on the line during the drift. The light needs to move in the same direction and at the same speed as the leader during the drift. While it's not nearly as much fun as swinging mouse patterns or large streamers, the black light technique has saved me from getting a giant goose egg on those slow nights.

NIGHT-FISHING PRESENTATIONS

At night, I like to cover water, especially when throwing large mouse or streamer patterns, and try to find the aggressive feeders. If fish activity is slow, then I slow down and vice versa. I think this is the reason why the Michigan crowd catches such a high volume of large trout at night: They cover more water by floating instead of wading. When wading, I may walk several miles each to hit the hot spots.

My mentor, Joe Humphreys, spent two years hunting a large trout that turned out to be a state-record fish. Joe heard the leviathan feeding one night in the head of riffle. At first he thought a deer had jumped into the water or a beaver had slapped its tail, but then he realized it was a fish. For almost two years, Joe hunted the waters where he heard the noise. Because large fish often consume large meals, Joe believed that a trophy trout might only feed once every few nights. He knew he had to put in time on the water before he could get his flies over the leviathan while it was on the feed. Two years later, the timing was right and Joe landed a trout of a lifetime; it is still the state-record trout caught on a fly in open water. I have yet to find a trout like Joe's, but I have located, stalked, and eventually caught trophy-class trout by concentrating my angling efforts into a smaller area.

Proper Depth for Flies

This is just a general rule, but I find the more moonlight there is hitting the water, the deeper you want to fish your flies. While fishing in the pitch-dark during a new moon, no ambient light penetrates to the stream bottom, which makes locating prey along the stream bottom more difficult. As a result, trout may look toward the sky, trying to locate prey silhouettes moving above. My best mouse nights have come during the dark of the moon or in heavily shaded areas that remain pitch-dark and where trout may be more oriented to look up for food because their horizontal view is limited. On dark nights I fish mice and unweighted wet flies or streamers high in the water column.

Surface patterns will work during a full moon, but my experience has taught me that finding the shaded spots offers

Matt Verlac from Gates Lodge in Grayling, Michigan, holds a brown trout taken on the South Branch of the Au Sable River. Matt spends countless nights each year stalking the Au Sable's night feeders.

Left: Trophy-size trout are notorious for feeding after dark. This is a side of fly fishing that few fly fishers ever witness. With rewards like this, it's surprising that more anglers don't give night fishing a shot. ALEX LAFKAS

When moonlight occurs, look for the shaded area of the stream that is protected from the moonlight. Find shade during moonlight, and you'll likely find a hunting trout. LANDON MAYER

better opportunities for fishing surface patterns. The opposite is true when the moon illuminates the stream bottom. These conditions allow the trout to locate food closer to bottom, and are looking horizontally, instead of vertically, for food. On bright moonlit nights, I fish the same-size wet flies or streamers as new-moon nights, but with added weight. When I recommend fishing deeper on moonlit nights, I'm not saying you have to bounce bottom, but you'll usually need a deeper retrieve. Use a top-down approach: Start high in the water column, and continue to fish deeper until you locate feeding fish.

ANGLE OF PRESENTATION

As with the daytime, I prefer to present my streamers up-and-across stream at night. I believe this angle provides better opportunities for a good hook set. I use this approach on small streams, where I know exactly where a fish is likely to feed at night. Josh Greenburg and Matt Verlac use the upstream approach to fish the Au Sable River at night. Over the years, these two guys have gotten a good handle on where trout feed at night, so they pick apart the water they know holds nighttime feeders. Instead of swinging their night patterns through the water, they keep the fly in the kill zone longer by casting directly upstream and leading the patterns downstream through the zone. By casting upstream and leading their pattern downstream slightly faster than the speed of the water, they create enough tension to feel the strike. A glow line can be helpful with this approach, but if done correctly, you can feel the fly being dragged along the surface and won't need to see it.

With this tactic, it's wise to listen to the water speed; faster-moving water creates a louder sound than slow-moving water. The louder the sound, the faster you should move the rod tip downstream and vice versa. If you're not feeling tension on the line, then you should move the rod tip faster downstream. The best tip I have for dead-fishing upstream during the night is to immediately move the rod tip downstream after presenting the fly. This immediate movement puts you in contact with your streamer from the very beginning of the presentation. On larger bodies of water or when I have no clear idea where the nighttime feeding areas are, I find myself fishing down-and-across, so I can swing my pattern through a wide arc to cover water.

Where Fish Feed at Night

Every river system has its own mannerisms, so the water types you target will depend on where you fish, even if the river systems are within an hour's drive of one another. While working on this project, I spent a good bit of time in northern Michigan fishing many of its famed waters. Two of my favorites are the

Brian Wilt with a White River brown trout. This trout took a small streamer on the swing when air temps were below freezing during a January night. This demonstrates that big fish feed year-round and will chase food during the coldest nights of the year.

Pere Marquette and Manistee Rivers. What's interesting to me is how opposite the fish behavior is on these two rivers during the night. When talking with guys like Tommy Lynch, Russ Madden, Josh Greenburg, and others, there's a consensus that many (though not all) larger trout hold on the inside bends on the Manistee; this is compared to the Pere Marquette, where trout more often position on the outside bend. There are a number of theories to explain this, but the point is that two rivers within roughly an hour's drive of each other can fish completely different during the night. This is why I hire a guide when fishing unfamiliar waters, and why I spend a good bit of time during the daylight scouting out water for the night session. After each night session, I often take ten or fifteen minutes to spotlight the water and see where fish may be holding.

I spend a lot of time spotlighting water with my 300-lumen flashlight to get a feel for where trout hold, especially on new waters. This gives me confidence in knowing that I'm covering likely holding areas. I learned long ago that you need confidence in your patterns, presentation, and the water you fish. I've felt this lack of confidence numerous times when arriving too late to the water to scout likely holding areas. Anglers new to the nighttime game often lose confidence and give up too soon because they cannot see the water, so it's important to first have confidence in knowing where trout are. This will keep you fishing during the slowest nights instead of heading home.

A welcome sight to any hardcore night fisherman. Some operations, including Gates Lodge on Michigan's Au Sable River, have guides that specialize in night trips. If you want to learn more about the night game, spend some time with a Michigan guide.

MOUSING

Mousing is by far the most exciting aspect of the night game. You're swinging a mouse in darkness, able to see the fly wake the water from a distance. Suddenly, you see the water erupt around the mouse, followed by a loud vacuuming sound—and then you feel the throb of a large fish on the line.

Mice feed mostly at night, are active almost year-round, and can live in just about any habitat. Hence, there are opportunities to mouse any stream bank anytime of the year. I've only seen a handful of mice swim across the river, but they move fast and don't stop. A mouse's natural environment is terrestrial, not aquatic, and its instinct is to move across the water fast to get back to dry land. While every guide has his or her particular approach to mousing, they are all keen on making sure the fly continues moving through the water.

My favorite night conditions for floating streamers or mice are dark nights when the stream bottom is not lit by any form of light. The darker the night, the better luck I have with surface flies. I say dark nights, not moonless nights, because mousing can be great during a full moon, as long as you can find shaded areas in which to swim your mouse. There's a few spots on my home waters where thick hemlock trees block out the brightest moonlight. While mousing with Tommy Lynch during a half-moon on the Pere Marquette, he was adamant about casting our mouse patterns into the shade and retrieving them until they reached the moonlit area. Once the mouse came out of the shadows into the bright moonlight, Tommy would immediately have us pick up our lines and cast back into the darkness.

Mousing is similar to dry-fly fishing in that trout need to be surface-oriented to feed, or your efforts may be futile. As much as I love to see an eruption around my waking mouse, I usually go with wet flies or a sunken streamer when trout are not surface-oriented. If trout are hugging the stream bottom at night, the mouse game may not produce a single strike.

Mouse Patterns

With the popularity of mousing increasing, many good mouse patterns are now available to the fly fisher. An effective mouse pattern needs to push enough water that it creates a wake on the surface. The keys to a good mouse pattern are that it creates a small disturbance when landing on the water, it creates a wake during the retrieve, and it's easy to cast. Some of the best mouse patterns may not look realistic at first, but they move through the water like the natural. Because trout often look up at night, the keys to any good night pattern are shape and movement.

My favorite mouse pattern of all time is Russ Madden's Softex Mouse, which he introduced to me in 2002. Extra-large pearl E-Z Body Braid is tied onto the hook shank to create the short and round profile of a mouse's body. Once the material is manipulated and tied on the hook shank to simulate a mouse's

Proof that mousing works year-round: Here Alex Lafkas and Tommy Lynch show off a monster brown trout that ate Tommy's White Belly Mouse pattern during a cold snap in February on Arkansas's White River.

Below: A hand-and-twist retrieve allows you to continuously move a mouse pattern across the stream. Mice are not aquatic creatures, and once they fall in the water, they will swim toward the other side without pause or hesitation. LANDON MAYER

Left: Night fishing from a moving boat requires a skilled and knowledgeable guide.

Amidea Daniel floats the South Branch of the Au Sable River in Michigan just before the night bite begins.

body, apply Softex over the body to seal it and create a large air chamber, like a balloon. Once covered and while still wet, dubbing is applied (not dubbed) onto the Softex by laying small clumps over the entire body. After you've applied all the dubbing, pull a wide foam strip over the body, and tie it in front of the hook eye, with a foam lip protruding past the eye to create a Gurgler effect. Tied with a long tail and two collars of hackled schlappen (rear and front), this pattern is easy to cast and moves smoothly through the water. Another advantage of this pattern's open air chamber is that you can insert a glass rattle inside the E-Z Body material before tying down, which will add a third dimension to the retrieve—sound. Some of my other favorite mouse patterns include Tommy Lynch's White Belly Mouse and variations of Gurglers.

While many anglers (including myself) tend to mouse by keeping the rod tip close to water's edge and either stripping or using a hand-twist retrieve, Tommy Lynch has a different approach for fishing a mouse. Using a RIO Glow Line for visibility, he fishes down-and-across but keeps the rod tip pointed upward at a 45-degree angle (similar to wet-fly tactics) after making a cast close to the bank. The bank shot is important since we are imitating a land-dwelling mammal, not an aquatic animal, and trout are looking for this prey immediately off the bank. Once he's made down-and-across to the bank, and after the rod tip is kept up at a 45-degree angle, the rod tip begins to drift downstream, as the current moves the mouse downstream. The line hanging off the rod tip creates a sag; the angler watching the glow line can see when the sag begins to tighten up to indicate a strike instead of feeling the strike. The sag creates enough slack in the system to allow a trout to inhale the fly without forcefully pulling it out of its mouth.

During the swing, Tommy will occasionally lift the rod tip up toward the sky and then drop it back to its original position. This movement shows a give-and-take profile of the mouse to the trout. This approach is similar to a cat chasing a string—the idea is to keep the trout interested in the pattern. As the trout is following the mouse on the swing, this give-and-take movement maintains the trout's attention and may trigger a reaction from the trout. Most of the strikes are seen by watching the sag of the line tighten or by hearing the trout erupt under the mouse, rather than feeling the strike. Once the line sag tightens or you hear the eruption, lift the rod as you would when indicator fishing or dry-fly fishing (aka a trout set). This approach has produced excellent results for Tommy and his clients for years. While I still prefer to keep the rod tip closer to water's surface while mouse fishing, I have witnessed this approach get great results.

WINTERTIME NIGHT FISHING

Big fish do feed at night during the coldest months. This is a fact, at least on the limestone streams near my home and on several Southern tailwater fisheries. The winter of 2013–14 was one of the coldest in central Pennsylvania. I would frequently go out at night and take a short hike with a powerful flashlight to spotlight fish. Even during the coldest nights, I spotted larger fish holding in shallow feeding lies. Although nighttime activity may be greatly reduced during the cold months, large trout will still feed at night.

When anglers think about winter nighttime fishing, they think slow and deep because a trout's feeding may slow during the coldest winter months. However, there are exceptions. Tommy Lynch has proven several times that large trout will chase mouse patterns on the surface during the coldest nights. Tommy has taken trout he refers to as "donkeys" on Arkansas's White River during cold snaps in February and March while fishing his favorite White Belly Mouse pattern.

This lesson took hold while I was fishing the White River in January 2013 with Lance Wilt and Brian Wilt. All generators were shut down during our entire six-day stay, leaving us with low flows and spooky fish. As soon as our lines and flies landed on the glassy water, trout shot in the opposite direction. Then we decided to sleep during midday and fish throughout the night in pursuit of larger fish.

The weather station was calling for a low of 20 degrees that first night. Given the cold temperature and the likelihood that trout were going to be sluggish, I decided to fish a large, heavily weighted streamer on a running line so I could feel the streamer bounce over every rock. Brian decided to stay with a standard weight-forward line rigged with two medium-size but lightly weighted streamer patterns. I fished first, bouncing bottom, and picked up three browns in the mid-teens—not bad for such a cold night. Once I worked 20 yards downstream, Brian dropped in and began swinging his streamer patterns high in the water column. He immediately began taking fish, including two fish over 20 inches, in the very same water where I was trying to bounce bottom.

This scenario played out all night long. I was certain that fishing large, heavyweight streamers near the stream bottom was the best way to take a large fish during the cold snap—and

It doesn't take long after the sun sets before trophy trout begin moving into their nighttime feeding lies.

During winter cold snaps, fishing at night requires the same adjustments as you'd make during the daylight. Josh Miller took this trout while nymphing his streamer at night after several weight adjustments.

I was wrong. This experience taught me that trout will chase food even during the coldest nights.

The only way we find out these things is by changing our approach when certain tactics fail to land fish and continuing to experiment until we figure it out. This is also why I prefer to spend time fishing with other anglers—I can compare notes, especially with those anglers who tend to catch more fish than I do. I like surrounding myself with anglers whose skills far surpass mine. Brian Wilt and Tommy Lynch spend more time night-fishing than anyone I know and have taught me many night lessons. Guys like them keep me humble and help me maintain a beginners' mind-set that is always open to new ideas.

While night-fishing during the winter can be just as fruitful as fishing during the summer, comfortable conditions are limited to a handful of nights when the air temperatures are 32 degrees or above. Most night fishing relies on keeping the rig under tension and feeling the strike, and when air temperatures reach 32 or lower, ice freezes in the guides and makes retrieving line difficult. I got a cool tip from Russ Madden while fishing Michigan's Manistee River during a snowstorm in 2003. I was fishing a 6-weight rod-and-line outfit in subfreezing conditions. Every thirty seconds, my guides would freeze up, forcing me to knock the ice out before continuing to fish. After thirty minutes of this, Russ told me to take the 6-weight line off my 6-weight rod and handed me his spare 9-weight rod to string up. Although it was more difficult to load the 9-weight rod with the 6-weight line, the 9-weight had significantly larger guides than my 6-weight. The oversized guides allowed me to cast several minutes before completely freezing over. The extra three or four minutes of fishing made all the difference and allowed me to spend more time with my fly in the water. If I were a rod builder, I would make a winter streamer rod with oversize guides to allow for longer fishing periods before having to break ice out of the guides.

Presentation

7

To be successful on the stream, all the pieces of the puzzle need to connect. Casting, presentation, line control, and retrieving all need to be in sync to have success with the streamer. Casting style, line-control management, and overall approach are personal choices. Not all anglers are physically built the same, fish the same water types, or fish the same techniques. You will need to use a wide range of styles, retrieves, and angles, even when fishing the same waters. If you are motivated to work toward small gains in your streamer game and have more fun while on the stream, it pays to study other successful anglers and continually try to improve technique. I don't have all the answers—far from it—but I attempt to maintain a beginner's mind-set every time I spend time with fellow anglers on the stream. This is what keeps me excited every moment I'm on the water. Keep an open mind when you begin playing around with some of these concepts, as you may find a better approach. If so, I would love to hear about it!

Streamer fishing requires casting accuracy, line control, and the correct retrieve. All three need to be working at the same time for fishing success.

CASTING

Anglers sometimes say, "It's too much work to fish streamers." I think that's a huge misconception. Granted, streamer fishing does require a little more energy on the angler's behalf than say, casting a dry fly. On most occasions we are using larger flies and heavier rods to present to the trout, but it doesn't mean you have to toss an 8-inch wind-resistant streamer on a 9-weight rod spooled with a 400-grain sinking line. I fish many of my 2- to 5-inch streamers with either a 4-weight or a 5-weight rod, and I've seen competitive anglers during the World Fly-Fishing Championships nymphing with a 10-foot, 3-weight, and then suddenly switch to fishing a 3-inch streamer. You don't always have to fish gigantic, heavy flies. Remember, many of the recent world-record brown trout were caught on light spin tackle.

With that said, when casting heavier rods, sinking lines, and weighted flies, you must adapt your casting style based on both the conditions and the equipment. I change my casting style from direct overhead (using nothing but the forearm/wrist) when nymphing or dry-fly fishing up-close to casting more to the side and rocking my body back and forth when throwing streamers (at least while wading; rocking in a boat can spook fish). This reduces fatigue because I am using my largest muscles. The key is to work smarter, not harder, with your body. The first step to working smarter is developing a casting approach that incorporates the largest muscle group—the legs.

Chad Johnson prefers easy-casting flies like the Double Deceiver when fishing large rivers like the White. This allows Chad to position the boat midstream and cast to both sides of the river. This unweighted Deceiver is thin in diameter and the bucktail body sheds water. This type of profile, coupled with a streamer line, makes casting distances easy.

Make sure not to drop your shoulders during the cast. Anglers commonly make the mistake of trying to use their legs to rock back and forth in the cast to create additional power. Rocking your shoulder back and forth adds power, but dropping your shoulders forces the rod tip to accelerate downward to the water and collapses the cast. You can drop your shoulder and lower the rod tip to prepare to retrieve line, but only after you have accelerated and stopped the rod tip at a higher plane.

When fishing low water, aim higher on the forward cast to allow your streamer to land softer on the water.

Obviously, your upper body is used to cast the streamer, but we need to use the legs to create the majority of the energy needed to present the fly.

While we still need the upper body in order to cast, using the legs to create energy for the cast will take a lot of wear off the body. And why not use the largest muscle group for casting? By simply rocking the body back and forth, you can create enough power to cast the heaviest rigs with ease, instead of trying to use only the upper body. This was a great lesson I learned from Rick Hartman, who is one of the best long-distance casters I've ever seen. Although Rick has a large upper body, so much of his power comes from rocking his body back and forth to create additional power.

When rocking the body, it's important that the motion is a smooth transition from the front foot to the back foot. It's not an erratic motion in which you're jerking your body back and forth to load the rod. Doing that is similar to using a jerky-wrist casting movement—both movements will quickly unload the rod. The key is to focus all the weight on your front foot while smoothly sliding the body backward, where you transfer all the energy of the cast to your back foot. The legs and upper body work in unison with the upper body. While the front foot is rocking backward, the rod hand is accelerating during the backcast movement. When the front foot has completed the backward-sliding movement, both the lower body and upper body come to a sudden stop, which unloads the line behind you. The process begins again as you rock toward the target to present the fly.

It's important to note that the body doesn't rock downward. Instead, you want to move the energy of your body outward toward the target instead of downward. The biggest hurdle I had to overcome while working on this movement was transferring the energy outward instead of down. This is why some people prefer to use the term "sliding" instead of "rocking." Regardless of your preferred terminology, this additional muscle movement will add power to your cast. This applies not only to streamer casts but to casting in general. If you drop your shoulder during the cast, this transfers the energy of the cast toward the water instead of out toward the target. You may be looking down to the water because the natural tendency is to aim downward during rod acceleration.

Again, this is a motion I use while wade-fishing and casting heavier rods at longer distances. For most streamer fishing, where I may be casting up to 40 feet away, all that is needed is a short rocking movement. However, if I'm trying to bomb out a big cast, a large rocking movement is necessary. It's a matter of simple casting fundamentals: A larger body movement is needed for long cast, and a smaller movement is needed for shorter cast.

If you make a bad cast, fish it out until the end. Do not pick up and recast. I've caught some of my best fish with my worst casts. Phil Croft holds a nice steelhead I took while executing the worst cast of the day. I overshot the target and the fly stuck in an overhanging tree. I eventually freed the fly, which came off the tree and landed 5 feet short of the target, but Phil told me to "fish it out." Then one of only three fish we caught all day committed to this poorly presented fly.

When working streamers near undercut banks, don't be afraid to slap the fly hard on the water. Such a disturbance will gain a trout's attention and pull it from the protection of the undercut bank. LANCE WILT

LOOP CONTROL

1. A wide loop occurs when the rod tip travels through a wide arc during the acceleration. Sometimes a wide loop is useful when casting heavily weighted streamers, as the wide loop keeps the fly higher above the rod tip and away from you.

2. A tighter loop occurs when the rod tip travels in a relatively straight line.

Sidearm Flip

There are no rules when it comes to fly fishing or casting. While I often use my leg muscles and upper body to cast streamers, there are casts that are better executed by using the wrist. For casting sinking lines, the sidearm flip is a useful tip I picked up from Tommy Lynch. Tommy showed me this tactic when he noticed the difficulty I was having when casting under the overhanging canopy along the Pere Marquette. Using the traditional overhead cast had my flies approaching the target in a downward manner, which is a tough angle if you want to cast the streamer underneath a target. After I hung up in the trees several times, Tommy showed me the sidearm flip in order to move my flies in a different plane. Instead of coming straight down, he had me casting off the side and using the wrist to make the cast.

The casting motion is similar to skipping stones. The elbow slides close to your body while the palm of your hand rides up and the wrist kicks upward at the end of the casting stroke. This propels your streamer line and pattern higher in the sky. Remember that many sinking lines are thinner in diameter and appear to drop faster in the air as they move toward their target. As a result, I prefer to cast in a higher trajectory to compensate for gravity's effect. While the wrist will create a shorter casting stroke, the acceleration needs to be smooth. Think about using the wrist to pull the rod tip through the air instead of trying to push it. Our bodies are designed to pull, not push.

The other major advantage of this sidearm flip is that you can shoot line under an obstacle instead of just casting under it. If I want to cast 15 feet and land my flip under an obstacle, the flip cast allows me to do this with a gentle presentation. Because the wrist kicks upward during the forward acceleration, the trajectory of both line and fly projects up and out, not downward. Again, this movement is akin to skipping stones.

Lance Wilt shows off a South Holston River brown trout. When drifting alongside a patch of overhanging trees, Lance switched to a skinny synthetic streamer pattern capable of being skipped across the surface. He was able to cast this pattern deep under the overhang and move this trout out of tight quarters.

Left: Small-stream streamer tactics can have good results. Guy Murray releases a beautiful brook trout that held underneath a overhanging hemlock tree. An underhand flip cast allowed Guy to present the fly deep under the tree and with a soft landing.

The way one gets distance when skipping stones is to keep the rock hand low to the water during the acceleration and kicking the wrist slightly upward at the very end. This upward trajectory will keep the rock skipping toward the opposite bank instead of dropping. The upward trajectory also allows the line and fly to fall easier on the water.

This brings up another idea for skipping your flies into a tight spot. There are times when the casting room is so tight that you may have only a few inches of overhead space to cast under. Such tight casting quarters only allow for you to literally skip their streamer under an obstacle. The casting principles are the same as for the sidearm flip; the only thing that changes is the height off the water the rod tip travels during the acceleration. Remember, the fly line will unload at the level the rod tip stops at the end of the acceleration. That means if you want to cast under an obstacle that is 8 inches off the water, you

This shot depicts why casting off your backhand is so important. I'm a right-handed caster and positioned tight to the bank on river right. I don't have the clearance to cast on my right side, so I need to cast the heavy rig off my opposite shoulder and present the fly with a backhand cast.

should keep the rod tip tracking 4 inches off the water before coming to a stop.

You should also think about the streamer design you use for skipping under obstacles. This again goes back to skipping stones—one simply doesn't attempt to skip any random rock. Instead, you look for a thin, round rock with smooth edges. This allows the rock to skip over the water with less resistance than a square-shaped rock. If you're in an area where skipping a streamer in the underbrush is going to be common theme, then you need to find a streamer design that allows the fly to be skipped over the water.

The first item I look at is the material used. I prefer to tie skipping streamers mostly with synthetic materials since they don't absorb water like natural materials (such as wool). Synthetic streamer brushes and Craft Fur are two good choices. One natural material that works is bucktail. The point is we want materials that repel water, not absorb it. The actual shape and diameter of the streamer is also crucial. What I'm looking for in a skipping streamer is a pattern with a conehead-style head (not a dumbbell). Conehead Clousers, Deceivers, and even Sparkle Minnows will skip over the water's surface with less resistance. The weighted front section gives the fly momentum as it's skipping over the water surface, similar to a bullet. Our job as anglers is to provide the correct direction and the right amount of momentum to the pattern. If we do this, a properly designed skipping streamer will do the rest.

When skipping streamers, we need to create enough energy so that the pattern doesn't stick to the water during initial impact. We need to keep the pattern moving after first contact with water. The haul plays a huge role in creating the additional energy needed to keep the fly moving after initial impact. I've found that a short but smooth acceleration provides additional momentum to the pattern. Note that unless you're fishing a streamer in the shape of a thin, rounded rock, it's not to going to skip multiple times on the water. I'm looking to skip the pattern only once or twice on the water before hitting the target.

BACKHAND CASTING

1. When casting backhand, position yourself as you would if you were making a traditional cast off your opposite shoulder, except the palm of your rod hand should face away from the target and your knuckles should face toward the target. As you wait for the rod to load on the backcast, your elbow slides out in front of your body (not away to the side). Note the approximately 90-degree bend between elbow and forearm.

2. After the line unrolls behind you, begin to accelerate toward the target by sliding your elbow away from your body but keeping the 90-degree angle between forearm and elbow. Maintain a stiff arm position as you drift forward—not wrist—during this stage of the movement.

3. When your elbow can no longer drift any further, snap your wrist toward the target to deliver the streamer. The snap will also unload the rod tip, so it's important to drift as far as you can before snapping your wrist. The longer the elbow slides, the more power you create for the cast.

INSIDE ELBOW POSITION

1. It doesn't matter if you're casting a dry-fly or a heavy streamer rig—you want to efficiently transfer all the power created by your body into the cast. Keeping your elbow close to your body will allow you to generate more power in the cast. Think about a boxer and how you rarely see an elbow positioned away from the body during a punch. Why? Because you lose power when the elbow is bent away from the body. So the first step to ensuring power during the presentation is to position the elbow close to the body. It doesn't remain locked into a single position, but can slide back and forth.

2. As you begin to accelerate, your forearm and wrist should remain in a locked position. This position will allow you to keep the heavy streamer rig tracking straight and smooth during the acceleration.

3. Continue to accelerate to a quick but smooth stop. The rod tip should point upward to allow the line to shoot out—not down. Notice how the butt section is tucked under my forearm. This position locks the rod into a fixed position, so it doesn't sway during the acceleration. Also, it helps me accelerate to a smooth stop, allowing the line to fully unload.

4. Only after the rod tip has come to a stop and the line begins to shoot, do I lower the rod tip to the water to start the retrieve. Shooting through the O-ring allows me to never let go of the line, which means I'm in control from start to finish.

ROLL CASTING A WEIGHTED STREAMER

1. The first step for roll casting a weighted streamer and/or a weighted line is to start with the rod tip lowered to the water, with the rod hand extended out. Make sure the line is under tension before making the next movement.

2. Before beginning the sliding movement, pick as much line as possible off the water by pointing the rod tip upward. This movement involves breaking the wrist upward to create a higher angle. Once the rod tip is in the correct location, keep your wrist and forearm locked in that position before making the sliding movement. Less line on the water will make it easier for you to slide the streamer toward its anchor point.

3. Use your forearm to begin sliding the line toward you. The idea is to keep the streamer sliding on the water's surface. If you break your wrist, the fly will likely break tension with the water and go airborne.

4. As the fly slides closer to your position, make sure the rod tip is angled away from you. In this case, I begin angling the rod toward the opposite stream bank. This will allow me to set up the D-loop away from my body and decrease the chance of it coming into contact with my body as I proceed to make the forward casting movement.

5. Continue to slide the fly with the rod tip off to the side. The rod tip needs to continue sliding until the fly is several feet in front of you. At this point, the accelerated sliding movement comes to a sudden stop. The entire slide should accelerate and then come to a smooth stop—just as with overhead casting.

6. Pause briefly (less than a second) to allow the D-loop to form off the rod tip. During the pause, angle the rod tip upward and away from your body. The idea is to keep the fly or fly line as close to the surface as possible. The longer the pause, the deeper the weighted streamer or line will sink and the more energy you'll need during the acceleration to break the surface tension. If the fly or line drops too deep in the surface, you may not have enough power to break the surface tension. With your hand positioned in front of your face at eye level, you are ready to begin the forward casting stroke.

7. Accelerate the rod tip. With a shorter cast, the rod tip should accelerate to a stop, where the rod is parallel to the current. When roll casting longer lengths of line, the rod tip needs to be angled upward to allow line to unroll toward the target.

8. After accelerating to a smooth stop, the loop will unroll and carry your streamer to the target.

9. The rod tip lowers toward the surface, just as the fly lands on the water. This gives you control and contact with your streamer the moment the fly lands. You want the line to be tight in a straight path as soon as it lands—no slack.

CASTING STREAMERS UNDER OBSTACLES

1. When casting under brush, you need to think about the level at which the rod tip travels during the casting stroke. The lower the path the tip travels, the lower you can cast under brush. This means you also need to think about lowering your body position to allow for the lowest possible rod tip path. It doesn't mean you have to crawl on your hands and knees. Often, all you need to do is bend your knees to create a lower profile for the rod tip to travel during the casting stroke. In this photo, I'm standing in a normal position before beginning the backcast.

2. As I begin the backcast, my knees bend and my shoulders drop to create a lower profile. The key is to make a slower backcast, which gives me time to set myself in a lower casting position. If you're a speedy caster, you'll likely not have enough time to set up.

3. I continue to bend my knees, and just before the cast begins to unroll, I drop my casting shoulder to the lowest point and hold that position until I'm ready to begin the forward casting stroke. Note how low I'm holding the rod tip on the backcast—this will allow me to accelerate through a straight-line path with ease on the forward casting stroke. If the rod tip is pointed up, the only path the rod can take (i.e., in a straight line) is downward. I keep my shoulders squared to the target. Once I begin to make the forward casting stroke, nothing but my hand will travel toward the target, meaning I don't twist my body or drop my shoulders.

4. When ready to begin the forward casting stroke, I lower my elbow to the water but keep it close to my body to apply power. The closer your elbow remains to your body during the acceleration, the more power you can create. This short cast only needs a short drift of the forearm before coming to a stop. The forearm simply accelerates forward before coming to a stop. Note how the rod tip accelerates upward, which forces the loop to carry your streamer pattern up and out rather than downward. The key to getting distance when casting under brush is to form a loop that opens upward rather than downward toward the water. If you aim down, the cast will likely collapse on you.

5. Once the fly lands on the water, the rod tip is already in position to begin the retrieve. Even though I'm casting off to my side, the rod tip still travels in a straight plane, which allows the line to land in a straight line.

STIFF ARM UNDER BRUSH

1. When you don't have the room to make a backcast in tight brush, using the water's surface to create tension in combination with a stiff arm cast is another option to consider. The first step is to let the current pull your fly and line downstream. You should feel the tension of the current wanting to pull your rig downstream. Second, position your streamer so you could draw a straight line from it to your target. This is important when casting heavily weighted patterns, as it will allow you to move the rod tip in a straight line to the target, allowing for an accurate presentation.

2. Once your flies are properly anchored, turn your attention to the target and keep your focus. For me, this is one of the keys to casting in tight quarters: Never take your eyes off the target once your backcast is complete. Once your attention is focused on the forecast, begin to slide the rod tip forward. This is a slow acceleration meant to bring your sinking line or streamer pattern closer to the surface before accelerating fast to the target. Maintaining a stiff forearm is key during this slide. This steady forearm movement creates tension as you pull the fly across the surface.

3. Continue to slide your forearm toward the target. Notice the amount of rod load. You want to deeply load the rod and slingshot the streamer deep under the brush. You don't want to cast several feet under the brush—you want to go under the brush and tight to the bank.

4. Your elbow can slide but should remain close to the body. This shot shows the forearm continues to slide toward the target while the rod continues to load deeper.

5. At the end of the sliding movement, your wrist pushes toward the target, with your thumb and knuckles pointed directly at the target. The rod tip must drift in a straight line below the level of the obstacle you want to cast under. For example, if you want to cast under a 3-foot limb, you need to track the rod tip in a straight line 2 feet above the water surface.

6. If the rod was properly loaded during the sliding movement, the weighted streamer should sling shot toward your target. Also, the rod tip must travel in a straight line path during the sliding movement. This will create a narrow loop. If your wrist breaks and the rod tip travels in a wide arc, the loop will open up, and the fly will travel into the obstacle instead of under it.

Reducing Kickback

Kickback occurs when you put too much power into a cast, causing the weighted fly or sinking line to kick back on itself. In dry-fly fishing, this is referred to as a shock cast or a slack-leader cast; the kickback in this cast imparts a series of S-curves into the line and leader. While you need slack in dry-fly fishing to create a natural drift, it becomes a detriment in streamer fishing because you lose contact with the fly and will not be able to sense a strike. This is unfortunate, since a feeding trout will strike a streamer when it first comes in contact with the water. Trout react fast; this is why you need immediate line control, especially when casting to shallow banks. I believe kickback is the number-one reason why so many streamer anglers never make contact when fishing right off the bank. We have a tendency to overpower the cast for the length of line we're using. When the streamer hits the bank with slack in the line, a trout can attack without the angler even knowing. You want to have contact with the rig the second it lands on the water. When fish are feeding on the flats or along banks, many takes will occur the moment the fly lands.

One tactic to reduce kickback is to moderate the power in the cast based on the length of line you use. You need less energy to make a short cast, but you'll need considerable power to make a long cast. I know this sounds like common sense, but time and again I see anglers create too much slack off the rod tip during the presentation. They overpower the cast and create slack in the line, and it takes several seconds to strip in all that slack before you are back in contact with the streamer.

EXAMPLES OF KICKBACK AND TUCKING THE CAST

1. Kickback occurs if you overpower the cast and force the streamer or line to kick back onto self. This is also known as an overpowered curve cast. While there is a place for this presentation in streamer tactics, most often it's an unwanted result, as it places excessive slack on the water. This kickback can occur from any position (such as casting to the side or overhead). Notice how the fly line tip is curving inward.

2. The result of an overpowered cast is curved line or slack on the water. It doesn't take much slack to put you out of touch with your streamer. If you're experiencing kickback, there's a good chance you're applying too much power for the length of line you're using. Decrease the power so the line doesn't kick back onto itself. You need less power for a shorter presentation, and vice versa for a longer presentation.

3. This is another example of an overpowered cast coming from the overhead position (also known as a tuck cast). This is the result of using too much power or stopping the rod tip at too high of an angle. The ideal presentation is to stop the rod tip high to allow line to shoot, but begin to drop the rod tip toward the water as the fly reaches its target. You want the rod tip to point toward water's surface and be ready to retrieve the moment the fly lands on the water.

Placing the Rod Tip Near the Surface

Another possible cause of kickback is forgetting to follow through with your presentation after coming to a stop. This is similar to bowing to a jumping trout in the sense that you want to reduce tension on the line so that it doesn't kick back. When an angler accelerates and stops the rod tip higher in the air, the line unloads and begins heading to the target. If you keep the rod tip high and don't lower the rod to the water for the presentation phase, kickback is likely to occur.

Lowering the rod tip accomplishes two things. First, it decreases the likelihood of the line kicking back and creating slack on the water. Second, lowering the rod tip close to the water allows for more sensitivity and a better connection to your streamer. My ideal scenario is having the rod tip at the water's edge before the fly hits the water, as this allows me to begin the retrieve the exact moment the fly lands. You'll be surprised how many fish you hook on the first strip. The goal is to reduce slack during the retrieve, and a low rod tip creates less slack between rod tip and fly line. A rod tip held several feet off the water would likely create significant sag in the line during the retrieve. One exception for keeping the rod tip higher off the water is if you desire to keep the fly riding higher toward the surface without having to change either the weight in the fly or the sink rate of the fly line. A higher rod tip will create additional slack in the line, but it will keep your streamer riding higher in the water column.

Curves

While curve casts are more important in dry-fly and nymph fishing, they do have their place in the streamer game. Ideally, I try to maintain a straight line during the retrieve for better contact and control. However, throwing a curve into a streamer presentation can initiate a strike. When attempting a curve cast, my preference is for a floating line, but you can also use sinking lines. I use a floater because the curved line remains at the surface where the currents keep tension on the line and help maintain line and leader control. It also helps maintain the shape of the curve. The streamer will follow the path of the line on the water; if the belly of the line is angled downstream, the streamer will follow.

Conversely, a sinking line will begin dropping toward the stream bottom where the currents are slower, which results in the curve not holding true to shape as long. The point is that any type of line can throw a curve, but what I like about curve cast is the unique path the streamer follows during the retrieve. And for that, I feel a floating line will maintain a longer curve shape and allow for a longer retrieve. A curve cast can be used to create a nonlinear movement of the fly in a large pool with no obstacles to work around. The movement of a baitfish is unpredictable. A curve forces the streamer to move in a nonlinear path, which provides a different-looking retrieve.

Curve casts are useful for working around obstructions, including boulders. At times, we have to cast and retrieve our flies around an object. Picture an angler fishing upstream while walking the left-side edge of a drop-off. He approaches a large boulder. The canopy along the left bank is too tall for the angler to make a cast from the side, and he can't wade around the

An angler searching for a target on Montana's Quake Lake. During the daylight, trout will hold deep and tight to the wooden structure. In this case, a full-sinking line along with a countdown is a must. The brighter the sun and the calmer the surface, the deeper your presentation needs to be.
CHRIS DANIEL

boulder because the water is too deep. The boulder is too large round to cast over with a reach cast, so one possibility is to curve-cast around the boulder.

When fishing streamers, I find an overpowered curve cast is easiest to make, as you can use either the weight of the fly or fly line to kick off to either side. Instead of casting the rig directly over your shoulders, you want the fly to travel off the side of the side—sidearm casting, if you will. A positive curve cast is a form of an overpowered cast. However, there's a difference between a curved line lying on the water and the undesired S-curves caused by slack in the line. A controlled "overpowered" movement can result in a tension-curved line lying on the water; it is not slack. The key is to overpower the line and/or weighted fly just enough to curve the path of the fly in a different direction without actually kicking back to the degree of creating slack.

Trout holding in flats are usually on the feed and will likely strike the moment your fly lands, so it's important to shoot through an O-ring. Doing so will allow you to make a hook set at any stage of the presentation, from the moment the fly lands to the end of the retrieve.

MENDS

Mending is an important part of my streamer game. Mends are used to direct the path of the retrieve. At times, mends are used to slow down the retrieve while at other times they are used to speed it up. I may also mend to strategically place the line on the water in a manner that forces the fly to move in particular path. We can look at mends in at least two ways: aerial mends and on-the-water mends.

Aerial mends are my first choice when mending. Since the adjustment is done in the air rather than on the water, when the line lands on the water I'm immediately in contact with my fly. Obviously this isn't always possible, but when given the choice, I prefer to make mends in the air. I often use aerial mends to lay line/leader parallel to a bank, which keeps the streamer riding parallel to the bank.

When making an on-the-water mend, you must do a few things to maintain as much control of your line as possible. I prefer not to kick out slack before making a mend, as one would kick slack out of the rod tip before mending an indicator rig. Continuous tension between rod tip and streamer is needed to detect a take, so I prefer to mend by maintaining a tight line from fly to rod tip and then raising the rod tip to position the mend. This movement, coupled with tensioned line, will create some drag on the streamer, but this keeps tension between rod tip and streamer.

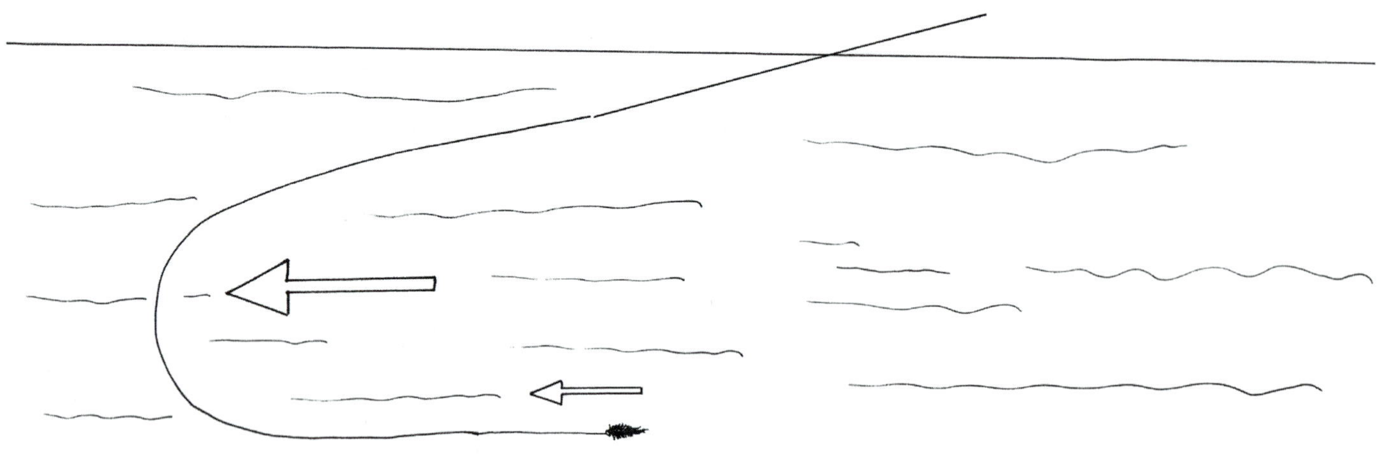

Take notice of the shape and position of the line belly lying on the water. The streamer will follow the path of the line belly during the retrieve and not necessarily move toward the angler. Think about the direction you want the streamer to move when you mend, and place the line on the water so it follows that direction.

There are two scenarios where I will intentionally throw slack into the line system. The first is when I make a mend parallel to the bank, as the goal is to reposition the slack laying off the rod tip and place it on the far bank in the formation of a tensioned loop. The second is when I am fishing a deep pool and I want to throw a little slack in the line to allow for a quicker sink rate. Remember, the greater the tension on any subsurface fishing rig, the slower the sink rate. These deep pools are the daytime resting areas where trout are likely to be hugging stream bottom. When fishing these deep runs, it's unlikely (but not impossible) that larger trout are suspended high up in the column.

The first step to mending is making sure you have ample slack line (the line you want to mend onto the water) pulled off the reel and ready to mend onto the water after the completion of the cast. You don't want to cast all the slack line coming off your reel, as this forces you to then strip line off the reel after the completion of the cast.

After you complete the cast, the rod tip stays low to the water and slides directly upstream. Moving the rod tip in against the currents pulls the slack off the water, moving it through the guides and then along the surface. The advantage of this approach is twofold. First, a long rod sweep will create enough slack to make a mend with only one rod movement

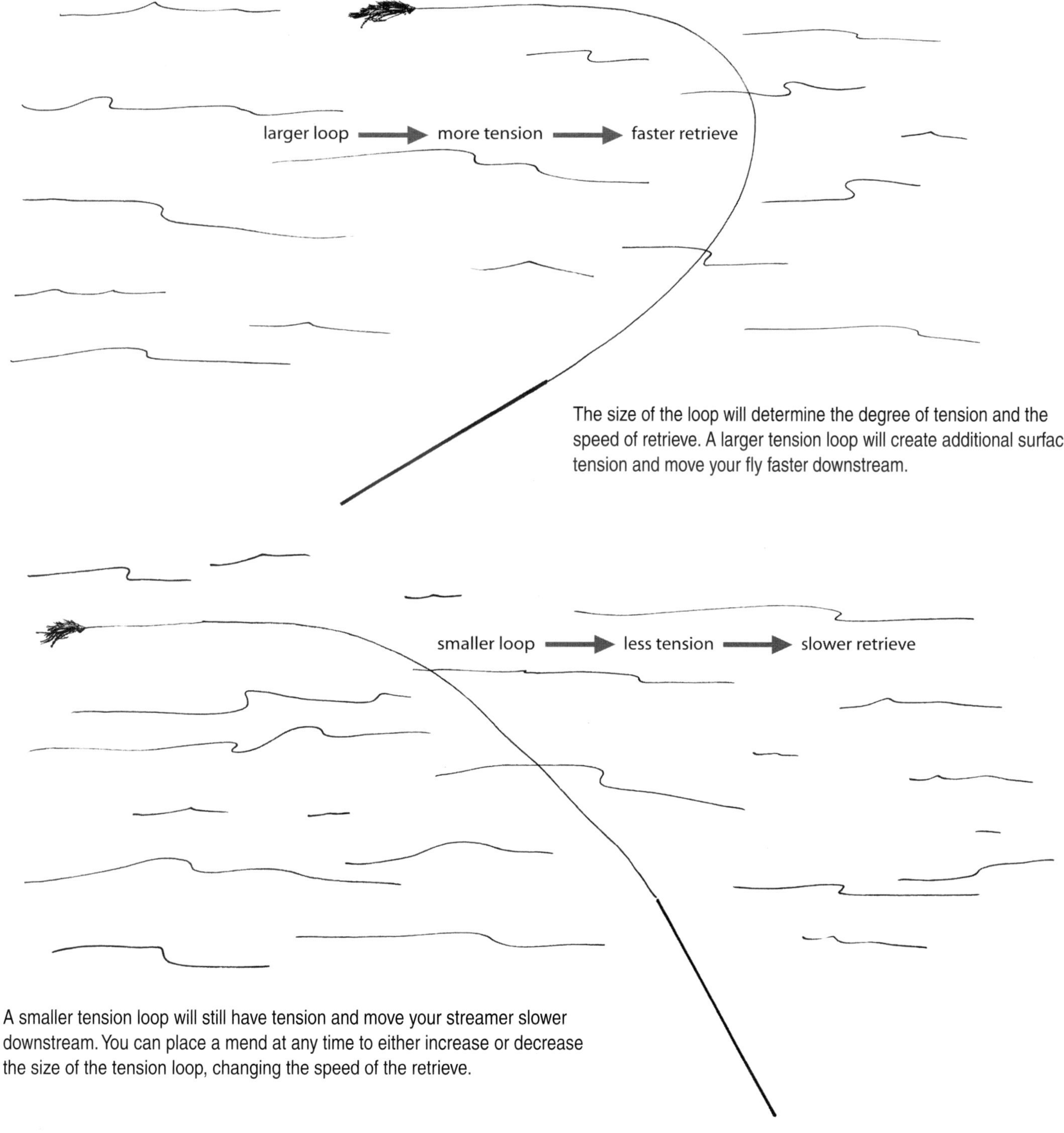

The size of the loop will determine the degree of tension and the speed of retrieve. A larger tension loop will create additional surface tension and move your fly faster downstream.

A smaller tension loop will still have tension and move your streamer slower downstream. You can place a mend at any time to either increase or decrease the size of the tension loop, changing the speed of the retrieve.

instead of multiple up-and-down motions commonly used with stack mending. Second, instead of having a pile of slack under the rod tip, the slack is in the form of a straight line on the water and can quickly be positioned into a mend. After the rod tip is swept upstream and the straight line of slack is lying on the water, the rod tip lifts upward as it moves into a mending position. I find this mending setup takes less time and therefore creates fewer moments of vulnerability in which I'm out of contact with the streamer.

Parallel Mends

With well-placed mends, you can position the line on water, so the fly drifts longer along a potential ambush area, such as an undercut bank or fallen log. While there are periods when trout will move a long distance to chase down a streamer, there are just as many occasions when the streamer needs to be moved to within several inches of the trout's position, and mends can keep your fly swimming through the prime zone for a longer period of time.

As an example, let's look at a 40-foot log that is positioned parallel along the opposite side of the stream amid strong midstream currents. My first approach would be to wade to the other side where I could cast and retrieve the streamer, either directly upstream or downstream of the log. This would allow me to cover the entire 40-foot length with one cast. However, let's say the current is too strong to cross, so we have to present our flies across-stream. If we were to cast directly across

When fishing a slower retrieve, keep the rod tip several inches off the water and watch the loops of line off the rod tip. Strip-set if the line remains tight after a pause in the retrieve, as this means your fly is still under tension. Watching the loops allows you to actually see the strike before feeling it.

If I don't know where larger trout are holding while streamer fishing large flats on rivers like the main branch of the Delaware, I'll swing my patterns through a wide arc in an attempt to cover water with greater speed.

the strong current to the bank, our streamer would move several feel along the bank, but would quickly be pulled away as the midstream currents created a belly in the line, forcing the streamer to move away from the log instead of along it. Instead, you can cast across the stream, kick excessive slack in front of the rod tip, and then throw a downstream mend to where the line is lying parallel to the log. Remember, the path a streamer takes during the retrieve is determined by where the line is sitting on the water. If the line is lying directly across the water, the streamer will move directly across the water. If the shape of the loop is positioned tight to the bank, the fly will run tight to the bank. The key is to maintain a tensioned loop in the line, so the line is under constant tension by the water. This will aid in creating a stronger hook set.

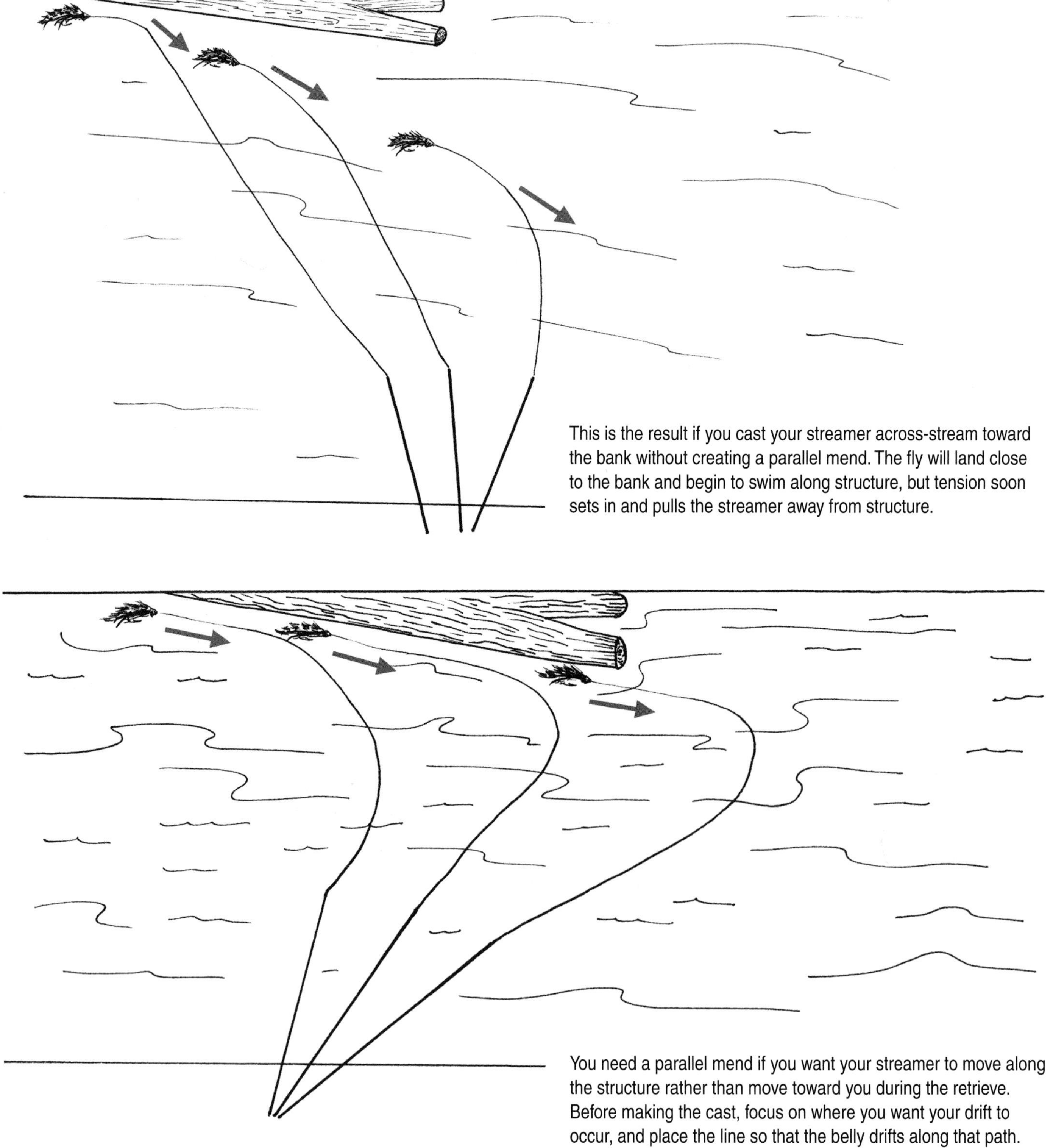

This is the result if you cast your streamer across-stream toward the bank without creating a parallel mend. The fly will land close to the bank and begin to swim along structure, but tension soon sets in and pulls the streamer away from structure.

You need a parallel mend if you want your streamer to move along the structure rather than move toward you during the retrieve. Before making the cast, focus on where you want your drift to occur, and place the line so that the belly drifts along that path.

PARALLEL MEND CAST

When casting directly across-stream, drag sets in and pulls your streamer away from the bank. While a streamer fleeing away from the bank is a useful approach, there are times when you'll need the pattern to remain moving parallel. In these cases, a parallel mend can be a useful tool. When line is lying on the water, look to see if there's a curve (aka belly in the line). If so, the fly will follow the path of this belly during the retrieve. Knowing this, you can control the direction of your streamer by intentionally repositioning the fly line on the water. Floating lines work best for this technique, as the line remains on the surface, where the stronger surface currents will maintain tension on the line. However, this technique can be used with sinking lines as well (especially with streamer-specific fly lines due to their taper). I do not recommend using the density-compensated sinking lines, as their thin diameter makes them difficult to roll cast. The only issue I see with sinking lines is that if the line sinks too fast, the line belly will sink below the stronger currents near the surface, which will decrease tension on the rig. Instead of getting pulled downstream by the current, the downstream belly will sink and pile up on the bottom—if the current isn't strong enough or if the line sinks too fast.

1. I cast my streamer across-stream and tight to the opposite bank. Notice the excess line on the water after I made the cast. This slack will be used for the next step.

2. Begin kicking the excess line in front of the rod tip, in preparation for the mend. Make this up-and-down acceleration of the rod tip with your forearm—not the wrist. You need to kick out enough slack to redistribute on the water in the form of a downstream mend.

3. When enough excess line is out in front of the rod tip, begin lifting the rod tip as you would when setting up a roll cast. This movement requires a short acceleration with the rod tip. The key is to create enough energy to create the D with the slack line you created off the rod tip without pulling the fly back toward you.

4. Accelerate to a stop and let a small D-loop form behind the rod tip. It's helpful to have the line hang off the rod tip, as it creates the tension needed to load the rod during the mend. Notice the height of the rod tip. The higher rod picks more line off the water, which allows me to create a mend without ripping too much line off the water and spooking the fish. Also, you don't need as much power during the acceleration of the mend, as you don't have to break the water's surface tension. Finally, as you begin setting up the D-loop, square your shoulders downstream and focus your eyes on where you want to create the loop.

5. Begin accelerating the rod tip toward the targeted area. Only use enough power during the acceleration to relocate the line downstream of the fly without moving the fly, just as you would if mending an indicator.

6. Accelerate the rod tip and stop high to position the slack downstream of the fly. Notice how the loop is moving in to the bank, as you want the fly to ride tight along the bank.

7. The loop will land on the water, the water tension begins moving the streamer downstream, and you can begin lowering your rod toward the surface.

8. The downstream loop is under tension—no slack from rod tip to fly. This is important in the event a trout eats the streamer. You want to create tension the moment you move the rod tip to set the hook. Also, notice that I'm pointing my rod tip toward the downstream side of the loop (not the fly) to have a better connection with my streamer.

9. Although I'm stripping line toward me, the streamer is following the path of the belly, which is running parallel to the bank. Stripping the line is optional. If you want to move your fly in a dead drift, keep the rod tip pointed at the belly, and let the current drag the streamer downstream. If you need additional movement, make short strips while keeping your rod tip pointed at the belly.

10. The drift can be extended by kicking slack onto the water, as you would when stack mending with an indicator. Just remember, the path of the streamer is determined by where the line belly is placed on the water. Knowing this allows you to not only move your streamer parallel to a log, but any direction you can imagine. You can also change the direction of the retrieve at any time of the retrieve. This means that if you see a trout following your streamer, you lift the rod tip up and reposition the line on the water so the fly changes direction during the retrieve, which is known to trigger a strike from any predatory fish.

Kicking Out Slack

Another method for extending the drift is an approach I call extending the leash. Let's say you're walking a dog along a trail and you come to a large mud puddle. You can't continue walking in a straight line, so you release the extendable leash so your dog can continue walking down the trail. The same scenario can occur when you are forced to fish down-and-across stream to a long undercut bank because you can't wade any farther downstream due to dangerous wading. This principle is the same as when kicking out slack to extend a suspender drifting downstream; instead of using a suspension device, though, we're using a downstream loop (under tension) to move the streamer downstream. Once the parallel mend is created and moving in a downstream position, you can extend the streamer drift by kicking slack into the same current, putting tension on the loop. This is a last-ditch effort for when significant line control is lost, but it may be your only chance to keep your streamer swimming parallel to a downstream holding lie.

Changing Direction and Speed

Even a small change in direction can trigger a strike. When a trout is following or chasing your streamer, so often the strikes occur the moment the fly begins rising to the surface or when the pattern changes direction during the retrieve. Sometimes during the retrieve, I'll mend the line so that the fly changes position and moves in. For example, halfway through a downstream presentation, I may create an upstream mend, so the fly suddenly goes from moving downstream to an upstream retrieve. I'll use this approach as a last-ditch effort to trigger a strike after I've seen numerous fish follow my streamer without committing. When trout are fully committed to chasing down a streamer, I'll fish a retrieve in one direction because this approach allows me to remain in constant contact as compared to a change of direction, where I lose contact for a moment as I lift the rod tip to reposition the line. Let the behavior of the trout dictate your approach.

Jigging a streamer may be your only fishing option during blown-out conditions, as wading may be restricted. If you're forced to fish during such conditions, be patient and don't be afraid to jig your streamer for several minutes in a specific spot. It may take a trout several minutes to find your pattern during low visibility.

Sometimes a change in retrieve speed is what you need to get a strike. I often vary my retrieve speed and rhythm to see what most appeals to the fish. Sometimes this means stripping faster, but you can also increase fly speed by mending line downstream so that the line downstream of the streamer creates tension and increases drag on the rig. The larger the overall diameter of the belly, the greater the tension and the faster the fly is pulled downstream. You can also use faster currents to your advantage. If you want to increase the drift speed, then position the downstream mend in the faster currents. A large-diameter tension loop placed in a faster seam, used in combination with a fast line-hand retrieve, will create a lightning-fast streamer retrieve. Slowing down the retrieve is often key, especially during cold snaps and when visibility is reduced. Make an upstream mend to eliminate a tensioned loop created by the current, just as you'd make an upstream mend to slow down a nymphing or dry-fly presentation.

When retrieving the fly, I've heard some anglers say you need to point the rod tip at the fly, while others believe you need to keep the rod tip pointed away from the fly. I think rod tip position depends on the direction you're fishing your flies, along with the current speed and the speed of your retrieve. For example, when fishing from a drifting boat and casting downstream, your should point the rod tip at the fly or line belly to create more contact. You have two items drifting in the water—

Jake Villwock from the TCO Fly Shop shows off a Mossy Creek brown trout caught on a bottom-bouncing streamer. When casting heavily weighted streamers, make sure you feel the weight tug on the backcast before proceeding with the forward casting stroke. Injury to rod or body may occur if you don't wait to feel this tug.

Jake Villwock holds a chrome steelhead taken on New York's Salmon River. Jake took this fish using a give-and-take technique in a staging pool (a holding area for steelhead before they continue their upstream voyage). The give-and-take is a tactic used more for irritating a fish than for provoking a hunger strike. The key is to keep the pattern within striking distance of the fish, pulling it away and then letting it slide back until it provokes a strike.

Jon Ray proves the switch rod has become a deadly tool for the streamer angler. On large rivers, a switch rod allows you to make longer casts with ease, enabling you to cover more water than with traditional single-handed rods. JON RAY

a boat and your fly line. Because the boat's larger diameter creates more surface tension, it moves downstream faster than the fly line, which is anchored with a weighted streamer or the line itself. In this situation I point the rod tip directly at the fly (if the line is straight) or directly at the downstream curve in the line (if downstream bow occurs), and this allows for better connection.

For another example, let's say you're casting upstream while drifting and retrieving your streamers downstream toward the drifting boat (aka trolling). In this case, I point the rod tip slightly downstream from the streamer to create a slight angle between rod tip and streamer. This allows the rod to act as a shock absorber during a strike. Because trolling creates a high degree of continuous tension, I prefer to position the rod tip in a manner that creates some give. This is similar to the old-school wet-fly fishermen, who fish downstream and keep a high rod tip angle (approximately 45 degrees) to act as a shock absorber.

Now let's think about wade-fishing and casting directly across-stream in a fast current, without mending. Let say trout

Ben Furimsky shows why a soft presentation is needed in shallow water. When water conditions are low, you need to employ less force to create less of a disturbance. BEN FURIMSKY

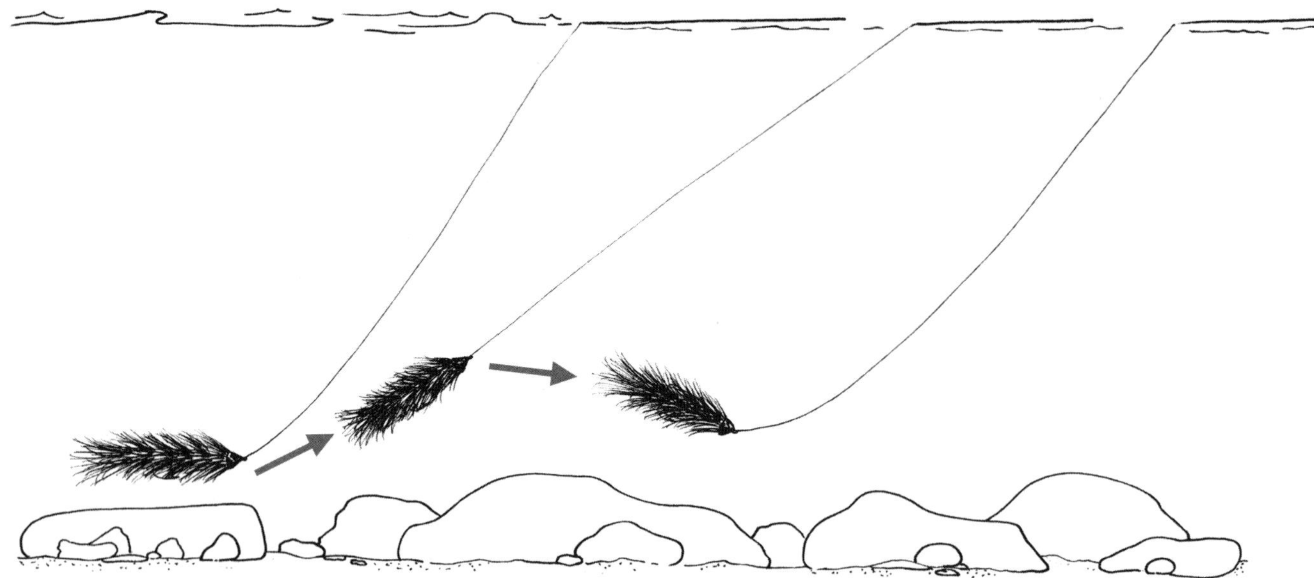

When fishing jig-style patterns, I prefer to use either a floating or intermediate line. The reason is that I want the line positioned above the streamer, as this will force the head of the fly upward during the strip, and it will fall back into position during the pause. The greater the upward lift of the fly's head, the more movement you'll create during the retrieve.

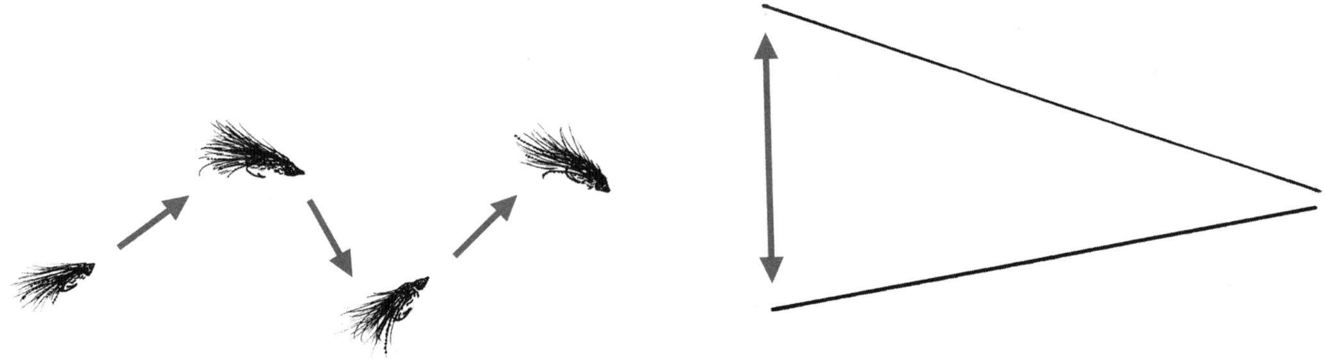

Another approach to retrieving your streamers is the side wiggle retrieve. When you look at a wounded baitfish, you often see it kick to the side. For the side wiggle retrieve, use a stiff forearm to sweep the rod tip to both sides while the line hand strips in the line.

are aggressively feeding on minnows but the water is low and clear, so you need to present the streamer in the fastest possible way and not allow the trout enough time to distinguish your pattern as a fake. After the fly lands, the strong currents will begin pulling your streamer downstream in a hurry. Then the angle of fly line landing on water will create a downstream bow, forcing your streamer to move even faster than the strong crosscurrents. This results in a high degree of continuous tension. Because of this, I prefer to point the rod tip slightly downstream of the bow—again, to create an angle to allow the rod tip to act as a shock absorber. The less tension there is in the rig, the straighter the angle I create between rod tip and streamer, and vice versa.

This angle is really important for detecting strikes. While some streamer takes are aggressive, just as many are soft. During my first few years of learning to streamer fish, I can recall countless times when I watched a trout come over and inhale my pattern without my feeling hesitation on the line—I had no contact with the fly. Poor line management was one reason for this lack of connection, but another reason had to do with the angle I was pulling the line through the guides. Instead of pulling the line straight through the stripping guide with my line hand (i.e., not touching any of the edges), I was pulling across the stripping guide. This increased friction caused my retrieve to slow down, and I lost a small degree of contact with the streamer. This happened because I kept the rod butt close to my right side during the retrieve (I'm a right-handed caster), which forced my left hand to pull directly across the stripping guide rather than directly through. While this small degree of friction will not negate the sensation of an aggressive strike, it will limit your ability to feel soft takes. And soft takes do happen while streamer fishing.

One way to fix this problem is to first move your rod hand farther away from your body during the retrieve. Once your

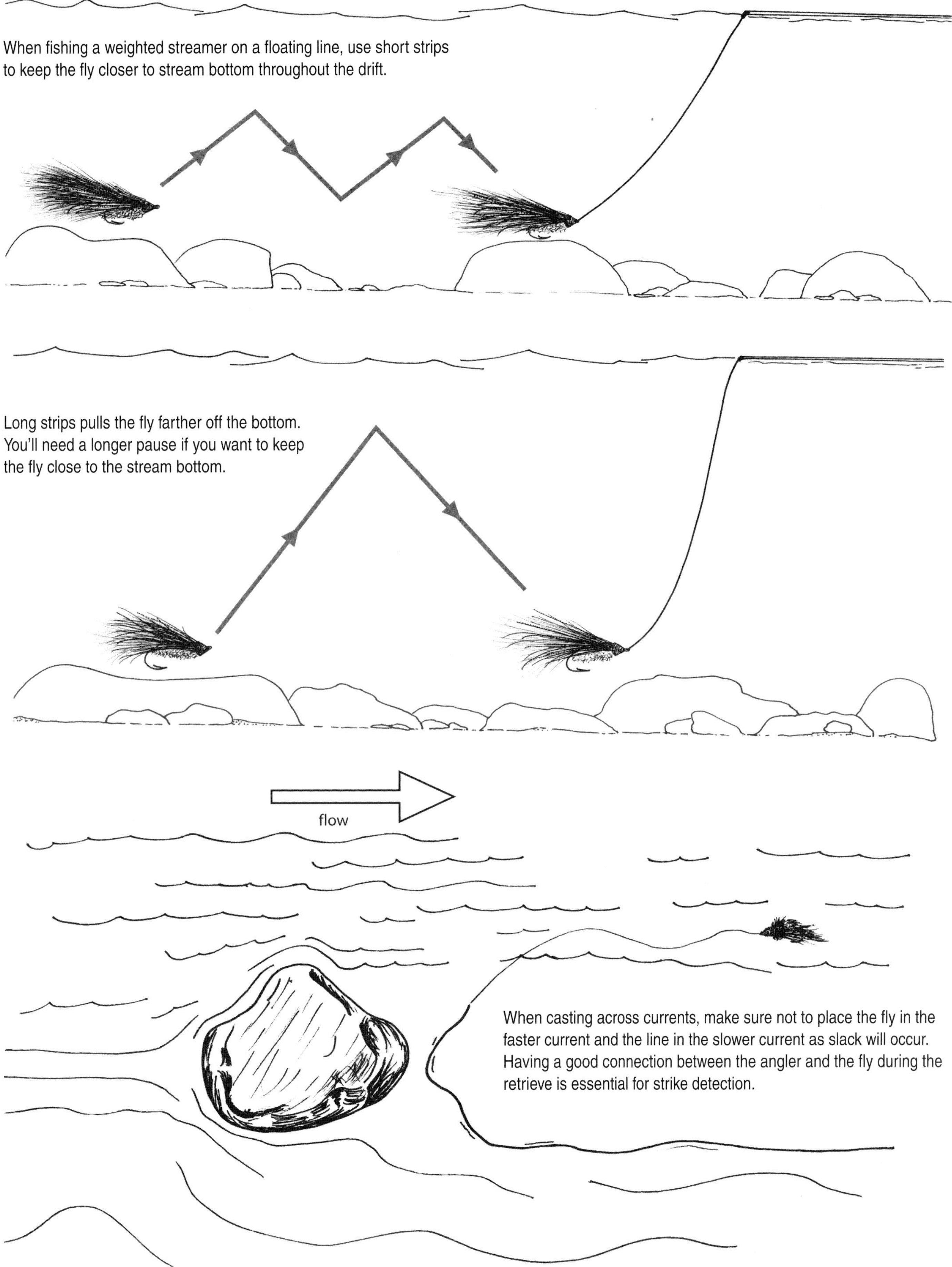
When fishing a weighted streamer on a floating line, use short strips
to keep the fly closer to stream bottom throughout the drift.
Long strips pulls the fly farther off the bottom.
You'll need a longer pause if you want to keep
the fly close to the stream bottom.
flow
When casting across currents, make sure not to place the fly in the
faster current and the line in the slower current as slack will occur.
Having a good connection between the angler and the fly during the
retrieve is essential for strike detection.

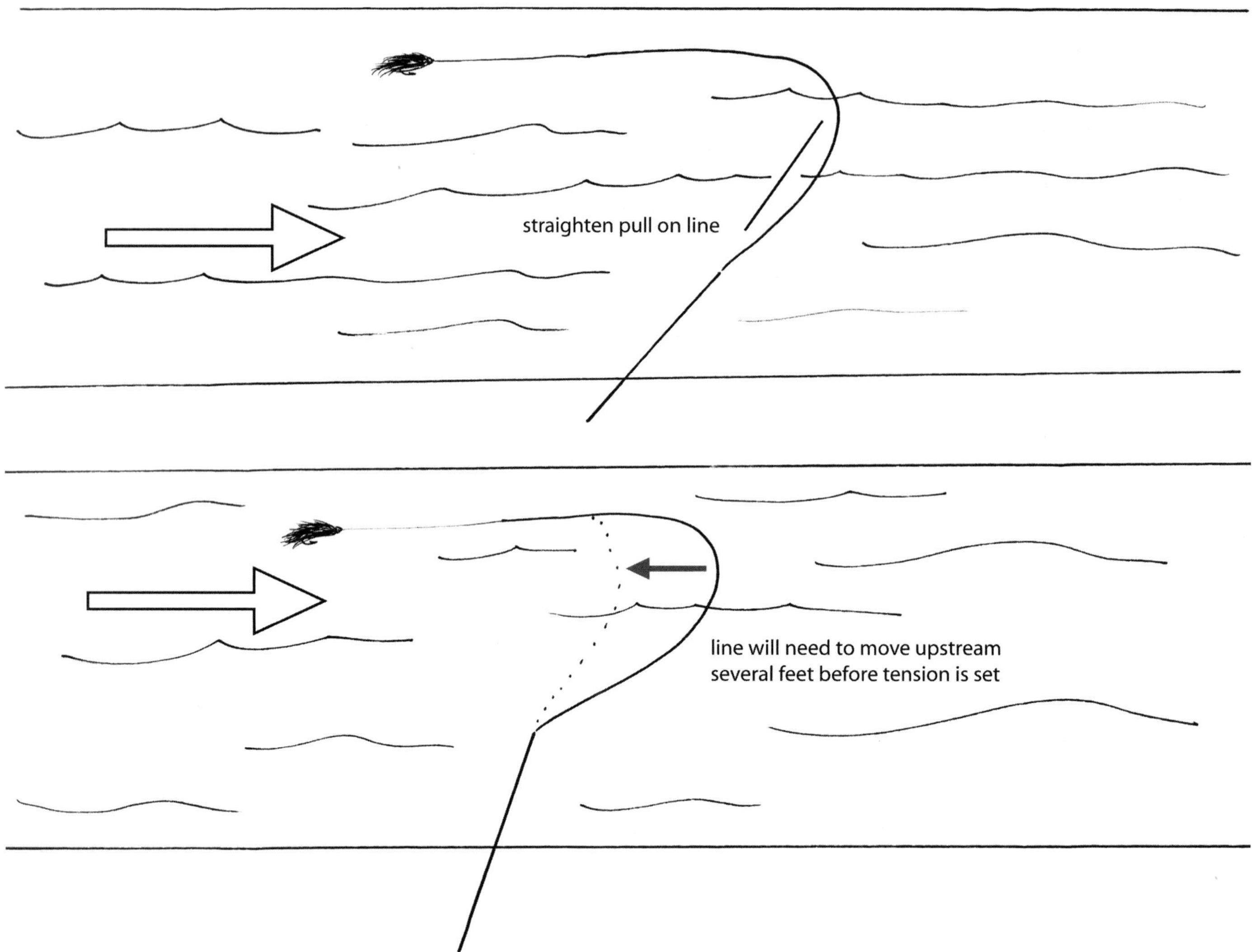

When fishing across-stream and a bow occurs in the line, point the rod tip at the bow instead of the fly to create a better connection with your streamer.

rod hand is extended outward, slide it toward the line-hand side of your body so the rod butt is pointing straight at your line hand. This will allow you to pull straight through the guides, which will reduce friction and allow you to have a better connection with the retrieve. The reduction in friction will create less wear and tear on the fly-line coating, allowing the line to last longer.

LINE MANAGEMENT

1. Line management is critical with streamer tactics, as you are continually casting out line and retrieving it back. This is especially true when casting and retrieving sinking lines, as these lines will sink and wrap around your feet if you don't have a system to manage the line out of the water. Creating large coils and storing them on your line hand is one line management method. After you make the first line strip, the line hand almost comes back together with the rod hand.

2. After your line hand joins your rod hand, store a loop of line on the top of the index finger of your line hand before pinching the line again to create a second strip. Once the loop is secure around your line hand, pinch the line immediately below the stripping guide to continue retrieving your fly.

3. Continue to strip as the loops of line are held in place by your thumb and index finger. At the end of the strip, pinch the line with the index finger on your rod hand in case a fish strikes on the pause while the line hand moves back toward the rod hand and creates another loop of line in hand.

4. Once the loop is secure, pinch the line again with your line hand (securing the loops) and begin the next strip of line. The key is to stack the loops next to one another (not on top of one another) so that they smoothly shoot off your line hand.

RETRIEVING AND SETTING THE HOOK

Much has already been written about the strip-set, so I will keep my points brief. Learning to set the hook with the line hand—known as a strip-set—rather than lifting the rod tip is an obstacle all fly fishers must overcome. The strip-set offers at least two advantages over lifting up the rod tip. First, it keeps the streamer within the strike zone after a fish has struck your streamer. The fact is, trout and other predatory fish can and may strike a baitfish several times before committing to eating. They may try to slow down or injure your pattern before attempting to inhale it. The problem with the lifting the rod tip in this scenario is that this motion pulls your fly out of the water and away from the fish. Using the strip-set keeps the fly in the strike zone, even after a trout has struck your pattern in an attempt to injure it. There have been a number of occasions when a trout has struck my streamer multiple times before committing.

The second advantage of the strip-set is the amount of power created during the set compared to lifting with the rod tip. When lifting with the rod, much of the power is absorbed by the rod bend. This is compared to pulling straight on the line, which generates more power. It's amazing to see how much power a single pull on the line creates. You can easily generate several pounds of pressure by pulling hard with the line hand. If you used the same energy to set the hook by lifting with the rod hand, the rod bend would absorb much of the power and result in less thrust.

While you need a strong hook set, I believe you can set the hook too hard. This is an issue I continue to deal with, especially when I see a large trout charge my streamer. I become overexcited and pull too hard and too long on the hook set, which rips the fly out of the fish's mouth. This is one reason why I feel it's sometimes better not to see the fish follow your fly, as any angler with a pulse gets an adrenaline rush. With today's quality hook points, it takes ounces of pressure, not pounds, to secure a hook set. I've noticed this several times when trying to retrieve my fly over a rock, only to have the hook point stick and hold onto the hard object. And that's not to mention how easy it is to accidentally embed a streamer hook into a fallen log. The point is, a short, quick burst of energy is all you need to secure a high-quality streamer hook into a fish's mouth. It's your responsibility not to rip the fish's

Toby Uppinghouse looks on while I hold my first steelhead caught while swinging a small fry pattern on California's Feather River. Switch rods are increasingly popular tools for covering large bodies of water. I prefer shorter switch rods such as the 11-foot, 7-weight H2, which allows you to use both the two-handed and single-handed option with ease. HUTCH HUTCHINSON

Lance Wilt pulls his elbow back to secure the hook set on a fish while floating the White River. Pulling the elbow back, combined with the strip-set, creates a powerful pull that secures the hook set.

When retrieving the line at a faster rate, I don't recommend keeping the rod tip off the water, as the line will rip off the surface. This ripping motion will create a disturbance on the water and likely spook fish, especially during low-water conditions.

mouth off. I've been guilty several times of ripping too hard on the line—to the point where I ripped part of the trout's mouth away. While this has only happened a few times to me, remember that this can and will happen if you apply too much power during the hook set.

Right: The figure-eight retrieve is a great tool for staying in touch with your streamers—without letting go of the line, as you have to with stripping line. Also, the speed of your retrieve is determined by how fast your fingers work, along with how many fingers you use to capture line. The more fingers you use during the retrieve, the greater the range of movement. Here, I'm using a four-finger figure-eight retrieve for faster results.

When retrieving the line, don't think one-dimensionally (i.e., moving the fly only with stripping in line). Instead, think about methods to move the fly side-to-side and up-and-down. In this instance, a sideward thrust will move the fly side-to-side during the retrieve. I prefer to use the line and rod hand in sync during this movement. For example, as I strip line with the line hand, my rod hand will slide away from my body simultaneously. This shot illustrates the beginning of the movement where the hands are close together and the rod hand is positioned straight in front of me.

During the retrieve, your line hand slides away from the rod hand while your rod hand slides away from the line—they pull apart from one another. Note that there's no wrist movement with either the rod hand or the line hand. Instead, your line hand pulls on the line while the forearm slides the rod tip away. The reason for using the forearm is to create a short, smooth, and powerful movement. Not only will you put more movement into the retrieve by using your forearm, but also the powerful movement will create a better hook set on the fish. After the movement is complete, bring your hands back together to repeat the process.

WADE-FISHING VERSUS DRIFT-BOAT FISHING

When I am moving in a boat and I only have one shot at a run, I'll guess where the trout are holding in the column and present the fly at that level. When wade-fishing, I'll fish the layers, starting with the top and working my way down to the stream bottom. A mistake I made for years when fishing deeper water was stripping in line immediately after placing the line on the water, instead of allowing the fly and line to sink to the correct depth before beginning the retrieve. When fishing shallower waters, I begin the retrieve immediately when my fly is within the striking level of the fish. The opposite is true when casting into deep waters where the trout are holding lower in the column. Because trout look up for food, my approach is to work from the top down. If you're floating and have only a single presentation, then you need to make a judgment call (based on conditions and fish behavior) about which level you will begin retrieving the flies at.

When casting from a drift boat, remember that you are moving downstream—that means leading the cast (based on the speed of the boat) so it doesn't fall short. Here Shawn Combs of the Orvis Company holds a quality New England brown trout.

STRIP TIPS

At times, the strike of a fish can be so forceful that it pulls the line straight from your fingers, which results in a hook set that won't be secure. Instead of simply pinching your thumb on top of your index finger, bend the index finger at roughly a 45-degree angle, and then proceed to pinch the line with your thumb. This forces the fly line to pass through your fingers at a similar angle. I feel this creates a more secure trap of line and doesn't allow line to be easily pulled from your hand.

When trapping the line under the finger of your rod hand, don't pinch the line during the retrieve. This is a common mistake many anglers make, as it creates friction during the retrieve and causes you to lose contact with your streamer. Instead, create an O-ring with your rod hand, which will help manage line and allow you to feel a better connection to the streamer. Remember, streamer takes can be subtle, so it pays to have a strong connection during your retrieve.

For ultimate sensitivity and a speedier retrieve, pull in line with the guides to reduce friction. While this isn't always possible, be conscious of the angle at which you're pulling the line through the guides. Remember that smooth is fast.

WATCH THE LOOP

1. When fishing a slow retrieve, the takes will also be softer because your line hand will create less force. As a result, keeping the rod tip several inches above the water will allow you to watch the loops directly off the rod tip. Here the rod tip is several inches above the water during a pause.

2. After a pause, the line coming off the rod tip should move back into this slight bend. However, if the line doesn't move immediately back into a bend, there's a chance a trout has taken the fly. Watching the loop off the rod tip was a trick I learned from British stillwater anglers, who tell me that great anglers are able to see the strikes occur before they feel them. Watching the loop off the rod tip will allow you to actually see the strike before feeling the connection.

ROLY POLY

1. The Roly Poly is the fastest retrieve I know. Instead of using a single hand to retrieve the line, you use both hands. After completing the cast, you need to shove the rod tip under your arm. If you're casting with your right hand, you'll shove the butt section under your right arm. The key is to make sure the rod is in a fixed position so the rod tip doesn't move around during the retrieve.

2. Once the rod is fixed underneath your arm, grab hold of the line coming off the stripping guide with both hands. One hand holds the line above the other by pinching the line with the thumb and index finger.

3. Use a hand-over-hand movement for the retrieve where each hand takes its turn pulling the line back through the guides.

4. Your hands move in an almost circular motion as they retrieve the line. A key to this retrieve is that the one hand always has control of the line. Due to the speed of the retrieve, the hand-over-hand motion also doubles as the hook set. When a fish is hooked, take the rod butt from your underarm and place it back in the rod hand.

DOWNWARD SWIPE RETRIEVE

Going back to the concept that there are three dimensions of retrieving (straight back, side-to-side, and up-and-down), the downward swipe is another way to present your flies. It's especially useful when fishing a wedge-style head streamer like Tommy Lynch's Drunk and Disorderly (aka Double D), where you want the pattern to dig deeper to the bottom. Due to the wedge-shaped design of the head, the pattern will go deeper in the water column every time you swipe downward. I find the best angle for this approach is either across- or downstream—then the line and rig are under constant tension.

1. Once the rig is under tension, swipe down with your forearm on the rod tip toward the water's surface in combination with a haul to help pull the fly deeper toward stream bottom. Again, there's no wrist with this movement but a forceful downward thrust with the forearm, as you would hit a nail positioned on the floor with a hammer. This is not a quiet approach since the rod tip will create a loud disturbance on the water, so it's not advised for slow and shallow water conditions.

2. After you thrust the rod tip below the surface, your forearm should make a short lift upward without the line haul. If you want the fly to continue diving deeper, pull during the downward movement. The rod tip movement is only a few inches. The short 3- or 4-inch movement creates less commotion and places less stress on the rod tip.

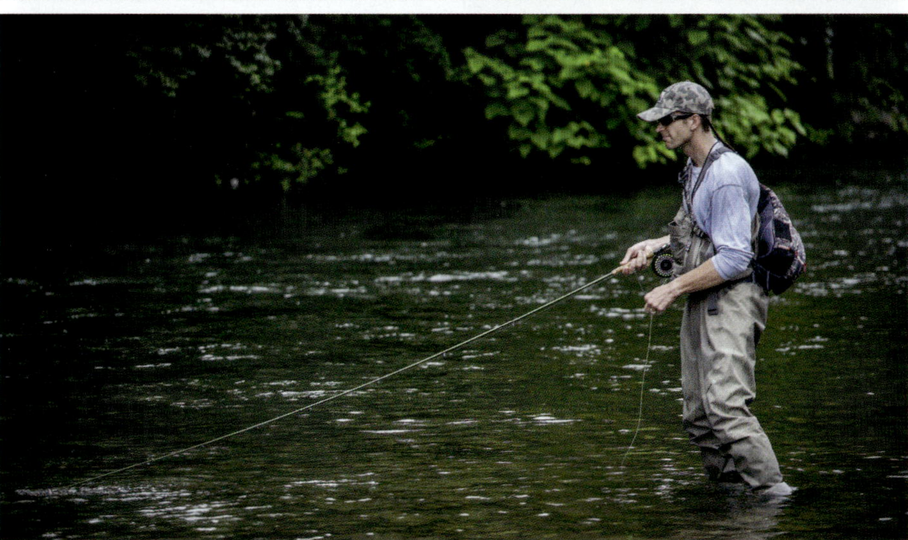

3. Repeat the process as your forearm forces the rod tip back toward the water, while implementing a short line strip. This short strip helps the wedge dig deeper toward stream bottom and also acts as a strip-set when a fish takes. Continue the process until your fly reaches the correct depth, then retrieve straight back toward you to level the plane of the retrieve.

PUMP RETRIEVE

One option during the retrieve is to use a pumping motion with the rod hand. This allows you to use your elbow during the retrieve, which provides greater speed and power. This means the rod hand slides away from your body and slides the rod tip toward the streamer. The rod tip doesn't actually stab the streamer, but the rod tip fully extends away from the body.

1. This is the beginning of a typical retrieve. Your elbow should be closer toward your body and begin to drift away while your line hand begins to pull away from the reel. The rod hand and line hand work together but move in opposite directions—the rod hand drifting toward the fly while the line pulls toward you. Also, during this motion your elbow pulls back. This means the elbow (not the hand) pulls back into the backcast.

2. The retrieve ends when the rod hand can travel no closer to the fly and where the line hand is almost fully extended. Try to stop 5 or 6 inches short of full line-hand extension to give you leverage on a hook set in the event a fish eats at the end of the drift. Also notice at the end of the retrieve, I pinch the line under the fingers of my rod hand before letting go and reaching higher on the line to begin the next retrieve.

3. Keep your elbow locked, with your hand fully extended away from your body. Pinch the line under your rod hand fingers while the line hand releases the line to move toward the reel and regain control of the line to begin the next retrieve. Even if a fish does strike in this position, the line pinched under the rod hand will not allow a fish to pull on the line without creating some tension. Also, the rod hand's elbow can always pull back and set the hook without having to use the line hand.

4. Begin to slide your elbow back toward you while your line hand pinches onto the line near the reel. The farther up the line hand can grab onto the line, the longer the retrieve. Also, notice my index finger on the rod hand—it's no longer pinching the line against the cork. Instead, it's opened up where I lay the line on top of the finger for line control. Note how my finger is curved upward to keep the line trapped between the finger and cork. A straight finger position will allow the line to slide off your finger.

5. Repeat the process as the rod tip slides away from your body toward the target. Remember to slide the elbow close to the body when moving to and from the target. An elbow that is positioned close to the body is capable of creating more power than an elbow position away from the body. Again, think about a boxer, a quarterback, or baseball pitcher.

THE FIGURE-EIGHT HAND RETRIEVE

1. Begin the figure-eight retrieve by pinching the line between your index finger and thumb. Notice the back three fingers' position over top the line to begin the next step.

2. Keeping the line pinched between your index finger and thumb, the back three fingers come over top and pull the line inward toward the palm of the hand.

3. The back three fingers continue to pull inward until the fingers touch the palm of your hand.

4. The back three fingers pinch the line against your palm, while your index finger and thumb release the line and reposition higher on the line to begin the process.

5. Your index finger and thumb pinch back onto the line. At this point, the back three fingers holding on to the loop release tension and begin to move above the thumb and index finger to begin pulling in the next loop of line.

6. The first loop of line remains inside the palm while the back three fingers begin pulling another loop of line toward the palm of your hand. Continue the process until your retrieve is done or until too many loops accumulate in your line hand. For example, after five or six retrieves, I'll let the coils slip from my hand onto the ground or water before continuing the retrieve.

THE VERTICAL JIG RETRIEVE

1. Line and leader control for the vertical jig are similar to other retrieves except for one difference—the rod tip will lift vertically in combination with the line strip. In this case, the rod tip points at the fly to keep a straight line. Because some slack will occur when you lift the rod tip out of the water, pointing the rod tip directly at the fly reduces slack and increases tension. Notice how I place both hands together before making the jigging retrieve, the line laying on the water is tight, and the rod tip is pointed at the water's surface.

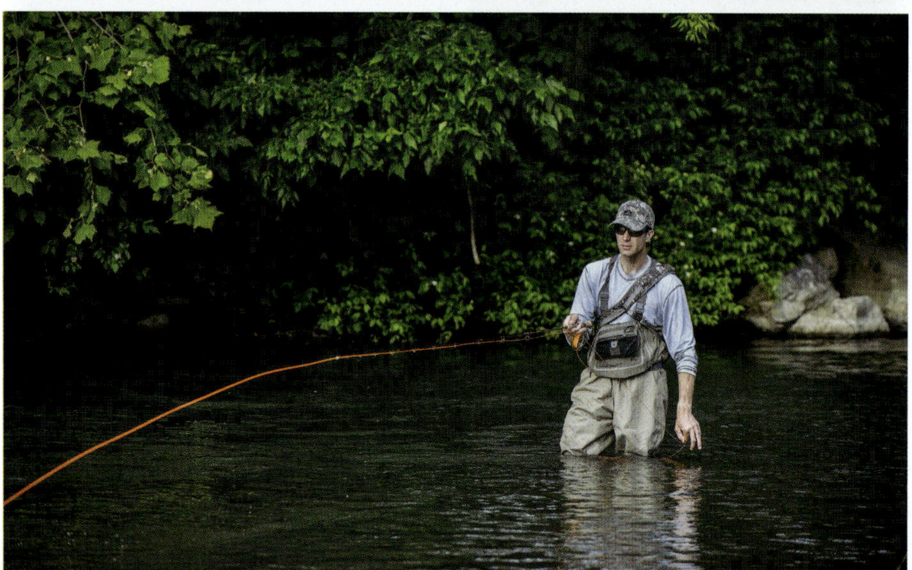

2. The first movement involves your line hand and rod hand working in combination. The rod hand lifts upward with the forearm controlling the movement. Don't use your wrist. Using the wrist to flip the rod tip upward creates too much slack and likely will rip the fly out of the water. Instead, all you want is to lift the rod tip upward and allow it to fall back down. While the forearm is lifting the rod tip upward, your line hand should make a stripping motion. Again, use your forearm (not your wrist) to pull downward on the line. At the end of the movement, pause.

3. After the pause, move your rod hand's forearm down and begin to place the line near the surface. You'll notice that slack is occurring during this downward movement. If you remember to use your forearm instead of your wrist during the downward movement, only a minimal amount of slack will accumulate. Lowering the rod tip is a smooth drop of the forearm toward the surface.

4. After the rod tip is back to the water's surface, pinch the line between your rod hand finger and the cork to maintain control as the line hand moves toward the reel hand to repeat the process. Notice there's little slack lying on the water—an ideal scenario. Pause to allow the streamer or sinking line to drop deeper into the water column. If you want the streamer to move in longer vertical movements, use a longer pause and a wider lift.

5. Repeat the sequence as your rod hand lifts upward while your line hand pulls downward. This smooth movement will lift your streamer vertically in the water column. Also, in the event of an unexpected strike, this forceful movement will create a secure hook set.

DEEP RETRIEVE

1. After you make the cast, shove the rod tip below the surface. The deeper the rod tip, the deeper the fly will ride.

2. After placing the rod tip at the correct depth, make several long strips. These strips will clean up any slack that you created while lowering the rod tip and allow you to be in touch with the streamer. Additionally, the tension created by the line hand draws the line deeper and breaks the surface tension, which allows for a quicker sink rate.

3. Once the line is tight, pause to allow the line to sink deeper. Notice my grip: The hand is choked higher on the cork, which allows the forearm to lie on top of the rod's butt section. Using the forearm is critical, as the water's current (especially if you face upstream) will want to lift the rod back toward the surface. Trying to hold the rod below the surface with only the wrist is tiresome and will quickly fatigue your rod hand. Instead, choke higher on the grip, laying your forearm on the rod, which will make it easier to keep the rod tip below the surface.

4. After the pause, keep the rod tip fixed below the surface, and make a second strip with the line hand. You'll notice the line forming an upside-down U. Continue to strip in line until the sunken line is straight. There will still be some curve in the line, but try to reduce the curve as much as possible, as a straighter line will afford better control.

5. Continue to allow the line to sink until it's reached the correct depth.

6. Now smoothly lift the rod tip from the depths toward the surface with your forearm.

7. Again, use your forearm to lift the rod tip above the surface. This is not a fast jerky motion but a smooth and steady upward lift. Note that the line is tight and that the line hand and rod hand are in a praying position. The hands need to be positioned together to begin the vertical jig movement.

8. Continue to lift the rod upward until the rod tip is above the surface. Again, the line and rod hand should be close together to begin the next movement. Notice how the rod tip is only a few inches above the surface. We don't want more than that, as greater separation between the rod tip and the surface will reduce the range of motion the rod tip has during the jig. In other words, keeping the rod tip closer to the surface will allow the rod tip to travel a longer range upward. The last thing you want is to creep the rod tip several feet above the surface before the upward lift.

9. Once the rod tip is several inches above the water, begin the upward movement. Just as with the traditional vertical jig tactic, your line and rod hand work in sync but move in opposite directions. The forearm lifts upward while the line hand pulls downward. Notice the bend in the rod. The deeper the line and streamer, the more bend you will place on the rod. If you see another angler on a lake or river getting better results than you, one of the first things I'd look at is the amount of bend in that angler's rod. If the rod is bent over during the retrieve, this may indicate the angler is fishing the streamer at a deeper level. You need to consider rod action when looking at rod bend, but it may provide a clue concerning the water depth the trout are feeding at on that particular section of water.

10. Continue to lift the rod tip upward with your forearm as the line hand continues to strip. The higher the rod tip lifts, the higher the streamer and fly line will lift toward the surface. When lifting, I try to keep the rod tip at a level plane, so the rod tip doesn't point downward or upward. The highest level I'll lift the rod tip is eye level, as anything above that places too much stress on my shoulders.

11. Now lower the rod tip back toward the surface with your forearm. You'll notice some slack, which is typical as you lower the rod downward. Pause to allow the sinking line and streamer to continuing dropping toward bottom. Make sure your line hand and rod hand are positioned together before making the next vertical jig retrieve.

12. Once again, use your forearm to lift upward while your line hand pulls the line downward. Notice the smaller degree of bend in the rod. The reason is the first lift pulled the streamer and sinking line higher in the water column. The second vertical jig movement begins with the line and leader higher in the water column, which creates less tension on the rod during the lift. The process continues until the sunken line section has been fully retrieved or until a strike occurs.

THE ELBOW SET

1. When you're holding a streamer immediately downstream, you can use your elbow (in place of your line hand) to make the hook-set. The elbow remains close to your body, but the hand should be slightly extended.

2. When a strike occurs, your elbow and forearm should maintain a 45-degree angle, but the elbow slides back in the opposite direction of the strike. During this movement, keep the rod tip positioned to the water.

3. Extend your elbow back until it can move no farther. If you miss the fish, the fly will remain in the water. This is a great tactic for fishing in cold weather conditions when you want to keep your line hand warm in your pocket. Although I prefer to use a set that incorporates both elbow and line hand, this set may also be useful to those with physical disabilities.

STOPPING SHORT OF A FULL HAND RETRIEVE

1. When stripping line, try not to move the line hand through the full range of motion. You want to be able to continue moving the line (i.e., setting the hook) if a fish takes the streamer at the end of the retrieve. Try to give yourself at least 4 to 6 inches of room to continue. This picture shows the line hand extended out, but allowing another 4 to 6 inches of movement in case a trout eats at the end.

2. If a fish does strike, your line hand can still move to set the hook.

3. To create additional leverage, your wrist can break upward once your hand is fully extended to provide another short movement. Every bit helps.

4. A mistake I frequently make during the retrieve is fully extending my hand on the strip. The problem is that when a trout eats the streamer when I'm at the end of the strip with my hand fully extended, my hand can't move any further to strip-set. So stop your strip shorter next time to allow the line hand to continuing stripping in line if a fish does take on the end of the strip.

Index

Page numbers in italics indicate photographs and illustrations.